"*These nineteenth- and early-twentieth-century biographies, now republished by Chelsea House, reveal an unsuspected significance. Not only are a good many of them substantively valuable (and by no means entirely superseded), but they also evoke a sense of the period, an intimacy with the attitudes and assumptions of their times.*"

— *Professor Daniel Aaron*

ANDREW HAMILTON

Other titles in this Chelsea House series:

JOHN PETER ZENGER
His Press, His Trial
LIVINGSTON RUTHERFURD

INTRODUCTION BY
STANLEY N. KATZ

American Men and Women of Letters Series
GENERAL EDITOR
PROFESSOR DANIEL AARON
HARVARD UNIVERSITY

CHELSEA HOUSE
NEW YORK, LONDON
1981

Library of Congress Cataloging in Publication Data

Rutherfurd, Livingston.
    John Peter Zenger, his press, his trial.

    (American men and women of letters)
    Reprint of the 1904 ed. published by Dodd, Mead,
New York.
    "A brief narrative of the case and tryal of John
Peter Zenger, printer of the New York weekly jour-
nal": p.
    Includes bibliographies.
    1. Zenger, John Peter, 1697-1746.   2. Liberty of
the press--New York (State)   3. New York weekly
journal.   I. Zenger, John Peter, 1697-1746, defendant.
A brief narrative of the case and tryal of John Peter
Zenger. 1981.   II. Title.   III. Series.
[Z232.Z5R9 1981]   342.73'0853   80-29427
ISBN 0-87754-150-7

Chelsea House Publishers
Harold Steinberg, Chairman & Publisher
Andrew E. Norman, President
Susan Lusk, Vice President
A Division of Chelsea House Educational Communications, Inc.
133 Christopher Street, New York 10014

TO

C. S. F. S.

PUBLISHER'S NOTE 1904

The Publishers make grateful acknowledgment to the New York
Public Library for permission to copy the portraits of Rip
Van Dam and Lewis Morris and to make use of its valuable collection of Zenger imprints; to the Pennsylvania Historical Society for permission to copy
the portrait of Andrew Hamilton, reproduced as frontispiece; and to other
persons and public libraries for
their assistance in the prepa-
ration of the bibliogra-
phy of the issues
of the Zeng-
er Press

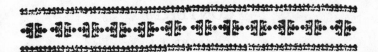

CONTENTS

CHAPTER I

PAGE

Political Conditions. Arrival of Cosby, His Character. Litigation with Rip Van Dam. Erection of the Court of Exchequer. The Removal of Lewis Morris from the Bench. Partisanship of DeLancey and Philipse. Termination of Van Dam's Case. Complaints against Cosby. His Increasing Unpopularity. Political Parties. . . 1

CHAPTER II

Extent of the City in 1734. John Peter Zenger. Commencement of the New York Weekly Journal. Contributors. Character of the Articles. DeLancey's first Charge on Libels. The Incident of Harison's Letter. Speeches before the Assembly. City Election. Songs on the Election. DeLancey's Second Charge on Libels. Burning of the Songs. Reward offered by Cosby. Burning of the Journals. Arrest of Zenger. Disbarment of Alexander and Smith. Their Complaint. John Chambers Appointed Counsel for Zenger. Andrew Hamilton Retained for Zenger. 25

CONTENTS

ILLUSTRATIONS

[All the initial letters and head- and tail-pieces used in these volumes are reproductions from issues of the Zenger Press.]

ILLUSTRATIONS

General Introduction

THE VISITABLE PAST
Daniel Aaron

THE TWENTY-FIVE BIOGRAPHIES of American worthies
reissued in this Chelsea House series restore an all but
forgotten chapter in the annals of American literary
culture. Some of the authors of these volumes—journal-
ists, scholars, writers, professional men—would be considered amateurs by today's standards, but they enjoyed
certain advantages not open to their modern counter-
parts. In some cases they were blood relations or old
friends of the men and women they wrote about, or at
least near enough to them in time to catch the contemporary essence often missing in the more carefully re-
searched and authoritative later studies of the same
figures. Their leisurely, impressionistic accounts—sometimes as interesting for what is omitted as for what is
emphasized—reveal a good deal about late Victorian assumptions, cultural and social, and about the vicissitudes
of literary reputation.

Each volume in the series is introduced by a recognized scholar who was encouraged to write an idiosyn-
cratic appraisal of the biographer and his work. The
introductions vary in emphasis and point of view, for
the biographies are not of equal quality, nor are the
writers memorialized equally appealing. Yet a kind of
consensus is discernible in these random assessments:
surprise at the insights still to be found in ostensibly
unscientific and old-fashioned works; in some in-

stances admiration for the solidity and liveliness of the
biographer's prose and quality of mind; respect for the
pioneer historians among them who made excellent use
of the limited material at their disposal.

The volumes in this American Men and Women of
Letters series contain none of the startling "private" and
"personal" episodes modern readers have come to expect in biography, but they illuminate what Henry
James called the "visitable past." As such, they are of
particular value to all students of American cultural and
intellectual history.

Cambridge, Massachusetts
Spring, 1980

INTRODUCTION
TO THE
CHELSEA HOUSE EDITION

Stanley N. Katz

This is a book about a pamphlet: *A Brief Narrative of the Case and Tryal of John Peter Zenger, Printer of the New-York Weekly Journal.* Since the pamphlet was originally published in 1736 and Rutherfurd's *John Peter Zenger* was not published until 1904, one might well ask why the report of a trial for a minor criminal offense remained of interest for such a long time. Why, indeed, does Rutherfurd's book deserve to be reprinted today?

The pamphlet is not brilliantly written, nor does it report a trial of any enduring legal value; the names of the people principally involved in the case have long been forgotten. The irony is that what does survive historically is the name of the printer, John Peter Zenger, whose role in his own trial was altogether marginal. Nevertheless, it seems quite clear that the pamphlet and the case *are* worth remembering, and it is necessary to explain why.

A Brief Narrative (as it has been called through the years) reports the trial of an immigrant German printer in colonial New York for the crime of seditious libel, or, in ordinary language, criminal criticism of the colonial government. Zenger was actually a nonpolitical artisan, printing a newspaper to earn a living, although the textbook tradition in American history still attributes a formative political role to him.

In fact, Zenger was merely the hireling of Lewis Morris, James Alexander and William Smith, New York politicians who were offended by the policy and behavior of a newly arrived royal governor, William Cosby. Morris, Alexander and their friends had dominated the politics and government of the colony during a hiatus between the terms of Cosby and his predecessor, and they were both insulted personally and excluded from power when Cosby turned to their local political antagonists for his base of support. Morris and his associates therefore organized themselves to combat Governor Cosby by opposing his legislative measures in the colonial assembly and by attempting to use the legal system to thwart his maneuvers. They also exerted themselves in England to have the governor's commision withdrawn. Cosby retaliated by forming a political faction of his own and by using his power over the judiciary to secure court judgments unfavorable to the Morrisites.

The response of Morris's "opposition"—a concept new in Anglo-American politics—was to create a newspaper, Zenger's *New-York Weekly Journal,* to represent its own interests and to criticize the behavior of the government. This strategy was novel in the colonies, and the *Journal* is rightly regarded as the first opposition newspaper in America. It seems quite clear that Cosby and his party were stung by the bitter criticisms Morris and Alexander wrote for the *Journal,* and that they determined to destroy the paper. Their counter-strategy

was to use the law of seditious libel to punish the printer, who was the only individual identified by name in
the newspaper; Alexander and the others who wrote the
inflammatory copy were pseudonymous, and their exis-
tence could not be proved legally. Zenger was thus left
to bear the brunt. The law employed by Cosby was the
English common law of seditious libel, the sole method
of restraining the press following the demise of formal
censorship in England at the end of the seventeenth
century.

The law of seditious libel made it a criminal offense
to publish criticism that endangered the government,
but it was left to the royal courts to determine what fell
into this category, and the precise definition of the
crime was by no means clear in the 1730s. Indeed, previous eighteenth-century seditious libel trials had almost
inevitably resulted in convictions, since juries were re-
stricted to deciding whether the accused had *published*
the allegedly libelous material and only judges could
rule on whether the statements so published were criminally libelous. Because contemporary judges were appointed "at the pleasure" of the Crown, there was an
overwhelming tendency for them to favor the government in its allegations of libel. The dice were further
loaded against defendants, for they were not permitted
to plead the truth of their publications. From the early
seventeenth century, English courts had recognized that
"the greater the truth, the greater the libel," since it was
ideas injurious to the government that were being punished rather than the publication of falsity. The law of
seditious libel proceeded, that is to say, on the assumption that the government had an absolute right to pro-

xviii   STANLEY N. KATZ

tect itself from provocative criticism, an assumption justified by the theory that the right of government flowed
from the Crown to the people rather than from the sovereignty of the people.

The Zenger trial thus represented the intersection of
two very different historical trends: the emergence of
modern factional politics and, in particular, the politics
of opposition to royal government; and the tradition of
government control of political speech by means of the
law of seditious libel. It is easy to see that these two
trends were moving in precisely opposite directions.
While the simple factionalism of early-eighteenth-centu-
ry New York politics was far from democratic populism,
it provided forms of political behavior that, when linked
to republican theories of government, would furnish the
basis for the revolutionary acts of 1776. The theory of
seditious libel, on the other hand, was an assertion of
prerogative power and authoritarianism only a generation prior to the era in which the Enlightenment would
make clear that freedom of expression was the critical
determinant of human progress. For the republican revolution to succeed, therefore, the law of seditious libel
would have to be destroyed. The basic premise of republicanism is that government is an expression of popular
sovereignty, and it is thus illogical to argue that the
people can be punished for criticizing themselves.

The unique historical interest of the Zenger trial is
that it seemed in 1735, and seems in retrospect, to be a
harbinger of the demise of seditious libel and the dawn
of republicanism, since the printer Zenger was acquitted
and the law of seditious libel severely criticized. Indeed,
this is precisely the interpretation given by Livingston
Rutherfurd. Rutherfurd accuses Governor Cosby of "ar-

bitrary acts which nearly produced a revolution" and
claims that the trial itself "established the freedom of
the press, . . . wrought an important change in the law
of libel, and marked the beginning of a new era in popular government." Rutherfurd contends that the trial represented the last hope of an oppressed people who, if
Zenger was convicted, would no longer have the capacity "to resist any hardship which their Governor might
see fit to impose. On the other hand, Zenger's acquittal
would mean a decided check to the evils from which
they suffered, a vindication of their demands and of the
principles for which they contended, and would give
them courage to continue their efforts to rid themselves
of their despicable Governor."

Rutherfurd sees the conclusion of the trial as a dra-
matic repudiation of the law of seditious libel and a
ringing assertion of freedom of the press: "The liberty
of the press was secure from assault and the people became equipped with the most powerful weapon for successfully combating arbitrary power, the right of freely
criticizing the conduct of public men, more than fifty
years before the celebrated trial of 'Junius' gave the
same privilege to the people of England." After the
death of Cosby in 1736, according to Rutherfurd,

. . . the old conditions were changed, the result of the trial had
imbued the people with a new spirit; henceforth they were united
in the struggle against governmental oppression, and as Gouverneur Morris has well said: "The trial of Zenger in 1735 was the
germ of American freedom, the morning star of that liberty
which subsequently revolutionized America."

This is elegant nonsense, but what ought to concern us
is why Americans for two hundred years have similarly

misconstrued the Zenger trial and exaggerated its significance.

The painful truth is that Morris and his friends were a characteristically narrow political faction largely motivated by personal political and economic ambition. They were neither premature republicans nor revolutionaries. In fact, when Lewis Morris subsequently became governor of New Jersey (the first independent governor of a colony that had always previously been linked to New York), he proved as repressive, bigoted and self-serving as Cosby. At the same time, as Leonard Levy has demonstrated, the Zenger case did not end either the law of seditious libel or the repressive behavior of colonial legislatures toward obstreperous newspaper printers and publishers. Indeed, Levy has correctly characterized eighteenth-century legal and political attitudes toward the press as a "legacy of suppression." So much for historical revisionism.

What, then, is all the fuss about? The *Brief Narrative* was, after all, reprinted fifteen times before the end of the eighteenth century, and there is no doubt that it was, as it has been called, "the most famous publication issued in America before the *Farmer's Letters.*" The bibliographic history Livingston Rutherfurd presents demonstrates the remarkable vitality of the pamphlet for about eighty years after its original publication, and it is notable that its popularity has revived since the Rutherfurd publication. The WPA reproduced the pamphlet in 1949, and the Rutherfurd volume was reprinted in 1941. New editions of the pamphlet were issued in 1954, 1957, 1963, and 1972. The Zenger case is clearly a case that will not die.

What is most interesting about the publication history of the pamphlet is the relative lack of attention to the Zenger trial from the early nineteenth century to the period just before the First World War. It is no accident that this corresponds precisely to the period in which civil liberties, and in particular the freedom of the press, were a submerged issue in American history, at least at the national level. It is striking that almost every one of the earlier reissues of the pamphlet can be associated with some notable controversy over freedom of the press. The 1752 London edition was part of the defense in a major British seditious libel case of that year, and the 1765 edition was brought out in connection with the persecution of John Wilkes. The same is true of most of the American editions, although not, I believe, of the edition at hand.

One must guess that Livingston Rutherfurd's motive in republishing the *Brief Narrative* was much more personal, for he was in fact a direct descendant of James Alexander. Curiously, although the evidence was available to him, he does not attribute *A Brief Narrative* to Alexander, but it seems quite clear that Rutherfurd's ancestor was the author. It is fitting that Alexander, also the principal editor of the *New-York Weekly Journal,* should receive credit for this famous pamphlet. He was not only one of the outstanding lawyers of eighteenth-century New York but certainly one of the most interesting political thinkers of the era, and a man who seemed much less devoted to his own advancement than Lewis Morris. The Rutherfurd edition can probably best be understood as both a family tribute and a glimpse of an early-twentieth-century Progressive view of pre-Revolutionary American politics. The exaggerated republican rhetoric with which Rutherfurd interprets the trial seems quite characteristic of the Progressive emphasis on legislative freedom, government responsiveness to the populace, and the power of the critical press. That all these attitudes were more to the point in the twentieth century than in the eighteenth did not occur to Rutherfurd, but that does not diminish the value of his edition for us.

In the end, the popularity of *A Brief Narrative* reflects a central dilemma in democratic theory, especially in the United States. That is, to what extent do our passionate commitment to freedom of the press and our belief (à la John Stuart Mill) that the free competition of ideas is central to republicanism conflict with the basic need of government to defend itself against potentially dangerous speech? Since the beginning of this century, at least, the debate over this subject has centered on Supreme Court interpretations of the First Amendment that have sometimes, especially in periods of international crisis, seemed more receptive to the requirements of government than to the claims of the people. The point is probably that crises are never the best moments for sober reflection on basic conflicts of value. For more than two centuries it has been the function of James Alexander's brilliant pamphlet to remind Americans of their duty to inquire into the conflict between free speech and governmental security. That there is no final or easy answer to the dilemma is not Alexander's fault, but it is much to the credit of the Morrisite party and subsequent publishers of the pamphlet that such an elegant statement of the problem is kept before the public eye. This, after all, is an issue that each generation must solve for itself.

Princeton, New Jersey
August, 1980

AUTHOR'S PREFACE
TO THE
1904 EDITION

HILE the events herein related are, perhaps, not as generally known as they should be, nevertheless, constituting as they do the earliest warning of the coming Revolution, they are of interest and importance in the study of the development of the Nation.

The editor wishes to state that he is under great obligations to the late Paul Leicester Ford for the loan of Charles R. Hildeburn's notes, which form the basis of the Bibliography of the different Zenger presses, and to Miss Robinson, of the American Antiquarian Society; Mr. Eames, of the New York Public Library, and Mr. Kelby, of the New York Historical Society.

The following abbreviations have been used in the Bibliography:

B.M. British Museum.

B.P.L. Boston Public Library.

C.E.N. Charles Eliot Norton, Cambridge, Mass.

C.H.S. Connecticut Historical Society.

E.D.C. E. Dwight Church, New York.

H.S.P. Historical Society of Pennyslvania.

L. New York Public Library, Lenox Collection.

L.C.P. Library Company of Philadelphia.

H.U. Harvard University.

N.J.H.S. New Jersey Historical Society.

N.J.S.L. New Jersey State Library.

N.Y.H.S. New York Historical Society.

N.Y.S.L. New York State Library.

W.N. William Nelson, Paterson, N. J.

Ed. Editor.

No effort has been made to locate all known copies.

ACCOUNT OF POLITICAL CONDITIONS, ZENGER'S PRESS AND TRIAL

CHAPTER I

POLITICAL CONDITIONS—GOVERNOR COSBY'S ARRIVAL
—HIS INCREASING UNPOPULARITY

FTER the English occupation of New York, in 1664, the inhabitants of the colony found themselves oppressed by a government that was arbitrary and despotic in its character. Grants of revenue were made generally for the use of the Crown, the revenues were disbursed by the governors, practically as they saw fit, and the people could not compel them to account. The governor was vested with power to convene and dissolve the Assembly at pleasure, and was given an absolute negative on the acts of the Assembly. The fiscal officer was the receiver-general, who was responsible only to his superiors in London. The salaries of royal governors and judges were fixed, and so long as they were promptly received these officials paid but little attention to the needs of the people and the development of the Colony.

The people, through their Assemblies, demanded that this state of affairs be radically changed. They

3

asked that revenue grants should be limited to specific purposes only; that the money levied should be confided to an officer responsible to the legislature; that the revenue should be granted from year to year, and that the salaries of governors and judges should be dependent annually upon popular contentment. These proposed changes constituted a great invasion of the prerogatives of the Crown, and were long and stubbornly resisted both by the governors and the colonial authorities in London. The people just as stubbornly insisted upon acquiescence in their demands, as they saw in this legislation their only safeguard against the avaricious character of the men appointed to govern the country, and the form of government which they administered.

The contest thus early commenced continued throughout the colonial period, and as the same questions came up for settlement in the other colonies the country gradually became united in its demands, and the spirit of the people grew bolder, until finally the unjust measures of Parliament were more than sufficient to kindle the long smoldering fires of revolt into the blaze of open rebellion.

The period covered by the administration of William Cosby as governor, from 1732 to 1736, was marked by a series of arbitrary acts which nearly produced a revolution, and which developed a hostility of political feeling almost as bitter as any which our generation has experienced. The oppressions culminated in the trial of John Peter Zenger, which was one of the most stirring incidents of colonial days. Its results were of greater magnitude than any

JOHN PETER ZENGER

of the participants could have imagined. It established the freedom of the press in North America,
it wrought an important change in the law of libel,
and marked the beginning of a new era in popular
government. It came about under the following
circumstances.

On the death of Governor John Montgomerie on
the first day of July, 1731, after an uneventful administration of about three years, Rip Van Dam as
senior councillor, according to a well-established cus-
tom, succeeded to the office of governor until the
arrival of the new appointee. Van Dam was a member of an old Dutch family, and was born in Albany
about 1662. He was bred to the sea and made
a voyage to Jamaica in 1686. For many years he
carried on a shipyard with his partner, James Mills,
in the rear of Trinity Church, and was interested in
several vessels. In 1690 he was one of the petition-
ers for relief from the arbitrary measures of Leisler.
He was Assistant Alderman from 1693 to 1696, and
was commissioned a member of King's Council in
1702 under Governor Cornbury, and held the office
for thirty-three years. He was appointed a master
in Chancery in 1711, and again in 1720. He married in 1684 Sara Vanderspeigel, and died June 10,
1749. He was the last native of New York of
Dutch extraction who presided at Council under
English rule, and to his Dutch blood may be attrib-
uted the pertinacity which he displayed in his contest with Governor Cosby. Smith, the historian,
says, " Van Dam was an eminent merchant of a fair
estate, though distinguished more for the integrity

of his heart than for his capacity to hold the reins of government." He performed the duties of governor for thirteen months, and his administration, though short, was peaceful and popular. At the close of his term warrants were passed by Council giving him the salary and fees of the office received during the period of his incumbency.

William Cosby, the new governor, was the tenth son of Alexander Cosby of Stradbally Hall, Queens County, Ireland. He had been Equerry to the Queen, and was Colonel of the Royal Irish Regiment, and retained his rank when he received his appointment as governor. He arrived in New York on the first day of August, 1732, on His Majesty's Ship, "Seaford." James Alexander had previously written Cadwallader Colden about him, saying:

" Our Doubts about our Governor are now Resolved, Coll. Cosby having kist the King's hand for New York and New Jersey in January Last, and has sent his private Secretary and some other servants to prepare the house and all things for him. The Governor was to Sail the tenth of this month, and proposes to be here in May. He is a man about 45 and gay—has the Earl of Halifax's Sister for his wife, 2 daughters almost women and a son."

Cosby wrote to Van Dam about this time, saying: " I shall be much obliged to you if you give Orders that care be taken of the Garden, and proper things be sow'n in for the Season; and care also be taken of Nutton Island and the Game preserved."

Cosby probably owed his appointment to the influence of the Duke of Newcastle. He had not long before been removed from the governorship of the Island of Minorca, where he had made himself intensely unpopular by his appropriation of the revenues, and where he had become involved in serious litigation by his arbitrary confiscation of the property of a Spanish merchant, made prior to a declaration of war between England and Spain. He sold part of the property and retained the proceeds, secreted the papers in the case and denied the injured merchant the right of appeal. He was a man of limited education; he lacked prudence and intelligence, and did not distinguish between power and right. He was avaricious, and his only idea of diplomacy was superior force. His disposition was haughty and pompous, and he was possessed of a violent temper, over which he exercised little or no control.

In colonial days the arrival of a governor was a most important event; he was the direct representative of the King, his influence and authority were all-powerful, and the prosperity of the people was directly dependent upon his policy. We can, therefore, understand the anxiety with which the people awaited Cosby's coming, especially as they had heard rumors of his maladministration at Minorca. Yet he was warmly welcomed. The Boston Weekly News Letter says:

"On Tuesday last his Excellency WILLIAM COSBY, Esq; Governour of this Province, arrived at Sandy Hook in his Majesty's Ship Seaford, Capt. Long, Commander, in seven Weeks from Great Britain, and landed here about 10 o'Clock, in the evening, and was received at the Waterside by several Gentlemen, who attended

7

JOHN PETER ZENGER

him to the Fort. The next Day between the Hours of 11 & 12 his Excellency walked to the City Hall, (a Company of Halbertiers & a Troop of Horse marching before, and the Gentlemen of this Majesty's Council, the Corporation, and a great number of Gentlemen and Merchants of this City following, the Streets being lin'd on each side with the Militia) where his Commission was published, and then his Excellency returned (attended as before) to the Fort. The Militia then drew up on the Parade and saluted him with three Vollies."

The Assembly met and voted him a salary of fifteen hundred pounds and gave him a gratuity of seven hundred and fifty pounds for his alleged services in procuring the repeal of a sugar bill which was considered detrimental to the interest of the middle colonies.

The affairs of the Colony were peaceful and the people hoped for a quiet administration. But they were soon disappointed. When Cosby was told by Lewis Morris, Chief Justice of the Supreme Court, about his present from the Assembly, he became angered at the smallness of the gift and shouted violently, " Damn them, why didn't they add the shillings and pence? Do they think I came here for money? I'll show them."

The Assembly afterwards raised the amount to one thousand pounds. This incident showed the real character of the man, for it seems extremely doubtful whether he contributed in any way to the repeal of the bill, and by the King's instructions he was forbidden to take any presents whatsoever from the Assembly.

Within a short time after his arrival Governor Cosby produced a royal order dated May 31, 1732, which gave him one-half of the salary, perquisites and emoluments of the office from the time of his appointment until he arrived in America. He served a copy on Van Dam, who conceived he had a right to retain what he had collected, and at first refused to pay over anything unless compelled by due course of law. It was alleged by Van Dam that the salary and perquisites annexed to such an office passed with the office, and that the person on whom, by law, the burden of the office was laid, was entitled to its benefits. The people considered the order a piece of favoritism in behalf of a royal appointee against a native of the Colony, and their sympathies were immediately aroused in favor of Van Dam.

Later, Van Dam expressed his willingness to comply with the order provided that Cosby would account for what he had received, alleging that Cosby had collected some six thousand pounds more than had come into his hands, and really owed him three thousand pounds. Cosby declined to accept this proposition, and Van Dam retained what he had collected. Cosby then determined to sue, but he was puzzled to know just how to proceed. The matter was one of account and could not be brought in the Supreme Court, as it possessed no equity jurisdiction. He could not sue in Chancery as he himself was chancellor, while a suit at common law would admit of a set-off by Van Dam, and he was afraid lest a jury would render a popular verdict against him. Cosby, therefore, by an ordinance dated December 4, 1732, attempted to give the Judges of the Supreme Court authority to hear causes as Barons of the Exchequer, and directed Richard Bradley, the Attorney-General, to bring an action there in the King's name, although Cosby was the person beneficially interested in the result. The people had always been most firmly opposed to the erection of a court of Equity without consent in general Assembly, and former assemblies had in 1702, 1708, 1711 and 1727 passed resolutions condemning in the strongest terms the erection of such a court. Therefore, the passing of this ordinance merely to serve the purpose of an avaricious governor, became at once the basis of union for the opposition to Cosby's administration.

The proceedings which followed are interesting not only as leading directly to the trial of Zenger, but from the prominence of the persons connected with them.

Lewis Morris, who was Chief Justice of the Supreme Court, was a son of Richard Morris of Morrisania, and one of the most distinguished men of his time. He was born in 1671, and early entered upon an active public career. He represented the Borough of Westchester in the Assembly from 1711 to 1738, or twenty-seven years, a much longer period than any other citizen has ever been returned to that body by his constituents. He was a member of Council from 1721 to 1729, Boundary Commissioner in 1723 and Chief Justice of the Supreme Court from 1715 to 1733, Judge of the Court of Admiralty for nearly fifteen years and Governor of New Jersey from 1738 to 1746. He was a man of great intellectual power, bold and fearless in his manner, and his temper, though hasty, was well con-

trolled.   He married, in 1691, Isabella, daughter of
James Graham, who was Attorney General and a
member of Council.   Their many descendants have
always been prominent in state and national affairs
for their ability and patriotism.

James Delancey, second justice of the Supreme
Court, born in 1703, was a son of Etienne DeLancey and Anna Van Cortlandt.   He was appointed a
member of Council in 1729 on the death of his
uncle, John Barbarie, and held office for twenty-
four years.   He was Chief Justice of the Supreme
Court from his appointment in 1733 until his death,
Lieutenant Governor in 1753, and Governor in
1755.   He was a man of education and ability, and
his arbitrary rulings in the Van Dam and Zenger
cases can scarcely be reconciled with his subsequent
conduct as Governor, except on the score of the
most bitter partisanship.

Frederick Philipse, third justice, also held his
position from his appointment for the remainder of
his life.   He was born in Barbadoes and married a
daughter of Anthony Brockholst.   He died in 1751.
He is said to have been a worthy gentleman of
plentiful fortune, "though with no pretensions to
learning of any kind."

James Alexander, counsel for Van Dam and later
for Zenger, was born in Scotland in 1691, and came
to New York in 1715, where he began the study of
the law.   By his industry and application he soon
rose to a high place in the profession.   He was Attorney General in 1721, and member of Council
from 1721 to 1737, and from 1750 to 1756.   He

was elected to the Assembly in 1737, and was a member of Council for New Jersey from 1722 until his death. He was one of the founders of the American Philosophical Society and was prominently connected with every public enterprise of his day. Smith says, "Though no speaker, he was at the head of his profession in sagacity and penetration, and in the application of business no man could surpass him."

He was a man of great depth of mind, and boldly espoused the side of the people in their fight against Cosby. Though he was well known as a man of ability and integrity in both New York and New Jersey, yet Cosby wrote the London Board of Trade urging his removal from Council, saying, "He is very obnoxious to most in the Council as well as to every honest man in both Provinces having the character of a very tricking dishonest man, and therefore very unfit to sit in King's Council."

William Smith, also counsel for Van Dam and Zenger, was born in England in 1697, and it is said that he came to New York in the same ship with Alexander. He too became prominent in the profession of the law as a man of talent and integrity. He was appointed Recorder September 30, 1736, and one of the incorporators of Princeton College in 1746. He was appointed Attorney General in 1751, member of Council from 1753 to 1767, and Justice of the Supreme Court from 1763 to 1769.

Richard Bradley, the Attorney General, was appointed in 1723, and held office until his death in 1752. But he early fell under the displeasure of the Assembly, as they considered " he was in the habit of filing informations on his own notion with a view rather to squeeze money from those he prosecuted than from any just cause."

When the action was commenced by the Attorney General, Van Dam was advised by his counsel, Alexander and Smith, to bring suit against Cosby for the half of what Cosby had received over and above the amount collected by Van Dam. But, to his astonishment, the clerk of the court refused to affix a seal to the summons, and Cosby would not answer the declaration. Accordingly, Van Dam was put on his defense in Cosby's action and his counsel, by way of plea, offered the following exceptions to the being and jurisdiction of the court:

" 1*st*. For that (Your Honours being applyed to as Justices of the supream Court) the supream Court was erected and established by Ordinance, in the Time of His late Majesty King *George* the first, and in His Name, and that that Ordinance expired by His Death, at least before exhibiting this Bill; and that there has been no Ordinance or other Act or Thing done, in the present King's Time, to re-establish that Court; and therefore no such Court now existing.

2*dly*. For that His present Majesty, by His Commission to Governour *Montgomerie*, under the great Seal of *Great Britain*, having commanded him to execute all Things in due Manner, according to the Powers granted by that Commission, and the Instructions therewith given; and by the 39*th* of these Instructions, His Majesty having required the said Governour *Montgomerie* to *grant Commissions, with the*

Advice of the Council, to Persons fit to be Judges in this Province, as by the Instructions proffered; and yet the said Governour granted Your Honours Commissions, without such Advice; and therefore not pursuant to the Authority aforesaid; And it's put to Your Honours Judgment, Whether, after Knowledge of this Defect, You will take upon You the Power of judging in this Cause?

3dly. For that the Defendant says, Your Honours have not any Authority or Jurisdiction to compel the Defendant to answer upon Oath, touching the Matters in the Bill: And that there is no Prescription, Act of Parliament, nor Act of Assembly, to establish any supream Court, nor to impower any Court or Person to hold Cognizance of Pleas, in a Course of Equity, in or for this Province: And therefore pray Your Honours Opinion, whether the Defendant ought to be compelled to answer you in a Course of Equity."

It was further alleged that it was the business of an equity court to grant relief where it could not be had by common law, and not to deprive the subject of the right to trial by jury; and that the King was not a person interested in the proceeding, having by his order given his interest in the salary and fees to the Governor.

Rule to argue the plea was filed February 1st, 1733, and the argument was set down for April 9th, 1733. Lewis Morris, at the opening of the court, delivered a long and exhaustive opinion against its jurisdiction in equity causes, and then left the bench, declining to have anything further to do with the case. The closing sentence of his opinion was as follows:

"And as I take it the giving of a new Jurisdiction in Equity by Letters Patent to an old Court, that never had such Jurisdiction before, or Erecting a new Court of Equity by Letters Patent or Ordinance of the Governor and Council, without Assent of the Legislature, are equally unlawful, and not a sufficient Warrant to justify this Court to proceed in a Course of Equity. And therefore by the Grace of God, I, as chief Justice of this Province, shall not pay any Obedience to them in that Point."

Cosby was intensely angered by the opinion and wrote Morris a savage letter, impugning his integrity and demanding a copy of what he had said in court. Morris sent him a copy, together with a letter, a part of which reads as follows:

"As to my Integrity, I have given You no Occasion to call it in Question. I have been in this Office almost twenty years, my Hands were never foul'd with a Bribe; nor am I conscious to myself, that Power or Poverty hath been able to induce me to be partial in the Favour of either of them. And as I have no Reason to expect any Favour from you, so am I neither afraid nor ashamed to stand the Test of the strictest inquiry you can make concerning my Conduct. I have served the Public faithfully and honestly, according to the best of my Knowledge; and I dare and do appeale to them for my Justification."

He was then summarily removed from his office without the advice of Council, although he had served for nearly eighteen years without complaint.

His opinion was published and ran through two editions. In the following August DeLancey was commissioned Chief Justice and Philipse second Justice. The number of the judges of the Supreme Court was thus arbitrarily reduced from three to two, for Daniel Horsemanden was not appointed third judge until 1737.

DeLancey and Philipse, however, decided that they had jurisdiction to determine matters in equity in a court of Exchequer and proceeded to hear counsel. Yet, although the whole case was set down, they heard argument on the third exception only, and then ordered that the plea in the case be set aside without further argument. At the time of the argument, counsel for Van Dam handed up a further exception to the commission of the judges, "that they were not granted for life nor during good behaviour." The clerk read it, endorsed it and noticed it as filed, when Philipse, without argument, ordered the minute to be blotted out, the endorsement to be razed, the exception to be taken off the file, and handed back to counsel, nor would he allow a bill of exceptions for use on appeal.

On November 30, 1733, Van Dam wrote a letter to Cosby's representative, in which he submitted three articles as a basis for the settlement of their troubles. But it was returned the next day, "it being such a Heap of INTELLIGIBLE (sic) Stuff, as I think very IMPROPER to trouble myself or the Governor with. - - - - *and doubt not but I shall hear that those will prove your best Friends* on *the End, who advised you* TO MAKE PEACE ON ANY TERMS."

JOHN PETER ZENGER

Van Dam published his case as it progressed, saying, " As the Wellbeing of the People of this Province, and their Posterity, is much concerned in the Consequences of that Opinion on my Demurrer, I think it my Duty, for their Sakes as well as mine own, to publish it at large, ... in order that they may, before it is too late, see the Bondage and Slavery, which may possibly follow from it. . . . . But as the Press here is so weak-handed and slow, it will be a Work of some Time, before that Argument and Opinion can be printed, which makes me chuse the publishing these short Proceedings first."

He comments on the answer to his letter as follows: "Here the Reader will also see the modern Doctrine of *Keeping in with Governours ON ANY TERMS* wound up to a higher Pitch, *even to make Peace ON ANY TERMS*, and movingly inculcated. The meaning of which Doctrine seems to be this, If Governours have a Mind to any Part or all of your Estate, by all means give it to them; for if you offer to keep it when they demand it, that is not making of Peace on any Terms. This Doctrine I take it to be that of passive Obedience and Non-Resistance, which every Lover of Liberty and the glorious Revolution ought strenuously to oppose."

After the court overruled Van Dam's plea he decided not to appear again until Cosby had answered his declaration. The Attorney-General then took out a commission of rebellion against him and a return was filed stating, "The said Rip Van Dam is not found." This proceeding rendered his estate liable to sequestration. The following affidavits show

the remarkable way by which the return to the commission was made. They are reproduced as showing
the spirit which animated this litigation.

"William Spinks, *Mariner on Board His Majesty's Ship the* Seaford, *aged about Twenty six Years,
being duly sworn on the holy Evangelists of Almighty
God, on his Oath doth declare, that on or about the Tenth
or Eleventh day of this instant* January, one Queen Marsh,
*formerly belonging to the said Ship, but now he believes
out of all Employ, and who lodges at Mr.* Hammonds,
next Door to the Coffee-house, came to Mrs. Hawkins's,
a publick House upon the Dock, where this Deponent and
William Fearn *lodge, and got into Company with the
Deponent and the said* William Fearn, *and called for
Liquor to treat them with, and after some Hours Drink-
ing, he told the Deponent and the said* Fearn, *that he had
a Paper concerning* Van Dam, *that he would be obliged
to them if they would set their Hands to, he said there was
no Harm in it, and confirmed it with many Oaths, and
that the Captain knew of it, and that it would oblidge the
Captain as much as the Governour. Then he took out a
Parchment, which he never opened to them, but shewed
them upon the back of it some Words to this Purpose,* the
within mentioned is not to be found. *And the said*
Marsh *said it was only to put their Names to that after
him, and he would sign it first, and swore many Oaths,
they would never be called to an Account for it: Whereupon the said* Marsh *signed his Name under the said
Words, and the Deponent and the said* Fearn, *signed after
him. The Deponent says, he has since heard and believes
that the above Parchment was a writ against Mr.* Van

Dam *to take him ; but the said* Marsh *did never tell them so at that Time, nor to this Deponent never before, and he believes not to* Fearn *neither. And this Deponent doth say, that he verily believes the Capt. knew nothing of the said Writ ; for that he has expressed a great Deal of Anger and Resentment at this Deponent and the said* Fearn, *for signing, as before, and ordered them this Morning to go and declare the Truth, and their concern for the doing thereof; which this Deponent hereby does : And farther saith not.*

William Spinks.
Sworn this 19th *Day of* January 1733–4. *Be-fore* - - - - - - -

William Fearn, *Mariner, on Board his Majesty's Ship* Seaford, *being duely sworn on the holy Evangelists, on his Oath doth declare, that he was present and heard the above* William Spinks *declare on Oath as before; and so far as relates to this Deponent of his the said* Spinks' *Affidavit, is true; and the rest he believes to be true; and farther saith not."*

William Fearn.
Sworn this 19th *Day of* January 1733–4. *Be-fore* - - - - - - - -

In his printed case Van Dam says : " The above Affidavits make it plain what low Means have been taken to bring my Estate into the Hands of a Governour, that he may cut and carve for himself. Here are Men plied with Drink, deceived by Falsehoods and Lies, and their Hands fixt to a Return, *That I am not to be found,* when these Men never stir'd from their Seats to seek me. - - - I am always to be found at my own House, and am able and willing to pay my own Debts: - - - I have already shown in Print the Account, upon which I think a very great Balance due to me from the Governour, when even the whole of what is demanded of me is deducted, which shows the unjust Design of this Prosecution, and these last Affidavits evidence the scandalous and base Methods with which it is carried on. - - - My Case published has been called Libelling; for my Part I don't pretend to understand Law, but I am sure it is Truth. And if I am to fall a Sacrifice to arbitrary Power, I have this Comfort left, that I have not deserved it, and hope I may be the last Example in this Province."

Another writ against Van Dam was directed to the sergeant-at-arms returnable on February 7th, but it was not executed. This is the last record in the case which Smith says was never settled, and that the court took cognizance of no equity causes after Van Dam's.

It is easy to understand what a ferment these proceedings caused. Here was a native of the Colony, a man who was rich, influential and popular, who was well known and respected, forced into expensive litigation by a grasping and unscrupulous governor who denied him common justice, who was, in reality, attempting to help himself to the property of a private citizen, and who hesitated at nothing which he thought would aid him in accomplishing his purpose.

The people had a long list of grievances against

their governor. They had been disgusted from the very first with the form and ceremony he affected when he received their representatives. Then, shortly after his arrival, while making a visit at Albany, he deliberately destroyed a deed to the corporation made by the Mohawk Indians. The deed had been made by the Indians for their protection against the rapid settling of the country, and was not to take effect until the dissolution of their tribe. It was destroyed because Cosby expected to receive certain fees when a new grant was executed.

They had heard, too, that in several instances Cosby had refused to grant lands to settlers unless he was permitted to retain a third for his personal use.

They had seen the Chief Justice of their Supreme Court deposed from his office, because his opinion on a matter of law differed from the wish of the governor, and they rightly inferred that any other official who attempted to stand in his way would be dealt with in the same summary manner.

Another serious complaint against Cosby was that at the assembly election held in Westchester in October, 1733, the Quaker voters were challenged on the ground that they were not freeholders, although they were all men of known estates. The sheriff required them to qualify by the usual oath. This they refused to do, but offered to affirm, as was their right, under the statute. Nevertheless, they were not permitted to affirm, and thirty-eight of them were arbitrarily disfranchised. These tactics were resorted to by Cosby's orders in the hope of defeating Lewis Morris, who was running against

William Foster, clerk of the Common Pleas, and who, it was said, paid Cosby one hundred pistoles for the appointment.

They knew that only such members of the Council were summoned to the meetings as were favorable to Cosby's designs, and they therefore began asking themselves if such a man as Van Dam could be wronged, how would a poor man fare? What security did the Province offer for a man's person or property? There were people living who could remember Andros, cruel and despotic; Fletcher, avaricious and fanatical; Cornbury, a bankrupt who came to New York to escape from his creditors; Hunter, timid and weak; and now they were cursed with a Cosby, worse in many ways than his predecessors. How long were they to serve as the prey of unprincipled men? Truly their position was indeed perilous, and they were rapidly realizing the truth of Van Dam's words when he said, "We are Tenants at Will to Governors, and exposed to be fleeced by them from Time to Time at their Pleasure."

The practical effect of Cosby's conduct was the division of the people into two political parties, one the court party with Cosby as its leader, with James DeLancey, Frederick Philipse, Richard Bradley and Francis Harison as the principal members. They also had with them George Clarke, a member of Council, who succeeded Cosby as Governor in 1736; Daniel Horsemanden, another member of Council, afterwards Justice of the Supreme Court, and author of the rare "Narrative of the Negro Plot;" Archibald Kennedy, later Earl of Cassillis, and Receiver

General of the Province for more than forty years; Joseph Murray, John Chambers, and a small following among the citizens at large.

The opposition or popular party had a majority in the Assembly and a large following among the people. The principal men were Lewis Morris, Lewis Morris, Jr., James Alexander, William Smith, Rip Van Dam, Vincent Mathews, Gerardus Stuyvesant, Philip Livingston, third Lord of the Manor, and Cadwallader Colden, who was member of Council for fifty-five years, Surveyor General of the Province, and later Lieutenant Governor. The following bit of gossip was found among the papers of an intimate friend of Colden:

"In '61 on Gov. Monckton's appointment to the Expedition against Martinico he (Colden) took the reins of Government which he held till the end of '65 when Sir H. Moore arrived. On Sir Harry Moore's arrival he retired to a Farm on Long Island, where I took my leave of him in '73. Tho far advanced he still retained all his Faculties and annually a set of his friends went from the City to celebrate his Birth-Day, when he cheerfully took his Bottle till 2 in the Morning."

The following is an extract from a letter written by Philip Livingston to James Alexander, which shows the state of feeling towards Cosby and his party. Alexander had previously written to Livingston complaining of the seizure of his letters.

"If Mr. Van Dam had suffered himself tamely to be devoured certainly another Morcell, as you say, would have followed, no person could expect to have escaped. If you and a few more had not opposed the arbitrary proceedings, they had been established to the Ruin of the whole Province. . . . It's very shocking that your letters have been intercepted. There can nothing bad enough be expected or apprehended from such Vile Varlets who are guilty of such Felony."

Vincent Mathews, who was a prominent man in Orange County, being at different times County Clerk, Assemblyman and Boundary Commissioner, also wrote as follows to Alexander:

"If the Hand of Providence does not arrest and give us some relief very quickly, I cannot see that any one Man of Honour and Honesty can remain in this Province without falling a Sacrifice to the basest and vilest of Villains."

It is not surprising, therefore, to find a letter from Alexander to a friend in London, describing the situation of the Province in the following language:

"The people of this Province had deservedly gained the character of being as easily governed as any in the King's dominions. They are generally industrious, the greatest number of them Dutch, and seldom trouble their heads with politics, but such people generally are most violent when they apprehend their liberties and properties to be in danger, and indeed we were lately afraid of their breaking out into open violence."

JAMES ALEXANDER

RIP VAN DAM

Engraved by Charles Burt, from an original sketch, by John Watson, in the Possession of Mr Wm A Whitehead.

Lewis Morris

TANDEM VINCITUR

A Song made upon the Election of
new Magistrates for *****,

To the tune of, To you fair Ladies now
on land

To you good lads that dare oppose
  all lawless power and might,
You are the theme that we have chose,
  and to your praise we write:
You dar'd to shew your *** brow
In spight of every abject slave,
                          with a fa la la.

Your votes you gave for those brave men
  who feasting did despise;
And never prostituted pen
  to carress the ***
That were drawn up to put in chains,
As well our ****** as happy ******;
                          with a fa la la.

And tho the great ones frown at this,
  what need have you to care?
Still let them fret and talk amiss,
  you'll shew you boldly dare
Stand up to save your Country dear,
In spight of usquebaugh and beer;
                          with a fa la la.

They beg'd and pray'd for one year more,
  but it was all in vain:
No welewants you'd have, you swore;
  By jove you made it plain:
So sent them home to take their rest,
And here's a health unto the best,
                          with a fa la la.

A Song made upon the foregoing
Occasion.

To the Tune of, Now, now, you ****
  all shall sleep.

Come on brave boys, let us be true
  for liberty and law,

**

*** despise the haughty Knave,
  that would keep us in aw,
Let's scorn the tools bought by a fop,
  and every cringing fool,
The man who basely bend's a fop,
  a vile insipid tool.

Our Country's Rights we will defend,
  like brave and honest men;
We voted right and there's an end,
  and so we'll do again.
We vote all *igners out of place,
  *** who did ***
Who sold us by a false ***,
  I'm sure we're right ***

Exchequer courts, as void by law,
  great grievances we call;
Tho' great men do assert no flaw
  is in them; they shall fall,
And be contemn'd by every man
  that's fond of liberty.
Let them withstand it all they can,
  our Laws we will stand by.

Tho' pettyfogging knaves deny
  us Rights of Englishmen;
We'll make the scoundrel raskals fly,
  and ne'er return again.
Our Judges they would chop and ***
  for those that serve their turn,
And will not surely think it strange
  if they for this should mourn.

Come fill a bumper, fill it up,
  unto our Aldermen;
For common-council fill the cup,
  and take it o'er again.
While they with us resolve to stand
  for liberty and law,
We'll drink their healths with hat in hand,
  whoraa! whoraa! whoraa!

By his Excellency

William Cosby, Captain General and Governour in Chief of the Provinces of *New-York*, *New-Jersey*, and Territories thereon depending in America, Vice-Admiral of the same, and Colonel in His Majesty's Army.

A PROCLAMATION.

Whereas Ill-minded and Disaffected Persons have lately dispersed in the City of *New-York*, and divers other Places, several Scandalous and Seditious Libels, but more particularly two Printed Scandalous Songs or Ballads, highly defaming the Administration of His Majesty's Government in this Province, tending greatly to inflame the Minds of His Majesty's good Subjects, and to disturb the Publick Peace. *And Whereas* the Grand Jury for the City and County of *New-York* did lately, by their Address to me, complain of these Pernicious Practices, and request me to issue a Proclamation for the Discovery of the Offenders, that they might, by Law, receive a Punishment adequate to their Guilt and Crime. *I Have* therefore thought fit, by and with the Advice of his Majesty's Council, to issue this Proclamation, hereby Promising *Twenty Pounds* as a Reward, to such Person or Persons who shall discover the Author or Authors of the two Scandalous Songs or Ballads aforesaid, to be paid to the Person or Persons discovering the same, as soon as such Author or Authors shall be Convicted of having been the Author or Authors thereof.

GIVEN under My Hand and Seal at Fort-George in New-York this Sixth Day of November, in the Eighth year of the Reign of Our Sovereign Lord G EORGE the Second, by the Grace of G O D of Great-Britain, France and Ireland, KING, Defender of the Faith, &c. and in the year of Our LORD, 1734.

By his Excellency's Command.
Fred. Morris, *D. Cl. Conc.*

W. COSBY.

GOD Save the KING.

By his Excellency

William Cosby, Captain General and Governour in Chief of the Provinces of *New-York*, *New-Jersey*, and Territories thereon depending, in America, Vice-Admiral of the same, and Colonel in His Majesty's Army.

A PROCLAMATION.

WHereas by the Contrivance of some evil Disposed and Disaffected Persons, divers Journals or Printed News Papers, (entitled, *The New-York Weekly Journal*, containing the freshest Advices, Foreign and Domestick) have been caused to be Printed and Published by *John Peter Zenger*, in many of which Journals or Printed News-Papers (but more particularly those Numbred 7, 47, 48, 49) are contained divers Scandalous, Virulent, False and Seditious Reflections, not only upon the whole Legislature, in general, and upon the most considerable Persons in the most distinguish'd Stations in this Province, but also upon His Majesty's lawful and rightful Government, and just Prerogative. Which said Reflections seem contrived by the wicked Authors of them, not only to create Jealousies, Discontents and Animosities in the Minds of his Majesty's Liege People of this Province, to the Subversion of the Peace & Tranquility thereof, but to alienate their Affections from the best of Kings, and raise *Factions*, *Tumults* and *Sedition* among them. *Wherefore* I have thought fit, by and with the Advice of His Majesty's Council, to issue this Proclamation, hereby Promising a Reward of *Fifty Pounds* to such Person or Persons who shall discover the Author or Authors of the said *Scandalous*, *Virulent* and *Seditious Reflections* contained in the said *Journals* or *Printed News-Papers*, to be paid to the Person or Persons discovering the same, as soon as such Author or Authors shall be Convicted of having been the Author or Authors thereof.

GIVEN under My Hand and Seal at Fort-George in New-York this Sixth Day of November, in the Eighth Year of the Reign of Our Sovereign Lord GEORGE *the Second, by the Grace of GOD, of Great-Britain, France and Ireland,* KING *Defender of the Faith, &c. and in the Year of Our LORD* 1734.

By his Excellency's Command,

         W. COSBY

Fred. Morris, D Cl. Conc.

GOD Save the KING.

CHAPTER II

EXTENT OF THE CITY IN 1734—THE BEGINNING
OF ZENGER'S NEWSPAPER—INCIDENTS
LEADING TO THE TRIAL

N 1734 the City of New York con-
tained about 10,000 inhabitants, of
whom fully 1,700 were negro slaves.
On the west side of the island, above
what is now Cortlandt street, there
was only an occasional house to be
met with, and the same was true of the east side north
of Frankfort street. South of this, however, the town
was far from being solidly built up. In 1731 there
were only 1,500 houses in the city, and in the same
year it is recorded that quail could be killed in the
brush east of the present Broadway.

There was but little business carried on, and it
was principally in the direction of importing from
abroad the supplies necessary for the Colony. The
Fort, the Governor's House, the City Hall, and the
churches were the principal buildings. Little devo-
tion was paid to the arts and sciences and there were
no indications of the controlling power which the
city was destined to exert. There was but one newspaper, "The New York Weekly Gazette," the first

paper published in the Colony, founded by William Bradford in October, 1725. At first it was merely a half sheet of foolscap, but in 1726 and 1727 it was occasionally issued with four pages. It was printed in a crude and rough fashion and its columns were filled principally with foreign news and advertisements, yet small and poor as it was it was amply sufficient for the needs of the public.

As Cosby became day by day more and more unpopular, one can almost see the citizens of New York gathering at their favorite meeting places, the Black Horse Tavern and the market place, and discussing the latest actions of their Governor. It was really the only way they had for ascertaining what was going on, for Bradford was a conservative man, and being public printer his paper was, naturally enough, devoted to upholding Cosby's position.

There was, however, in New York at this time, beside Bradford, a poor German printer, John Peter Zenger by name, who was carrying on a struggling little business. The records of Zenger's life are very meagre and but little is known of him.

He was born in Germany, the name of the place is unknown, in 1697. He was one of a large company of Palatines who were sent to America in 1710 by Queen Anne. With him came his mother Johanna, his sister Anna Catharina, and a brother Johannes. The father of the family died on shipboard. After their arrival in New York the boy John was apprenticed to William Bradford on October 26, 1711, for a term of eight years. At the expiration of his apprenticeship he went to Maryland, probably with the expectation of finding better opportunities for practicing his trade, and settled at Chestertown in Kent County. In April, 1720, he petitioned the Maryland Assembly to be allowed to print the session laws. His petition was granted and it was suggested that he be given seven hundred pounds of tobacco for doing the work, but no trace of these session laws can be found, and it is doubtful if he ever printed them. At a later session of the Assembly Zenger applied for naturalization; his bill was the first to pass and it cost him a fee to the Speaker of £1, 10s., and 15s. to the Clerk.

He saw but little chance of success in Maryland and returned to New York, where on September 11, 1722, he married Anna Catharina Maulin, who is said to have been one of the first persons interested in Sunday School work in the city. The records of the Dutch Church state that Zenger was a widower at the time of this marriage, and it is known that his son John was born in 1719, but it is impossible to discover where the first marriage took place or who his first wife was. On September 10, 1723, Zenger was made a freeman of the city, having been naturalized July 6 of the same year.

In 1725 he formed a partnership with Bradford, but it was of short duration, and there is but one book extant bearing the imprint of their joint names.

In 1726 Zenger started in business for himself. His shop was on Smith street, which was that portion of the present William street lying between Maiden Lane and Pearl. In May, 1734, he moved to Broad street near the Long Bridge. He printed a few political tracts and a number of unimportant books, principally theological in character and written in Dutch. In 1730 he brought out "Vanema's Arithmetica," which was the first arithmetic printed in the Colony.

After Cosby's erection of the Court of Exchequer and his removal of Morris, the popular party determined that the people of the Colony should see him in his true character. For this purpose it was necessary that they should have a newspaper. Accordingly they selected Zenger for their printer and probably aided him financially in starting the "New York Weekly Journal, containing the freshest Advices, Foreign and Domestic," the first number of which appeared November 5, 1733.

The idea of the popular party was, that a printed account of Cosby's actions would arouse such a storm of indignation that he would surely be recalled. The following extracts are from letters written about this time to former Governor Robert Hunter by James Alexander:

"Our Governor who came here but last year has long ago given more Distaste to the People than I verily believe any Governor that ever this Province had during his whole government. . . . . Nothing does give a greater lustre to your and Mr. Burnet's administrations than the being succeeded by such a man."

"Inclosed is the first of a newspaper designed to be continued Weekly and chiefly to expose him and those ridiculous flatteries with which Mr. Harison loads our other Newspaper which our Governor claims and has the privilege of suffering nothing to be in but what he and Mr. Harison approve of."

A censorship of the press had been established by the commission and instructions issued to Governor Bellomont in 1697 as follows:

"For as much as great inconveniences may arise by the liberty of printing within the province of New York, you are to provide all necessary orders that no person keep any press for printing, nor that any book, pamphlet or other matter whatsoever be printed without your especial leave and consent first obtained."

But it does not seem to have been continued in the commissions of subsequent governors, or Cosby would certainly have taken this means of suppressing the new paper.

Lewis Morris, Lewis Morris, Jr., James Alexander, William Smith and Cadwallader Colden were the principal contributors to the columns of the new paper. Indeed, they wrote practically everything but the news notices. Alexander seems to have been editor in chief and to have passed on most of the contributions prior to their publication, as many manuscript articles designed for the "Journal" are found among his papers. Zenger was poorly educated, and he possessed little experience or skill in his trade. His business ventures up to this time had been failures and, with a large family to support, he was very poor. It seems certain that he went into the newspaper scheme from a commercial point of view only, and without any adequate idea of the results which were to be accomplished.

JOHN PETER ZENGER

The "Journal" was a folio in size, with four pages. The press work was better than that of the "Gazette," but there were many grammatical errors, Zenger's knowledge of English being very limited. The paper sold for three shillings per quarter, and advertisements cost three shillings for the first insertion and one shilling for each insertion thereafter.

The "Journal" immediately proved to be a very popular paper, and some of the earlier numbers ran through as many as three editions. Supplements, which up to that time had only been used on rare occasions for governor's addresses and fiscal statements, became common. The articles were written with spirit and cleverness, and they were eagerly read.

In the second number there appeared an article on the liberty of the press, which was used as the text of many others. The articles were filled with direct allusions to Cosby and his conduct. For instance, in number four there is an article on civil government and its obligations, with the following : "A supream Magistrate may be conceived to injure his Subjects, if in his Dealings with them, he treats them either not as Subjects, or not as Men. The Duty of a supream Magistrate respects either the whole People, or particular Persons ; and thus much he owes to the whole People, that he procures the Good and Safety of the Community, according as Laws direct and prescribe. Therefore he injures the whole People, if he evades or suffer these LAWS to be evaded to their hurt."

JOHN PETER ZENGER

In the same number appeared the following advertisement:

"A Large Spaneil, of about Five Foot Five Inches High, has lately stray'd from his Kennel with his Mouth full of fulsom Panegericks and in his Ramble dropt them in the NEW-YORK-GAZETTE; when a Puppy he was mark'd thus ⌐F⌐, and a Cross in his Forehead, but the Mark being worn out, he has taken upon him in a heathenish Manner to abuse Mankind, by imposing a great many gross Falsehoods upon them. Whoever will strip the said Panegericks of all their Fulsomness and send the Beast back to his Kennel, shall have the Thanks of all honest Men, and all reasonable Charges."

This is directed at Francis Harison, who, as an ardent adherent of Cosby, wrote many articles to the "Gazette" supporting his actions.

In number five there is an article on "Trial by Jury," with an allusion to Cosby's depriving Van Dam of a jury trial in their disputes. A quotation from it is as follows:

"Deservedly therefore is this Tryal by Juries, ranked amongst the choicest of our fundamental Laws, which whosoever shall go about openly to suppress, or craftily to undermine, does ipso facto, ATTACK THE GOVERNMENT, AND BRING IN AN ARBITRARY POWER, AND IS AN ENEMY AND TRAYTOR TO HIS COUNTRY."

In number eight is an article by Lewis Morris, purporting to be an interview with a magician, in which he says that from the initial letter of the surname of a Governor, one might form a judgment as to his character and conduct. "Provinces have also their *Cabala* Letters, and *York* and *Jersey* seem pretty much under the same Influence, the *H's* and *C's* pertain to them. The *H* seems to be a fortunate Letter, witness *Hamilton*, *Hurley*, and *Hunter*, Men of amiable Characters. On the contrary *C* has always proved unhappy, either to the Government, or to themselves, or both: He instanced *Campbell* and *Cartaret* in *Jersey*, and *Coot* and *Cornbury* in *New-York*."

Then follows an account of Cornbury's administration, and a parallel is drawn between it and Cosby's by implication, and the article concludes with, "What has once been may be again."

In number nine we learn that, "*The Spaniel strayed away is of his own Accord returned to his Kennel, from whence he begs Leave to assure the Public, that all those fulsome Panegirics were dropt in the* New York Gazette *by the express Orders of His Master. That for the gross Falsehoods he is charged with imposing upon Mankind, he is willing to undergo any Punishment the People will impose on him, if they can make full Proof in any Court of Record that any one Individual Person in this Province (that knew him) believed any of them.*"

In number ten the articles begin to take the form of letters apparently written by the subscribers, and replies were made to the articles in the "Gazette." It can readily be seen that the new paper and the radical tone of its articles created great excitement, as nothing like it had before appeared in the Province. Both parties read it, and everybody wondered what the next number would disclose. About this time Van Dam's case, which was printed in sections, was brought out, and for a while Zenger probably had more work than he could attend to. In fact Zenger says in number twelve in a card to his patrons, "*I must acknowledge my Obligations to you to be such, that you do so plentifully supply me, that tho for some Weeks past I have used my smallest Letter, and to put as much into a Paper as was in my Power, yet I have now Supplies sufficient to fill above seven weekly Papers more. . . . I have thought of publishing a* Thursdays Journal *weekly for the next Quarter.*"

At the opening of court on January 15, 1734, Justice DeLancey, referring to Van Dam's case, charged the grand jury on libels, saying, "You must have observed, that of late there have been served Papers printed, with a Design and a Tendency to alienate the Affections of His Majesty's Subjects of this Province from the Persons whom His Majesty had thought it fitting to set over them; and in particular, some Men with the utmost Virulency have endeavored to asperse his Excellency and vilify his Administration; they have spread abroad many seditious Libels, in order to lessen in the People's Minds the Regard which is due to a Person in his High Station. . . . The Authors are not certainly known, and yet it is an easy Matter to guess who they are, that by making Use of Mr. *Van Dam's* Name, have gain'd some credit among the common People, which they were not wont to have, and never thought to have deserved."

He concluded by saying, "I know most of you

Personally, and I make no doubt but that you will discharge your Duty." The charge covered six folio pages, but the grand jury returned no indictments.

This was followed by a pamphlet entitled, " Some Observations on the Charge delivered to the Grand Jury by the Honourable James DeLancey," written by Lewis Morris, in which the new Chief Justice was severely criticised for his application of the law.

The court party then found themselves in a quandary: the case against Van Dam had been dropped on account of the rising indignation of the people. But now they were stung by the attacks of the " Journal," which were sharper than ever since the failure of the Grand Jury to indict, though ordered to do so by the Chief Justice in the plainest language possible. They were sullen and revengeful, and denounced Alexander and Morris at every opportunity, as they were the head and front of the movement against Cosby.

Cosby again complained to the London Board of Trade, saying:

" Cabals were form'd against the Government and a meeting of their factious men is still held several nights in a week at a private lodging which I have discover'd Alexander always prsent and Morris."

The Governor's wife had been heard to say that her highest wish for Alexander and Smith was to see them strung up on the gallows at the gate of the Fort. Accordingly, their next step was a more desperate one.

On the evening of Friday, February 1, 1734, as some of James Alexander's friends, Mr. and Mrs. John

JOHN PETER ZENGER

Hamilton and Mrs. Ann DePeyster, were leaving his house, they picked up a letter outside the door directed to Mrs. Alexander. On being read, it proved to be an anonymous demand for money coupled with a threat to destroy the members of the family in case of a refusal. James Alexander at once recognized the address as being similar to the handwriting of Francis Harison. William Smith and Colonel Lurting, the Mayor, also recognized the writing as similar to Harison's. Alexander was summoned to attend before a committee of the Council appointed to investigate the matter, but declined to appear, since Harison was one of the committee. The matter was brought to the attention of the grand jury. After deliberation they declared that there was a similarity of hands, refusing to say to whose, and asked the Governor to offer a reward for the discovery of the writer. The Governor accordingly offered a reward of fifty pounds for the discovery of the author of the letter and fifty pounds to any accomplice who would come forward and make known the truth of the matter.

From a letter written soon after this time by James Alexander to Lewis Morris, we get his idea of the motive for the anonymous letter. He says : " By comparing the ' Spectator ' in Bradford's ' Gazette ' of Jan. 28, the Monday before Friday the First of February when the incendiary Letter was found in my Entry, in which it's advanced that the taking away the good name of another was to be punished by Death ; that a good name is equal in value to Life itself, the words good name being several times in Italicks there, and the papers published in the 'Gazette' Feb. 4, which must have been in the press before the incendiary letter was found, in which it's said a good name ought to be maintained by the Sacrifice of Life, and the next article in that paper concluding, 'Cut off the Causes and the Effects will cease.' I say comparing these two Gazettes with the Report of the Council and Harison's Address, in which a good name is spoke of in the same way, they give not a small Light into the plot and design of the incendiary Letter and of the author or authors of it. For how could they expect, as the handwriting of the Letter was not much disguised, but that I should have proclaimed to all the author of it. As I did not, they were in their Committee in Harison's presence to oblige me to say it. And then according to the papers in these two Gazettes, he was justified in destroying me at once, and a pety jury could have been found to have brought it in manslaughter from the heat of blood a man must be put into by hearing himself charged with such a villany. His motives to this murder are obvious for he found himself so pushed in Truesdell's two cases that there was no averting his disgrace but by mine or Smith's destruction, and possibly they expected the Murder of me would cause all the rest of us to fly to save our Lives. You or Mr. Paris have those Gazettes which if You'll view with these Hints I believe this matter will appear plainer to you than I can point it out. There's a great satisfaction that he has left this Country but a Dread that he may assassinate You, or have some ruffians do it, and You cannot be too much upon Your guard against so execrable a villain and his plots."

It is needless to say that the rewards offered by the Governor were never claimed. Harison afterwards died in great poverty in London.

In the meantime there had been a great outcry against the new court, many petitions complaining of it had been presented to the Assembly together with Van Dam's printed case. Finally the Assembly decided to hear counsel, and on June 7, 1734, William Smith delivered a long opinion against the jurisdiction of the court. He was followed on the twelfth by Joseph Murray, who spoke in favor of its procedure, but the Assembly seem to have taken no action in the matter.

Smith's speech before the Assembly won so much support for the popular party that the Governor, seeing the danger of the situation, invited persons of inferior station to the Fort and dined them at his table, many of whom signed an address applauding the mildness and merit of his administration. This sudden change of front on the part of Cosby, who had previously been very pompous in his bearing towards the citizens, is thus commented on in a letter to the "Journal":

"Mr. *ZENGER:* I Am a poor Man and have been Tenant to several Landlords since I came into this Country, I have Paid my Rents to all of them tho' some Times not on quarter Day, and have been well used by all my Landlords, except the Last, who has given me several gross Affronts, altho I have paid him by far the greatest Part of his Rent and made him several handsom Presents. But now of late he grows extremely Civil, I am invited, and (when Business allows me to come) entertained after the elegantest Manner.

I desire you to Publish this for I am at a Loss to know the Reason of this late and extraordinary Civility, is it not to Cajole me to sign a new Lease, or to give him more Rent?"

Among the signers of the address were the Aldermen and Common Councilmen of the city. At the election held on St. Michael's day, 1734, the popular party put up opposition candidates to the signers. A bitter contest ensued, but the new candidates were all elected.

The "Journal" said : "*Simon Johnson* and *Edie Myer* (aldermen in South ward elected by four majority) carried it against the Governour's Interest notwithstanding there voted against them a considerable Merchant who was an Inhabitant of another Ward, and about 15 of the Soldiers of His Majesty's Garrison, besides the Recorder of the City and his Interest. . . . . All the Members that are chosen were put up by an Interest opposite to the Governour's except *John More*, (Dock ward 1 maj.) in whose Favour a great many of the City joyned, or he would have lost his Election. All those that were Aldermen and Common-Councilmen before signed the Address to the Governour that is printed in Mr. *Bradford's Gazette* No. 449 except Alderman *Styvesand*, for which Reason he had no Opposition in the new Choice."

In the evening there was great rejoicing over the popular victory; houses were illuminated and speeches were made. The next day a couple of ballads were circulated through the town commemorating the occasion, containing many sarcastic allusions to the Governor and his party. It would be interesting to know who the author of the ballads was, but he has left no trace of his identity.

On October 15, 1734, Chief Justice DeLancey delivered another charge to the Grand Jury for New York county on the subject of Libels. Among other things he said, " I shall conclude with reading a Paragraph or two out of the same Book, concerning Libels; they are arrived to that Height that they call loudly for your Animadversion; it is high Time to put a Stop to them; for at the rate Things are now carried on, when all Order and Government is endeavored to be trampled on; Reflections are cast upon Persons of all Degrees, must not these Things end in Sedition, if not timely prevented ? Lenity you have seen will not avail, it becomes you then to enquire after the Offenders, that we may in a due Course of Law be enabled to punish them. If you, Gentlemen, do not interpose, consider whether the ill Consequences that may arise from any Disturbances of the publick Peace, may not in part, lye at your Door ?"

He further said, " You must have heard of two *Scandalous Songs* that are handed about, it is your Duty to enquire the Author, Printer and Publisher of them. Sometimes heavy, half-witted Men get a knack of Rhyming, but it is Time to break them of it, when they grow Abusive, Insolent, and Mischievous with it."

JOHN PETER ZENGER

The jury returned a presentment of the songs on the election when the Supreme Court issued the following order :

" *At a Supreme Court of Judicature held for the Province of* New-York, *at the City of* New-York, *Octob.* 19, 1734. *Present the Honourable* James DeLancey, *Esq; Chief Justice, the Honourable* Frederick Philipse, *Esq; second Justice.*

" THe Grand Jury having yesterday Presented two Scandalous and Seditious Songs or Ballads, lately dispersed about this City, one entitled, *A Song made upon the Election of New Magistrates for this City ;* the other entituled, *A Song made on the foregoing Occasion*, both highly defaming the present Administration of His Majesty's Government in this Province, tending greatly to inflame the Minds of His Majesty's good Subjects, and to disturb and destroy that Peace and Tranquility which ought to subsist and be maintained in this Colony and in all other well governed Communities ; of which *Virulent, Scandalous* and *Seditious Songs* or *Ballads*, they have not been able, on a strict enquiry, to discover either the Author, Printer or Publisher. *It is therefore Ordered by the Court* That said *Virulent, Scandalous* and *Seditious Songs* or *Ballads* be burnt before the City-Hall, sitting the Court, by the hands of the *common Hangman*, or *Whipper*, on *Monday*, ted 21*st* of this Instant, at 12 o'Clock, and that the High-Sheriff of this City and County do take Order accordingly."

The fact that out of the nineteen members of

this grand jury five had served on the first one, was probably the reason they returned no indictment. This method of procedure, having thus been found to be barren in results, on October 17th, the Council sent a message to the Assembly, saying that they had several of Zenger's Weekly Journals laid before them and other scurrilous papers tending to alienate the affections of the people of the Province from His Majesty's Government, and asked for a conference with a committee from the Assembly to examine into said papers and their authors. A committee was appointed and the concurrence of the Assembly was asked for in the following:

"That Zenger's Papers No. 7, 47, 48, 49 which were read, and which we now deliver, be burnt by the hands of the common Hangman, as containing in them many Things derogatory of the Dignity of His Majesty's Government, reflecting upon the Legislature, upon the most considerable Persons, in the most Distinguished Stations in the Province, and tending to raise Seditions and Tumults among the People thereof. That you concur with us in Addressing the Governour to issue His Proclamation, with a Promise of Reward for the Discovery of the Authors or Writers of these Seditious Libels. That you concur with us in an Order for Prosecuting the Printer thereof. That you concur with us in an Order to the Magistrates, to exert themselves in the Execution of their Offices, in order to preserve the public Peace of the Province."

On October 22, the House took the matter into consideration and after several debates it was "*OR-*

DERED THAT THE SAID PAPERS AND RE-
QUEST LYE ON THE TABLE."

On November 2, the papers and request were
returned to Council, and on the fifth the Sheriff delivered the following order of Council to the court
of Quarter Sessions directed "To *Robert Lurting*,
Esq ; Mayor of the City of *New-York*, and the Rest
of the Magistrates for said City and County."

"*Whereas by an Order of this Board, of this Day,
some of* John Peter Zenger's *Journals, entitled*, The
New-York weekly Journal containing the freshest
Advices, foreign and domestick, No. 7, 47, 48, 49,
*were ordered to be burnt by the Hands of the common
Hangman, or Whipper, near the Pillory in this City,
on* Wednesday, *the 6th Instant, between the Hours of
Eleven and Twelve in the Forenoon, as containing in
them many Things tending to Sedition and Faction, to bring
His Majesty's Government into Contempt, and to disturb
the Peace thereof, and containing in them likewise, not
only Reflections upon His Excellency the Governour in particular, the Legislature in general, but also upon the most
considerable Persons in the most distinguished Stations
in the Province. It is therefore ordered, That the Mayor,
and Magistrates of this City, do attend at the Burning
of the several Papers or Journals aforesaid, Numbered as
above mentioned.*"

Upon reading the order, the court forbade its
entry in the records at that time, and some of the
members declared that if it was entered they would
at the same time enter their protest against it.

On the sixth of November Governor Cosby
issued two proclamations, one offering a reward of

fifty pounds for the conviction of the author of the articles in the " Journal ; " the other offering a reward of twelve pounds for the conviction of the author of the scandalous songs.

On the same day the sheriff, John Symes, moved the court for compliance with the order, when one of the Aldermen read the following protest, which was approved by all the Aldermen, either expressly or by their not objecting to it :

" And whereas this Court conceives, they are only to be commanded by the King's Mandatory Writs, authorized by Law, to which they conceive they have the Right of shewing Cause why they don't obey them, if they believe them improper to be obey'd, or by ORDERS, which have some known Laws to authorize them; and whereas this Court conceives, THIS ORDER to be no Mandatory Writ warranted by Law, nor knows of no Law that authorized the making of the Order aforesaid ; So they think themselves under no Obligation to obey it : Which Obedience, they think, would be in them, an opening a Door for arbitrary Commands, which, when once opened, they know not what Dangerous Consequences may attend it. Wherefore this Court conceives it self bound in Duty, (for the Preservation of the Rights of this Corporation, and as much as they can, the Liberty of the Press, and the People of the Province, since an Assembly of the Province, and several Grand Juries, have refused to meddle with the Papers, when applied to by the Council) *to protest against the ORDER aforesaid and to forbid all the Members of this Corporation, to pay any Obedience to it*, until it be shown to this Court, that the same is Authorized by some known Law, which they neither know nor believe that it is."

On reading the protest Francis Harison, the Recorder, who was one of the Council present at the making of the order, was called on to show by what authority the order was made. He cited in its support the case of Dr. Sacheverel's sermon, which was ordered burnt by the hangman, and said the Mayor and Aldermen of London were ordered to attend. To this one of the Aldermen replied that the cases were not parallel, that Sacheverel and his sermon had been impeached by the House of Commons and prosecuted before the House of Lords, which had cognizance of such affairs, and that he had a fair hearing for his defense; and after such hearing he and his sermon had been justly and legally condemned; that the judgment did not direct the Aldermen but only the Mayor and Sheriffs of London and Middlesex, to be present at the burning, and that the order on the judgment did not include the Mayor.

It was further said that if the Recorder could show that the Council had the same authority as the House of Lords in the matter and that the papers had been legally condemned the case of Sacheverel would be in point. And he was asked to produce his authorities warranting this order, to which he made reply, that " he did not carry his Books about with him." It was suggested that he could send a constable for them. He then arose and cited the case of Bishop Burnet's Pastoral Letter which was ordered burnt by the High Bailiff of Westminster, "upon which he abruptly went away, without waiting for an Answer or promising to bring his Books, and did not return sitting the Court."

It was then moved that the protest be entered, but this was objected to on the ground that the order would then have to be entered and that " it was not fit to take any Notice of IT," and the court then agreed no entry should be made of either. The sheriff then asked that the court would direct their Whipper to perform the order, but they replied that as he was the officer of the Corporation they would give no such order.

Zenger says: "Soon after which the Court adjourned, and did not attend the Burning of the Papers. Afterwards about Noon, the Sheriff after reading the Numbers of the several Papers which were ordered to be burnt, delivered them into the Hands of his own Negroe, and ordered him to put them into the Fire, which he did, at which Mr. Recorder, *Jeremiah Dunbar*, Esq ; and several of the Officers of the Garrison attended."

On Sunday, November 17th, Zenger was arrested under the following warrant of the Council:

"It is ordered that the Sheriff for the City of *New-York*, do forthwith take and apprehend *John Peter Zenger*, for printing and publishing several Seditious Libels dispersed throughout his Journals or News Papers, entitled, *The New-York Weekly Journal, containing the freshest Advices, foreign and domestick;* as having in them many Things, tending to raise

Factions and Tumults, among the People of this Province, inflaming their Minds with Contempt of His Majesty's Government, and greatly disturbing the Peace thereof, and upon his taking the said *John Peter Zenger, to commit him to the Prison or common Goal of said City and County*.

Fred. Morris, *D. Cl. Con.*"

The issuing of this warrant by the Council was an extraordinary proceeding. In the first place, it was extremely doubtful if the Council had power to issue such process, especially as with the Governor they constituted a court for the correction of errors and appeals. And in the second place, the warrant by its terms was merely the expression of the opinion of the Council, supported by no evidence, and with no opportunity offered to the accused to defend himself.

Zenger was for several days denied the use of pen, ink and paper, and liberty of speech with any person. The Monday after his arrest the "Journal" did not appear, and in the next number he issued the following notice:

"*To all my Subscribers and Benefactors who take my weekly* Journall. *Gentlemen, Ladies and Others;*

"AS you last week were Disappointed of my Journall, I think it Incumbent upon me, to publish my Apoligy which is this. On the Lords Day, the Seventeenth of this Instant I was Arrested, taken and Imprisoned in the common Goal of this City, by Virtue of a Warrant from the *Governour*, and the Honorable *Francis Harrison*, Esq; and others in Council of which (God willing) Yo'l have a Coppy whereupon I was

46

put under such Restraint that I had not the Liberty of Pen, Ink, or Paper, or to see, or speak with People, till upon my Complaint to the Honourable the Chief Justice, at my appearing before him upon my *Habias Corpus* on the *Wednesday* following.   Who discountenanced that Proceeding, and therefore I have had since that time the Liberty of Speaking through the Hole of the Door, to my Wife and Servants by which I doubt not yo'l think me sufficiently Excused for not sending my last weeks *Journall*, and I hope for the future by the Liberty of Speaking to my servants thro' the Hole of the Door of the Prison, to entertain you with my weokly *Journall* as formerly.   *And am your obliged Humble Servant.*"

A habeas corpus was procured by his counsel returnable on the 20th, when it was insisted that the prisoner should be admitted to reasonable bail.   Zenger made affidavit that he was not worth forty pounds over and above his debts, wearing apparel, and the tools of his trade.   But, nevertheless, it was ordered by De Lancey that he might be admitted to bail in four hundred pounds with two sureties, each for two hundred pounds.   Zenger says, " And as this was Ten Times more, than was in my Power to counter-secure any Person in giving Bail for me, I conceived I could not ask any to become my Bail on these Terms ; and I returned to Goal, where I lay until *Tuesday*, the 28*th* of *January*, 1734, 5 ; . . . . and the Grand Jury having found nothing against me, I Expected to have been discharged from my Imprisonment; But my Hopes proved vain; for the Attorney General then charged me by *Information*, for Printing and publishing Parts of my Journals No. 13 and 23 as being *false, scandalous, malicious, and seditious.*"

There was no attempt made to justify DeLancey's arbitrary refusal to admit Zenger to reasonable bail. It was done in the hope that if he was imprisoned the "Journal" would be discontinued. No further action was taken until the 15th of April, when Alexander and Smith, in behalf of Zenger, offered the following exceptions to the commissions of DeLancey and Philipse:

"1*st*. For that the Authority of a Judge of the King's Bench, in that Part of *Great Britain* called *England*, by which the Cognizance of this Cause is claimed, is by the said Commission granted to the Honourable *James DeLancey*, Esq; aforesaid, only *during Pleasure*; whereas that Authority (by a Statute in that Case made and provided) ought to be granted *during good Behaviour*.

2*d*. For that by the said Commission, the Jurisdiction and Authority of a Justice of the Court of Common Pleas at *Westminster*, in that Part of *Great Britain*, called *England*, is granted to the said *James DeLancey*, Esq; which Jurisdiction and Authority, cannot be granted to, and exercised by, anyone of the Justices of the King's Bench.

3*d*. For that the Form of the said Commission, is not founded on nor warranted by the Common Law, nor any Statute of *England*, nor of *Great Britain*, nor any Act of Assembly of this Colony.

4*th*. For that it appears by the Commission aforesaid, that the same is granted under the Seal of this Colony, by His Excellency, *William Cosby*,

JOHN PETER ZENGER

Esq.; Governour thereof; and it appears not, that the same was granted, neither was the same granted, by and with the Advice and Consent of His Majesty's Council of this Colony; without which Advice and Consent, His Excellency could not grant the same."

Counsel then asked that their objection be filed. To which DeLancey said, "That they ought well to consider the Consequences of what they offered." To which they both replied they had well considered what they offered and all the consequences, and Smith added that he was so well satisfied with the right of the subject to take an exception to the commission of a judge, if he thought such commission illegal, that he dared venture his life on that point. Argument on the exceptions was postponed until Wednesday, the 16th, when counsel asked to be heard on,

1st. That the subject has a right to take such exceptions if they judge the commissions illegal.

2nd. That the exceptions tendered were legal and valid.

The Chief Justice then replied, "That they would neither hear nor allow the Exceptions; *for* (said he) *you thought to have gained a great Deal of Applause and Popularity by opposing this Court, as you did the Court of Exchequer; but you have brought it to that Point, That either,* We must go from the Bench or you from the Barr : *Therefore We exclude you and Mr.* Alexander *from the Barr.*" An order was then delivered to the clerk as follows:

"At a Supream Court of Judicature held for the

JOHN PETER ZENGER

Province of *New-York* at the City Hall of the City of *New-York* on *Wednesday*, the 16*th* Day of *April*, 1735:

PRESENT,

The Honourable *James DeLancey*, Esq.; Chief Justice.

The Honourable *Frederick Philipse*, Esq.; Second Justice.

James Alexander, *Esq., and* William Smith, *Attornies of this Court, having presumed* (notwithstanding they were forewarned by the Court of their DISPLEASURE if they should do it) *to sign, and having actually signed, and put into Court, Exceptions, in the name of* John Peter Zenger; *thereby denying the Legality of the Judges their Commissions;* tho' *in the usual Form,* and the being of this Supreme Court. *It is therefore ordered, that for the said Contempt, the said* James Alexander, *and* William Smith, *be excluded from any farther Practice in this Court, and that their Names be struck out of the Roll of Attornies of this Court.*"

per Cur'. JAMES LYNE, *Cl.*

After the order was read Alexander asked if it was the order of Justice Philipse as well as of the Chief Justice, that they might know how to have their relief. They both replied it was their order. Counsel then said that the court were mistaken in the wording of the order, that the exceptions were only to their commissions and not to the being of the court and asked that it might be altered accordingly. Smith said that the court might well exist

50

though the commissions of all the judges were void, which the Chief Justice confessed to be true, but the order was not amended. It was then asked whether the court overruled or rejected the exceptions. The Chief Justice said that he did not understand the difference. To which it was replied that if they were rejected they could not appear upon the proceedings, but the defendant was entitled to have them made so by a bill of exceptions; if they overruled them they only declared them not sufficient to hinder them from proceeding by virtue of those commissions and the exceptions would remain as records of the court and ought to be entered on the record of the case as part of the proceedings.

The Chief Justice then replied, "They must remain upon the File, to warrant what we have done; as being Part of the Record of the Proceedings in that Cause, he said, you may speak to that Point tomorrow." But on the eighteenth the court would hear neither Alexander nor Smith insisting that they had said they could get some person to speak for them. Counsel also expressed a doubt as to whether they had been disbarred as attornies as well as counselors, but were informed by the court that their order meant to exclude them from their whole practice at the bar.

This remarkable order of disbarment well illustrates the intense and bitter partisanship which characterized the actions of the government party. It is the only instance in legal history of such an order being issued for such a reason. As Alexander and Smith said subsequently in their complaint to the Assembly:

JOHN PETER ZENGER

" . . . We would humbly ask, whether any Thing can be more Arbitrary, than these Gentlemen's pretending to make the Notification of their *Displeasure* to be the Rule of our Conduct?"

"We ever thought it lawful for any of our Clients to bring the Commissions of the Judges to the Touchstone of the Law: But we never thought it so necessary as in this Case. We conceived the Innocency of our Client, no sufficient Security, while we esteemed the Governour his Prosecutor, who had his Judges in his Power. We had too much Reason for Caution from the Conduct of the Chief Justice. We heard, how His Honor had vented his Displeasure against him, when he accidentally met him in the Streets, on a *Sunday* before his Arrest. We had been near Witnesses to sundry warm Charges, and moving Addresses, to several Grand Juries, plainly levelled against *Zenger*, and with Intention to procure his Country to Indict him. And we saw his Name amongst that Committee of Council, which conferred with a Committee of this House, in order to procure a Concurrence to condemn some of *Zenger's Journals*, without giving him Opportunity to defend them. We heard that the Chief Justice was a principal Manager upon that Conference, and spoke much on that Occasion. We saw his name among those who issued that Order of the Council, which commanded the Magistrates of this City to attend the Burning of some of those *Journals*; and which sets forth; *that they had been condemned by the Council to be burnt by the Hands of the common Hangman*. We much doubted of the Legality of these Extraordinary Proceedings, of the Chief Justice, and the Rest of the Council. We saw the Chief Justice's Name, among those, who issued that Extraordinary Warrant, by which our Client was apprehended. We had seen his Want of Moderation, in demanding Security in *Eight Hundred Pounds*, when *Zenger* was brought before him, on his *Habeas Corpus*, tho' the Act only required Bail to be taken, *according to the Quality of the Prisoner, and the Nature of the Offence.* - - - - We had heard the Chief Justice declare, in the fullest Court we had ever seen in that Place, *That if a Jury found Zenger Not Guilty, they would be perjured*; or Words to that Effect; and even this before any Information in Form was lodged against him. As for Justice *Philipse*, we had been told, how vigorous and Active he had been, in the General Assembly, to procure the Concurrence of that House, with the Council, in the Order for Burning of *Zenger's* Papers; even before they were legally Condemned; and Addressing the Governour to issue a Proclamation with Promise of Reward for the Discovery of the Writers of them; and in an Order for Prosecuting the poor Printer. We wish we had no Occasion to repeat these Things, to shew the Motives of our Conduct; had we not been obliged thereto, in Order to vindicate our selves, we had much rather that they had been buried in Silence: But under these many Forewarnings, what could we, what ought we to do for our Client? Surely every Thing that was lawful and likely to contribute to his Safety. And in taking the Exception, we conceived some Benefit would accrue: For, had the Exception been allowed, the Dependence of the Judges on the Governour (which we thought dangerous to our Client) would be in some Measure removed, and the Judges have stood more indifferent between the real Parties; Had it been over-ruled, yet we had Reason to think, that it might have proved some Check to an exorbitant Stretch of Power; because, That *dernier RE-SORT*, the Commissions had been judged illegal, any Abuse offered, after Exceptions taken, might have rendered the Judges, not only civilly, but criminally, answerable for their Conduct."

"It was then full *two and Thirty Years*, since one of us had first applied to the Study of Law (a Time near equal to the whole Age of either of these Judges) and who for several Years had been one of the oldest Practitioners at the Barr here; the other of us did not want *two* months of *Ten* Years standing there, and had a good Share of Practice for several Years, before either of these Judges were known to have had any knowledge of the Law, or pretended to have made it a Part of their Study. What has been our Character and Reputation for Ability, or Integrity, in our Practice, and Morals, belongs not to us to declare: But we hope, our being employed in almost all the Causes within this Colony, of any Importance, that have depended for several Years last past, may, as to those Points, in some Measure, witness in our Favour."

"That we were perfectly innocent, and did our Duty in the Case of *Zenger*, is what we have the clearest Sense of. That the Law was with us, *in the Right of the Subject to take an Exception*, is what we will steadfastly maintain ; and challenge these Gentlemen to prove the Contrary. Had we err'd ; must a Man loose his Livelihood for an innocent Mistake ? Must his Brains be beat out, because they are not cast in the same Mould with another Man's ? Had we been guilty of *Contempt*, as is groundlessly pretended ; is there no Proportion between Offences ? Is there no Distinction between Punishments ? Must we be put to starve, or to seek our Bread in a new Country, or in a new Manner of Life, for one Contempt ? If these Things are to be tolerated, . . . hard will be the case of Lawyers, who are sworn *To use their Offices according to their Learning and Discretion.* Yet, by this Rule, we must not be permitted the Use of either. Instead of consulting our Law Books, and doing what we think consistent therewith, for the Benefit of our Clients, we must study in GREAT MEN'S CAUSES, only *what will PLEASE the Judges, and what will most flatter Men in Power."*

"We are loath to declare what we think these Gentlemen deserve : We wish their Amendment, not their Destruction. But we humbly request, that this House would come to such Resolutions upon this Case, as they shall think just and necessary, for the Preservation of the Rights and Liberties of the People ; and such Measures may be taken, as, that we may be restored to the Liberty of our Practice ; that our Clients may have that Service from us, which they have a Right to demand ; and the Publick Administration of Justice, that Help which we are able to afford ; and that we may have the Means of common Justice, for Recovering such Damages from the Gentlemen as we have suffered, or shall suffer, until we are restored to our Employments."

The real reason for the order of disbarment was that by means of it the court party expected to be victorious at the trial as they well knew there were no attorneys in the Province who would be so vigorous and bold in defense of the printer as Alexander and Smith. John Chambers was assigned by the court as counsel for Zenger; he entered a plea of not guilty to the information but as Zenger says, "But as to the Point. *Whether my Exceptions should be a part of the Record - - - - thought not proper to speak to it.*"

Chambers then moved for a struck jury and a day for trial. The court allowed his motion for a jury and set the trial for August fourth. The clerk drew the jury on the evening of July 29th, and was attended by some of Zenger's friends. Instead of producing the freeholders' book, he made a list of forty-eight names which he said had been taken from the book. The list was objected to on behalf of Zenger as containing the names of many persons who were not freeholders, of others who were holding office at the Governors' pleasure, of some who had been defeated in the recent city election and of still others who "were the Governours' Baker, Taylor Shoemaker, Candlemaker, Joiner &c."

But in spite of these objections the clerk refused to strike the names out of the freeholders' book, nor would he hear objections to any of the persons on his list, saying the defendant could strike out any objectionable persons; to which it was replied there would not be twelve men left, and by law they could only strike out twelve names. The following day, however, on motion the clerk was ordered to take forty-eight names from the freeholders' book as usual, and to allow of such objections as were just.

John Chambers was a young man without much experience in the law, and had been one of the signers of the address complimenting Cosby's administration, and was really affiliated with the court party. Accordingly Alexander and Smith had, immediately upon their disbarment, begun to look for a capable man to try the case. They first wrote to John Kinsey, a Pennsylvania attorney, and a prominent man in Philadelphia, but he replied, saying, "I have inclination enough to serve you in any just Cause in which I am at Liberty, but as I stand Circumstanced at Present And in the Case you mention I think, I cannot do it. Divers Letters have lately passed between the Governor and myself, which, tho' they do not relate to this Affair, are of such Import that I cannot undertake against him without subjecting myself to be reflected on as doing what is dishonorable. And for that Reason must desire your Excuse for not appearing in Zenger's Cause."

They then selected Andrew Hamilton, also of Philadelphia; and Lewis Morris, Jr., wrote to Alexander as follows about securing his services:

"On Saturday morning, according to my promise, I met at Smith's with Captain Norris, where I was in hopes of seeing you. We then talked of writing to Andrew Hamilton, which I consented to do as well as Norris. Smith acquiesced with us. I think it absolutely necessary that he be wrote to to come to plead Zenger's cause. I declare to you I shall be willing to contribute my part to so Necessary an Expense, and if you think it of service that I subscribe the Letter you send joyntly with you and Smith, I hereby give you full power and Authority to affix my name when you and Smith have signed."

Andrew Hamilton had long been prominent in Pennsylvania affairs. He is said to have been born in Scotland in 1656. There is some uncertainty about his real name as at one time he was called Trent. He was Attorney General of Pennsylvania, 1717–26; Recorder of Philadelphia, 1727; Vice Admiralty Judge, 1737; Speaker of the Assembly from 1729 to 1739, with the exception of one year. He and Alexander had long been associates in many cases. In 1726 when Hamilton was in London probating the will of William Penn in Chancery, he wrote Alexander of the delays and difficulties of the practice, saying : " Could ye Devil be obliged to appear to a Bill of Chancery, and to bear ye Costs and attend ye Issue of ye Cause, I would for any ill turn he should do me, doom him to endure this Curse instead of going to Hell."

On being written to, Hamilton promptly expressed his willingness to come on and try the case. He was at that time nearly eighty years of age. He was a great sufferer from gout, and for a while it was quite uncertain whether he would be able to appear. His intellect, however, was vigorous and unclouded. He had the reputation of being the

JOHN PETER ZENGER

best advocate in North America, and was probably
the only American who was ever admitted a bencher
of Gray's Inn.

CHAPTER III

THE court party up to this time had in a certain way carried everything before it. Van Dam had not secured the payment of his debt from Cosby, Morris had been removed from the bench, Zenger's counsel were disbarred, Zenger himself was in prison and soon to be tried, and all these things had come about in an hitherto vain attempt to oppose the aggressions of arbitrary power. The situation was disheartening, indeed, to the leaders of the popular party. But, on the other hand, the "Journal" still made its appearance every Monday, the business being ably managed by Zenger's wife, who received her instructions from her husband through the hole in the door of his cell, and the spirit of the people raged more violently and with an increased bitterness as they realized how completely they were at the mercy of Cosby and his judges.

There were then considerably less than one thousand men in New York County possessing the necessary qualifications for jury duty, so the articles in the " Journal " during Zenger's imprisonment were carefully written with the intention of thoroughly instructing all possible jurors not only on the real questions at issue, but also to acquaint them with their rights and duties in cases of libel.

The day appointed for the trial was August 4, 1735. The place, the City Hall, built in 1700, on the corner of Nassau and Wall streets, the finest building in the city. Long before the opening of the court the little room was crowded to its utmost capacity. Every class in the community was represented. The majority of the people felt that they had assembled not merely to witness the trial of the printer for libel, but that here the last fight was to be made against the administration which was so arbitrarily oppressive. If Zenger should be found guilty, surely their last hope of relief would be gone, they would be powerless to resist any hardship which their Governor might see fit to impose.

On the other hand, Zenger's acquittal would mean a decided check to the evils from which they suffered, a vindication of their demands and of the principles for which they contended, and would give them courage to continue their efforts to rid themselves of their despicable Governor. In fact, the result of the trial would be so far-reaching in its consequences, and of such momentous importance to every inhabitant of the Province, that it is doubtful if any trial ever held in America had a more thoroughly interested and attentive audience.

After the entry of the judges, clad in their dignified court robes of the period and wearing their elaborate wigs, the following jury was obtained:

Thomas Hunt, Foreman,	Harmanus Rutgers,
Samuel Weaver,	Benjamin Hildreth,
Stanly Holmes,	Edward Man,
John Bell,	Andries Marschalk,
Egbert van Borsom,	Abraham Keteltas,
John Goelet,	Hercules Wendover.

As these men took their seats the leaders of the popular party must have had an intimation of their final success. Harmanus Rutgers had served on the first grand jury in January, 1734, while at least seven of the twelve were of Dutch ancestry; and though the old feeling of animosity on the part of the Dutch towards the English was practically extinguished, yet Cosby's conduct served to keep alive the few remaining sparks. If the way were pointed out, these men could be relied on for a favorable verdict for this reason alone.

The retention of Hamilton for Zenger's defense had been kept very quiet and was known to but few people. Consequently, his appearance in court produced a great dismay among Cosby's friends, and a corresponding degree of security in the popular party, as they had known that Chambers was unequal to the task imposed upon him. Hamilton was equipped with the careful study and research of Alexander and Smith, who sat near him in court, and a reference to Alexander's brief shows that Hamilton followed the line of defense there set forth. It might have been supposed that the court, judging from its previous conduct, would have found some pretext for excluding Hamilton from the case, but on account of his reputation they did not dare to proceed to such an arbitrary length.

It has seemed proper to give the trial in detail, and it accordingly is given, using the text of the First Edition printed by Zenger in 1736. The only change from the printed text is that all reference to the matters and proceedings had before the trial and leading up to it, have been left out, as they are fully treated in other parts of this work.

The articles embodied in the Information were taken from Numbers 13 and 23 of the " Journal." It would be interesting to know who the authors of these articles were, but the only clew is to be found in their respective styles. Judged by this, the first was written by James Alexander, and the second by Lewis Morris.

The Attorney General opened the case by reading the Information.

Mr. *Attorney.* May it please Your Honours, and you Gentlemen of the Jury; the Information now before the Court, and to which the Defendant *Zenger* has pleaded *Not Guilty,* is an Information for printing and publishing *a false, scandalons and seditious Libel,* in which his Excellency the Governour of this Province, who is the King's immediate Representative here, is greatly and unjustly scandalized, as a Person that has no Regard to Law nor Justice; with much more, as will appear upon reading the Information. This of Libelling is what has always been discouraged as a Thing that tends to create Differences among Men, ill Blood among the People, and oftentimes great Bloodshed between the Party Libelling and the Party Libelled. There can be no Doubt but you Gentlemen of the Jury will have the same ill Opinion of such Practices, as the Judges have always shewn upon such Occasions: But I shall say no more at the Time, until you hear the Information, which is as follows.

' *New-York*, Supream Court.

' of the Term of *January* in the Eighth Year
' of the Reign of our Sovereign Lord King
' GEORGE, the second, &c.

' *New-York*, ss. BE it remembered, That *Rich-*
' *ard Bradley*, Esq; Attorney General of Our Sover-
' eign Lord the King, for the Province of *New-*
' *York*, who for Our said Lord the King in this
' Part prosecutes, in his own proper Person comes
' here into the Court of Our said Lord the King
' and for our said Lord the King gives the Court
' here to understand, and be informed, That *John*
' *Peter Zenger*, late of the City of New-*York*,
' Printer, (being a seditious Person, and a frequent
' Printer and Publisher of false News and seditious
' Libels, and wickedly and maliciously devising the
' Government of Our said Lord the King of this
' His Majesty's Province of *New-York*, under the
' Administration of His Excellency *William Cosby*,
' Esq; Captain General and Governour in Chief of
' the said Province, to traduce, scandalize and vilify,
' and His Excellency the said Governour, and the

' Ministers and Officers of Our said Lord the King of
' and for the said Province to bring into Suspicion
' and the ill Opinion of the Subjects of Our said
' Lord the King residing within the said Province)
' the Twenty-eighth Day of *January*, in the seventh
' Year of the Reign of Our Sovereign Lord *George*
' the second, by the Grace of God of *Great Britain*,
' *France* and *Ireland*, King, Defender of the Faith,
' &c. at the City of *New-York*, *did falsely, seditiously*
' *and scandalously* print and publish, and cause to be
' printed and published, a certain *false, malicious, se-*
' *ditious, scandalous* Libel, entituled *The New-York*
' *Weekly Journal, containing the freshest Advices for-*
' *eign and domestick*; in which Libel (of and concern-
' ing His Excellency the said Governour, and the
' Ministers and Officers of Our said Lord the King,
' of and for the said Province) among other Things
' therein contained are these Words, " *Your Appear-*
" *ance in Print at last*, gives a Pleasure to many, tho'
" the most wish you had come fairly into the open
" Field, and not appeared behind *Retrenchments* made
" of the supposed Laws against Libelling, and of
" what other Men have said and done before; these
" *Retrenchments*, Gentlemen, may soon be shewn to
" you and all Men to be weak, and to have neither
" Law nor Reason for their Foundation, so cannot
" long stand you in stead : Therefore, you had much
" better as yet leave them, and come to what *the*
" *People of this City and Province* (the City and Prov-
" ince of *New-York* meaning) think are the Points
" in Question (*to witt*) *They* (the People of the City
" and Province of *New-York* meaning) *think as Mat-*

" *ters now stand, that their* LIBERTIES *and* PROP-
" ERTIES *are precarious, and that* SLAVERY *is like*
" *to be intailed on them and their Posterity, if some past*
" *Things be not amended, and this they collect from many*
" *past Proceedings.*" (Meaning many of the past Pro-
' ceedings of His Excellency the said Governour, and
' of the Ministers and Officers of our said Lord the
' King, of and for the said Province.) And said the
' Attorney General of Our said Lord the King, for
' Our said Lord the King, likewise gives the Court
' here to understand and be informed, that the said
' *John Peter Zenger* afterwards (*to wit*) the eighth Day
' of *April,* in the seventh Year of the Reign of Our
' said Lord the King, at the City of *New-York* afore-
' said, did *falsely, seditiously and scandalously* print and
' publish, and cause to be printed and published, an-
' other *false, malicious, seditious and scandalous* Li-
' bel, entitled *the New York Weekly Journal contain-*
' *ing the freshest Advices foreign and domestic.* In which
' Libel (of and concerning the Government of the
' said Province of *New-York,* and of and concerning
' His Excellency the said Governour, and the Minis-
' ters and Officers of Our said Lord the King, of and
' for the said Province) among other Things therein
' contained, are these Words, " *One of our Neighbors*
" (one of the Inhabitants of *New-Jersey* meaning)
" *being in Company, observing the Strangers* (some of the
" Inhabitants of *New-York* meaning) *full of Complaints,*
" *endeavoured to persuade them to remove into* Jersey ; *to*
" *which it was replied, that would be leaping out of the*
" *Frying Pan into the Fire ; for, says he, we both are*
" *under the same Governour* (His Excellency the said

JOHN PETER ZENGER

" Governour meaning) *and your Assembly have shewn*
" *with a Witness what is to be expected from them; one*
" *that was then moving to* Pensilvania (meaning one
" that was then removing from *New-York,* with in-
" tent to reside at *Pensilvania*) *to which Place it is re-*
" *ported several considerable Men are removing* (from
" *New-York* meaning) *expressed in Terms very moving,*
" *much Concern for the Circumstances of* New-York (the
" bad Circumstances of the Province and People of
" *New-York* meaning) " *seemed to think them very much*
" *owing to the Influence that some Men* (whom he called
" *Tools*) *had in the Administration* (meaning the Ad-
" ministration of Government of the said Province
" of *New-York*) *said he was now going from them, and*
" *was not to be hurt by any Measures they should take,*
" *but could not help having some Concern for the Welfare*
" *of his Country-Men, and should be glad to hear that*
" *the Assembly* (meaning the General Assembly of the
" Province of *New-York*) *would exert themselves as be-*
" *came them, by shewing that they have the Interest of*
" *their Country more at Heart, than the Gratification of*
" *any private View of any of their Members, or being at*
" *all affected, by the Smiles or Frowns of a Governour*
" (His Excellency the said Governour meaning) *both*
" *which ought equally to be despised, when the Interest of*
" *their Country is at stake. You, says he, complain of*
" *the Lawyers, but I think the Law it self is at an End,*
" WE (the People of the Province of *New-York*
" meaning) SEE MENS DEEDS DESTROYED,
" JUDGES ARBITRARILY DISPLACED, NEW
" COURTS ERECTED WITHOUT CONSENT
" OF THE LEGISLATURE (within the Province

" *New-York*, meaning) BY WHICH IT SEEMS
"TO ME, TRYALS BY JURIES ARE TAKEN
"AWAY WHEN A GOVERNOUR PLEASES,
" (His Excellency the said Governour meaning)
"MEN OF KNOWN ESTATES DENIED
"THEIR VOTES, CONTRARY TO THE RE-
"CEIVED PRACTICE, THE BEST EXPOSI-
"TOR OF ANY LAW : *Who is then in that Prov-*
" *ince* (meaning the Province of *New-York*,) *that call*
" (can call meaning) *any Thing his own, or enjoy any*
" *Libery* (Liberty meaning) *longer than those in the*
" *Administration* (meaning the Administration of Gov-
" ernment of the said Province of *New-York*) *will*
" *condescend to let them do it, for which Reason I have*
" *left it*, (the Province of *New-York* meaning) *as I*
" *believe more will.*" To the great Disturbance of
' the Peace of the said Province of *New-York*, to the
' Great Scandal of Our said Lord the King, of His
' Excellency the said Governor, and of all others con-
' cerned in the Administration of the Government of
' the said Province, and against the Peace of Our
' Sovereign Lord the King His Crown and Dignity,
' &c. Whereupon the said Attorney General of Our
' said Lord the King, for Our said Lord the King,
' prays the Advisement of the Court here, in the
' Premises, and the due Process of the Law, against
' him the said *John Peter Zenger*, in this Part to be
' done, to answer to Our said Lord the King of and
' in the Premises, &c.

' *R. Bradley*, Attorney General.

To this Information the Defendant has pleaded
Not Guilty, and we are ready to prove it.

JOHN PETER ZENGER

Mr. Chambers *has not been pleased to favour me with his Notes, so I cannot, for fear of doing him Injustice, pretend to set down his Argument; But here Mr.* Chambers *set forth very clearly the Nature of a Libel, the great Allowances that ought to be made for what Men speak or write, That in all Libels there must be some particular Persons so clearly pointed out, that no Doubt must remain about who is meant; That he was in hopes* Mr. Attorney *would fail in his Proof, as to this Point; and therefore desired that he would go on to examine his Witnesses.*

Then Mr. *Hamilton*, who at the Request of some of my Friends, was so kind as to come from *Philadelphia* to assist me on the Tryal, spoke.

Mr. Hamilton. May it Please your Honour; I am concerned in this Cause on the Part of Mr. Zenger the Defendant. The Information against my Client was sent me, a few Days before I left Home, with some Instructions to let me know how far I might rely upon the Truth of those Parts of the Papers set forth in the Information, and which are said to be libellous. And tho' I am perfectly of the Opinion with the Gentleman who has just now spoke, on the same Side with me, as to the common Course of Proceedings, I mean in putting Mr. Attorney upon proving, that my Client printed and published those Papers mentioned in the Information; yet I cannot think it proper for me (without doing Violence to my own Principles) to deny the Publication of a Complaint, which I think is the Right of every free-born Subject to make, when the Matters so published can be supported with Truth;

and therefore I'll save Mr. Attorney the Trouble of examining his Witnesses to that Point; and I do (for my Client) confess, that he both printed and published the two News Papers set forth in the Information, and I hope in so doing he has committed no Crime.

Mr. Attorney. Then if Your Honour pleases, since Mr. *Hamilton* has confessed the Fact, I think our Witnesses may be discharged; we have no further Occasion for them.

Mr. Hamilton. If you brought them here, only to prove the Printing and Publishing of these News Papers, we have acknowledged that, and shall abide by it.

Here my Journeyman and two Sons (with several others subpoena'd by Mr. Attorney, to give Evidence against me) were discharged, and there was Silence in the Court for some Time.

Mr. Chief Justice. *Well Mr. Attorney, will you proceed?*

Mr. Attorney. Indeed, Sir, as Mr. *Hamilton* has confessed the Printing and Publishing these Libels, I think the Jury must find a Verdict for the King; for supposing they were true, the Law says that they are not the less libellous for that; nay indeed the Law says, their being true is an Aggravation of the Crime.

Mr. Hamilton. Not so neither, Mr. Attorney, there are two Words to that Bargain. I hope it is not our bare Printing and Publishing a Paper, that will make it a Libel: You will have something more to do, before you make my Client a Libeller;

for the Words themselves must be libellous, that is, *false, scandalous, and seditious*, or else we are not guilty.

As Mr. Attorney has not been pleased to favour us with his Argument, which he read, or with the Notes of it, we cannot take upon us to set down his Words, but only to show the Book Cases he cited, and the general Scope of his Argument, which he drew from those Authorities. He observed upon the Excellency, as well as Use of Government, and the great Regard and Reverence, which had been constantly paid to it, both under the Law and the Gospel. That by Government we were protected in our Lives, Religion and Properties; and that for these Reasons, great Care had always been taken to prevent every Thing that might tend to scandalize Magistrates, and others concerned in the Administration of the Government, especially the supreme Magistrate. And that there were many Instances of very severe Judgments, and of Punishments inflicted upon such, as had attempted to bring the Government into Contempt; by publishing false and scurrilous Libels against it, or by speaking evil and scandalous Words of Men in Authority; to the great Disturbance of the publick Peace. And to support this, he cited, 5 Coke 121. (Suppose it should be 125.) Wood's Instit. 430. 2 Lilly 168. 1 Hawkins 73. 11. 6. *From these Books he insisted, that a Libel was a malicious Defamation of any Person, expressed either in Printing or Writing, Signs or Pictures, to asperse the Reputation of one that is alive, or the Memory of one that is dead; if he is a private Man, the Libeller deserves a severe Punishment, but if it is against a Magistrate or other publick Person, it is a greater Offence; for this concerns not only the Breach of the Peace, but the Scandal of the Government; for what greater Scandal of Government can there be, than to have corrupt or wicked Magistrates to be appointed by the King, to govern his Subjects under him? And a greater Imputation to the State cannot be, than to suffer such corrupt Men to sit in the sacred Seat of Justice, or to have any Medling in, or concerning the Administration of Justice: And from the same Books Mr. Attorney insisted, that whether the Person defamed is a private Man or a Magistrate, whether living or Dead, whether the Libel is true or false, or if the Party against whom it is made is of good or evil Fame, it is nevertheless a Libel: For in a settled State of Government, the Party grieved ought to complain for every Injury done him, in the ordinary Course of the Law. And as to its Publication, the Law had taken so great Care of Men's Reputations, that if one maliciously repeats it, or sings it, in the Presence of another, or delivers the Libel or a Copy of it over, to scandalize the Party, he is to be punished as a Publisher of a Libel. He said it was likewise evident, that Libelling was an Offence against the Law of God. Act. XXIII. 5.* Then said *Paul*, I wist not, Brethren, that he was the High Priest: For it is written, thou shalt not speak evil of the Ruler of the People. 2 *Pet. X.* 11. Despise Government, presumptuous are they, self willed, they are not afraid to speak evil of Dignities, &c. *He then insisted that it was clear, both by the Law of God and Man, That it was a very great Offence to speak evil of, or to revile those in Authority over us; and that Mr. Zenger had offended in a most notorious and gross*

Manner, in scandalizing His Excellency our Governour, who is the King's immediate Representative, and the supream Magistrate of this Province: For can there be any Thing more scandalous said of a Governour than what is published in those Papers? Nay, not only the *Governour,* but both the Council and Assembly are scandalized; *for there it is plainly said, That* as Matters now stand, their Liberties and Properties are precarious, and that Slavery is like to be entailed on them and their Posterity. *And then again Mr.* Zenger *says,* The Assembly ought to despise the Smiles or Frowns of a Governour; That he thinks the Law is at an end; That we see Men's Deeds destroyed, Judges arbitrarily displaced, new Courts erected, without Consent of the Legislature; *And* That it seems Tryals by Juries are taken away when a Governour pleases; That none can call any Thing their own, longer than those in the Administration will condescend to let them do it. . . . *And Mr. Attorney added, that he did not know what could be said in Defense of a Man, that had so notoriously scandalized the Governour and principal Magistrates and Officers of the Government, by charging them with depriving the People of their Rights and Liberties, and taking away Tryals by Juries, and in short; putting an End to the Law itself. . . . If this was not a Libel, he said, he did not know what was one. Such Persons as will take those Liberties with Governours and Magistrates, he thought ought to suffer for stirring up Sedition and Discontent among the People. And concluded by saying, that the Government had been very much traduced and exposed by Mr. Zenger before he was taken Notice of;*

that at last it was the Opinion of the Governour and Council, that he ought not to be suffered to go on, to disturb the Peace of the Government; by publishing such Libels against the Governour, and the chief Persons in the Government; And therefore they had directed this Prosecution, to put a Stop to this scandalous and wicked Practice, of libelling and defaming his Majesty's Government and disturbing his Majesty's Peace.

Mr. Chambers *then sum'd up to the Jury, observing with great Strength of Reason on Mr. Attorney's Defect of Proof, that the Papers in the Information were* False, Malicious or Seditious, *which was incumbent on him to prove to the Jury, and without which they could not on their Oaths say,* That they were so, as charged.

Mr. *Hamilton.* May it please Your Honour; I agree with Mr. Attorney, that Government is a sacred Thing, but I differ very widely from him when he would insinuate, that the just Complaints of a Number of Men, who suffer under a bad Administration, is libelling that Administration. Had I believed that to be Law, I should not have given the Court the Trouble of hearing any Thing that I could say in this cause. I own, when I read the Information, I had not the Art to find out (without the Help of Mr. Attorney's *Innuendo's*) that the Governor was the Person meant in every Period of that News Paper; and I was inclined to believe, that they were wrote by some, who from an extraordinary Zeal for Liberty, had misconstrued the Conduct of some Persons in Authority into Crimes; and that Mr. Attorney out of his too great Zeal for Power, had exhibited this Information, to correct the Indiscretion of

JOHN PETER ZENGER

my Client; and at the same Time, to shew his Superiors the great Concern he had, lest they should be treated with any undue Freedom. But from what Mr. Attorney has just now said, *to wit*, That this Prosecution was directed by the Governour and Council, and from the extraordinary Appearance of People of all Conditions, which I observe in Court upon this Occasion, I have Reason to think, that those in the Administration have by this Prosecution some-thing more in View, and that the People believe they have a good deal more at Stake, than I apprehended: And therefore, as it is become my Duty, to be both plain and particular in this Cause, I beg Leave to bespeak the Patience of the Court.

I was in Hopes, as that terrible Court, where those dreadful Judgments were given, and that Law established, which Mr. Attorney has produced for Authorities to support this Cause, was long ago laid aside, as the most dangerous Court to the Liberties of the People of *England*, that ever was known in that Kingdom; that Mr. Attorney knowing this, would not have attempted to set up a Star-Chamber here, nor to make their Judgments a Precedent to us: For it is well known, that what would have been judg'd Treason in those Days for a Man to speak, I think, has since not only been practiced as lawful, but the contrary Doctrine has been held to be Law.

In *Brewster's* Case, for printing, *That the Subjects might defend their Rights and Liberties by Arms, in case the King should go about to destroy them*, he was told by the Chief Justice that it was a great

Mercy, he was not proceeded against for his Life; for that to say, the King could be resisted by Arms in any Case whatsoever, was express Treason. And yet we see since that Time, Dr. *Sacheverell* was sentenced in the highest Court in *Great Britain*, for saying, *That such a Resistance was not lawful*. Besides, as Times have made very great Changes in the Laws of *England*, so in my Opinion there is good Reason that Places should do so too.

Is it not surprising to see a Subject, upon his receiving a Commission from the King to be a Governor of a Colony in *America*, immediately imagining himself to be vested with all the Prerogatives belonging to the sacred Person of his Prince? And which is yet more astonishing, to see that a People can be so wild as to allow of, and acknowledge those Prerogatives and Exemptions, even to their own Destruction? Is it so hard a Matter to distinguish between the Majesty of our Sovereign, and the Power of a Governor of the Plantations? Is not this making very free with our Prince, to apply that Regard, Obedience and Allegiance to a Subject which is due only to Our Sovereign? And yet in all the Cases which Mr. Attorney has cited, to show the Duty and Obedience we owe to the Supreme Magistrate, it is the King that is there meant and understood, tho' Mr. Attorney is pleased to urge them as Authorities to prove the Heinousness of Mr. *Zenger's* offence against the Governor of *New-York*. The several Plantations are compared to so many large Corporations, and perhaps not improperly; and can any one give an Instance, that the

Mayor or Head of a Corporation, ever put in a Claim to the sacred Rights of Majesty? Let us not (while we are pretending to pay a great Regard to our Prince and His Peace) make bold to transfer that Allegiance to a Subject, which we owe to our King only. What strange Doctrine is it, to press every Thing for Law here which is so in *England?* I believe we should not think it a Favour, at present at least, to establish this Practice. In *England* so great a Regard and Reverence is had to the Judges,* that if any man strike another in *Westminster Hall,* while the Judges are sitting, he shall lose his Right Hand, and forfeit his Land and Goods, for so doing. And tho' the Judges here claim all the Powers and Authorities within this Government, that a Court of King's Bench has in *England,* yet I believe Mr. Attorney will scarcely say, that such a Punishment could be legally inflicted on a Man for committing such an Offence, in the Presence of the Judges sitting in any Court within the Province of *New-York.* The Reason is obvious; a Quarrel or Riot in *New-York* cannot possibly be attended with those dangerous Consequences that it might in *Westminster Hall;* nor (I hope) will it be alledged, than any Misbehaviour to a Governor in the Plantations will, or ought to be, judged of or punished, as a like Undutifulness would be, to Our Sovereign. From all which, I hope Mr. Attorney will not think it proper to apply his Law-Cases (to support the Cause of his Governor) which have only been judged, where the King's Safety or Honour was concerned.

---

*C. 3 *Inst.* 140.

JOHN PETER ZENGER

It will not be denied but that a Freeholder in the Province of *New-York* has as good a Right to the sole and separate Use of his Lands, as a Freeholder in *England*, who has a Right to bring an Action of Trespass against his Neighbour, for suffering his Horse or Cow to come and feed upon his Land or eat his Corn, whether inclosed or not inclosed; and yet I believe it would be looked upon as a strange Attempt, for one Man here, to bring an Action against another, whose Cattle and Horses feed upon his Grounds not inclosed, or indeed for eating and treading down his Corn, if that were not inclosed. Numberless are the Instances of this Kind that might be given, to shew, that what is good Law at one Time and in one Place, is not so at another Time and in another Place; so that I think, the Law seems to expect, that in these Parts of the World Men should take Care, by a good Fence, to preserve their Property, from the Injury of unruly Beasts. And perhaps there may be as good Reason why Men should take the same Care, to make an honest and upright Conduct a Fence and Security against the Injury of unruly Tongues.

Mr. Attorney. I don't know what the Gentleman means, by comparing Cases of Freeholders in *England* with the Freeholders here. What has this Case to do with Actions of Trespass, or Men's Fencing their Ground? The Case before the Court is, whether Mr. *Zenger* is guilty of Libelling His Excellency the Governor of *New-York*, and indeed the whole Administration of the Government? Mr. *Hamilton* has confessed the Printing and Publishing, and I think nothing is plainer, than that the Words in the Information are *scandalous, and tend to sedition, and to disquiet the Minds of the People of this Province*. And if such Papers are not Libels, I think it may be said, there can be no such Thing as a Libel.

Mr. Hamilton. May it please Your Honour; I cannot agree with Mr. Attorney: For tho' I freely acknowledge, that there are such Things as Libels, yet I must insist at the same Time, that what my Client is charged with, is not a Libel; and I observed just now, that Mr. Attorney in defining a Libel, made use of the Words, *scandalous, seditious, and tend to disquiet the People*; but (whether with Design or not I will not say) he omitted the Word *false*.

Mr. Attorney. I think I did not omit the Word *false*: But it has been said already, that it may be a Libel, notwithstanding it may be true.

Mr. Hamilton. In this I must still differ with Mr. Attorney; for I depend upon it, we are to be tried upon this Information now before the Court and Jury, and to which we have pleaded *Not Guilty*, and by it we are charged with Printing and publishing *a certain false, malicious, seditious and scandalous Libel*. This Word *false* must have some Meaning, or else how came it there? I hope Mr. Attorney will not say, he put it there by Chance, and I am of Opinion his Information would not be good without it. But to shew that it is the principal Thing which, in my Opinion, makes a Libel, I put the Case, the Information had been for printing and publishing a certain *true* Libel, would that be the same thing? Or could Mr. Attorney support such an Information by any Precedent in the *English* Law? No, the Falsehood makes the Scandal, and both make the Libel. And to shew the Court that I am in good Earnest, and to save the Court's Time, and Mr. Attorney's Trouble, I will agree, that if he can prove the Facts charged upon us, to be *false*, I'll own them to be *scandalous*, *seditious*, and *a Libel*. So the Work seems now to be pretty much shortened, and Mr. Attorney has now only to prove the Words *false*, in order to make us Guilty.

Mr. Attorney. We have nothing to prove; you have confessed the Printing and Publishing; but if it was necessary (as I insist it is not) how can we prove a Negative? But I hope some Regard will be had for the Authorities that have been produced, and that supposing all the Words to be true, yet that will not help them, that Chief Justice *Holt* in his Charge to the Jury, in the Case of *Tutchin*, made no Distinction, whether *Tutchin's* Papers were *true* or *false*; and as Chief Justice *Holt* has made no Distinction in that Case, so none ought to be made here; nor can it be shewn in all that Case, there was any Question made about their being *false* or *true*.

Mr. Hamilton. I did expect to hear, That a Negative cannot be proved; but every Body knows there are many Exceptions to that general Rule: For if a Man is charged with killing another, or stealing his Neighbour's Horse, if he is innocent in the one Case, he may prove the Man said to be killed, to be really alive; and the Horse said to be stolen, never to have been out of his Master's Stable. &c., and this, I think, is proving a Negative. But we save Mr. Attorney the Trouble of proving a Negative, and take the *Onus probandi* upon ourselves, and prove those very Papers that are called Libels to be *true*.

Mr. Ch. Justice. You cannot be admitted, Mr. *Hamilton*, to give the Truth of a Libel in Evidence. A Libel is not to be justified; for it is nevertheless a Libel that it is true.

Mr. Hamilton. I am sorry the Court has so soon resolved upon that Piece of Law; I expected first to have been heard to that Point. I have not in all my Reading met with an Authority that says, we cannot be admitted to give the Truth in Evidence, upon an information for a Libel.

Mr. Ch. Justice. The Law is clear, That you cannot justify a Libel.

Mr. Hamilton. I know that, may it please Your Honour, to be so; but, with Submission, I understand the Word, *justify*, there, to be a justification by Plea, as it is in the Case upon an Indictment for *Murder*, or an *Assault and Battery*; there the Prisoner cannot justify, but plead *Not Guilty*: Yet it will not be denied that he may, and always is admitted, to give the Truth of the Fact, or any other Matter, in Evidence, which goes to his Acquital; as in Murder, he may prove it was in Defence of his Life, his House, &c., and in Assault and Battery, he may give in Evidence, that the other Party struck first, and in both Cases he will be acquitted. And

JOHN PETER ZENGER

in this Sense I understand the Word *justify*, when applied to the Case before the Court.

Mr. Ch. Justice. I pray shew that you can give the Truth of a Libel in Evidence.

Mr. Hamilton. I am ready, both from what I understand to be the Authorities in the Case, and from the Reason of the Thing, to shew that we may lawfully do so. But here I beg leave to observe, That Informations for Libels is a Child, if not born, yet nursed up, and brought to full Maturity, in the Court of Star-Chamber.

Mr. Ch. Justice. Mr. *Hamilton*, you'll find your self mistaken ; for in *Coke's. Institutes* you'll find Informations for Libels, long before the Court of Star-Chamber.

Mr. Hamilton. I thank Your Honour ; that is an Authority I did propose to speak to by and by : But as you have mention'd it, I'll read that Authority now. I think it is in 3 *Co. Inst.* under Title *Libel;* it is the Case of *John de Northampton* for a Letter wrote to *Robert de Ferrers*, one of the King's privy Council,* concerning Sir *William Scot*, Chief Justice, and his Fellows ; but it does not appear to have been upon Information ; and I have good Grounds to say it was upon Indictment, as was the Case of *Adam de Ravensworth*, just mentioned before by Lord *Coke* under the same Title ; and I think there cannot be a greater, at least a plainer Authority for us, than the Judgment in the Case of *John de Northampton*, which my Lord has set down at large. *Et quia praedictus Johannes cognovit dictam Litteram*

---

* *Coke* 3 *Inst.* 174.

82

per se scriptam Roberto de Ferrers, qui est de Concilio Regis, qua litera continet in se nullam veritatem, &c. Now Sir, by this Judgment it appears the libellous Words were utterly false, and there the Falsehood was the Crime, and is the Ground of that Judgment: And is not that what we contend for? Do not we insist that the Falsehood makes the Scandal, and both make the Libel? And how shall it be known whether the Words are libellous, *that is, true* or *false*, but by admitting us to prove them *true*, since Mr. Attorney will not undertake to prove them *false?* Besides, is it not against common Sense, that a Man should be punished in the same Degree for a *true Libel* (if any such Thing could be) as for a *false one?* I know it is said, *That Truth makes a Libel the more provoking, and therefore the Offense is the greater, and consequently the Judgment should be the heavier.* Well, suppose it were so, and let us agree for once, *That Truth is a greater Sin than Falsehood;* Yet as the Offenses are not equal, and as the Punishment is arbitrary, *that is,* according as the Judges in their Discretion shall direct to be inflicted; is it not absolutely necessary that they should know, whether the Libel is *true* or *false*, that they may by that Means be able to proportion the Punishment? For, would it not be a sad Case, if the Judges, for want of a due Information, should chance to give as severe a Judgment against a Man for writing or publishing a Lie, as for writing or publishing a Truth? And yet this (with submission) as monstrous and ridiculous as it may seem to be, is the natural Consequence of Mr. Attorney's Doctrine, *That Truth makes a worse Libel than Falsehood,* and must follow from his not proving our Papers to be *false*, or not suffering us to prove them to be *true*. But this is only reasoning upon the Case, and I will now proceed to shew, what in my Opinion will be sufficient to induce the Court, to allow us to prove the Truth of the Words, which in the Information are called libellous. And first, I think there cannot be a greater Authority for us, than the Judgment I just now mentioned, in the Case of *John de North-ampton*, and that was in early Times, and before the Star Chamber came to its Fulness of Power and Wickedness. In that Judgment, as I observed, the *Falsehood* of the Letter which was wrote, is assigned as the very Ground of the Sentence. And agreeable to this it was urged by Sir *Robert Sawyer*,* in the Tryal of the Seven Bishops, *That the Falsity, the Malice, and Sedition of the Writing, were all Facts to be proved.* But here it may be said, Sir *Robert* was one of the Bishop's Council, and his Argument is not to be allowed for Law: But I offer it only to shew that we are not the first who have insisted, that to make a Writing a Libel, it must be *false*. And if the Argument of a Council must have no Weight, I hope there will be more Regard shewn to the Opinion of a Judge, and therefore I mention the Words of Justice *Powel* in the same Tryal, where he says (of the Petition of the Bishops, which was called a Libel, and upon which they were persecuted by Information), *That to make it a Libel, it must be false and malicious, and tend to Sedition;* and declared, *as he saw no Falsehood or Malice in it, he was of Opinion, that it was no Libel.*

---

* *State Tryals*, Vol. 4.

Now I should think this Opinion alone, in the Case of the King, and in a Case which that King had so much at Heart, and which to this Day has never been contradicted, might be a sufficient Authority, to entitle us to the Liberty of proving the *Truth* of the Papers, which in the Information are called *false, malicious, seditious and scandalous.* If it be objected, *that the Opinions of the other three Judges were against him,* I answer, That the Censures the Judgments of these Men have undergone, and the Approbation Justice *Powel's* Opinion, his judgment and Conduct upon that Tryal has met with, and the Honour he gained to himself, for daring to speak Truth at such a Time, upon such an Occasion, and in the Reign of such a King, is more than sufficient, in my humble Opinion, to warrant our insisting on his Judgment, as a full Authority to our Purpose, and it will lye upon Mr. Attorney to shew, that this Opinion has since that Time been denied to be Law, or that Justice *Powel* who delivered it, has ever been condemned or blamed for it, in any Law-Book extant at this Day, and this I will venture to say, Mr. Attorney cannot do. But to make this Point yet more clear, if any Thing can be clearer, I will on our Part proceed and shew, that in the Case of Sir *Samuel Barnardiston,* his Council, notwithstanding he stood before one of the greatest Monsters that ever presided in an *English* Court (Judge *Jefferies*), insisted on the Want of Proof to the *Malice* and *seditious Intent* of the Author, of what was called a *Libel*. And in the Case of *Tutchin,* which seems to be Mr. Attorney's chief Authority,

State Tryals, Vol. V. 549.

that Case is against him ; for he was upon his Tryal
put upon shewing the Truth of his Papers, but did
not, at least the Prisoner was asked, by the King's
Council whether he would say they were *true?* And
as he never pretended, that they were true, the Chief
Justice was not to say so. But the Point will still
be clearer on our Side from *Fuller's* Case, *For falsly
and wickedly causing to be printed a false and scandalous
Libel, in which (amongst other Things) were contained
these Words,* ' Mr. Jones *has also made Oath, That* ' he
' *paid* L. 5,000. *more by the late King's Order, to sev-*
' *eral Persons in Places of Trust, that they might com-*
' *pleat my Ruin, and invalidate me for ever. Nor is this*
' *all ; for the same Mr.* Jones *will prove by undeniable*
' *Witness and Demonstration, that he has distributed more*
' *than* L. 180,000. *in Eight Years last past, by the French*
' *King's Order, to Persons in publick Trust in this King-*
' *dom.*' Here you see is a scandalous and infamous
Charge against the late King ; here is a Charge no
less than High Treason against the *Men in publick
Trust,* for receiving Money of the *French King*, then
in actual War with the Crown of *Great Britain*; and
yet the Court were far from bearing him down with
that Star-Chamber Doctrine, *to wit, That it was no
matter, whether what he said was true or false*; no, on
the contrary, Lord Chief Justice *Holt* asks *Fuller, Can
you make it appear, they are true? Have you any Witnesses? You might have had* Subpoena's *for your Witnesses against this day. If you take upon you to write
such Things as you are charged with, it lies upon you to
prove them true, at your Peril. If you have any Wit-*

JOHN PETER ZENGER

nesses I will hear them. How came you to write those books which are not true? If you have any Witnesses, produce them. If you can offer any Matter to prove what you have wrote, let us hear it. Thus said, thus did, that great Man Lord Chief Justice *Holt*, upon a Tryal of the like Kind with ours, and the Rule laid down by him in this Case is, *That he who will take upon him to write Things, it lies upon him to prove them at his Peril.* Now, Sir, we have acknowledged the Printing and Publishing of those Papers, set forth in the Information, and (with the Leave of the Court) agreeable to the Rule laid down by Chief Justice *Holt*, we are ready to prove them to be true, at our Peril.

Mr. Ch. Justice. Let me see the book.

Here the Court had the case under Consideration, a considerable Time, and every one was silent.

Mr. Ch. Just. Mr. Attorney, you have heard what Mr. *Hamilton* has said, and the Cases he has cited, for having his Witnesses examined, to prove the Truth of the several Facts contained in the Papers set forth in the Information, what do you say to it?

Mr. Attorney. The Law in my opinion is very clear; they cannot be admitted to justify a Libel; for, by the Authorities I have already read to the Court, it is not the less a Libel because it is true. I think I need not trouble the Court with reading the Cases over again; the Thing seems to be very plain, and I submit it to the Court.

Mr. Ch. Just. Mr. *Hamilton*, the Court is of the Opinion, you ought not to be permitted to prove the Facts in the Papers: these are the Words of the Book. *' It is far from being a Justification of a Libel,*

' *that the Contents thereof are true, or that the Person*
' *upon whom it is made, had a bad Reputation, since the*
' *greater Appearance there is of Truth in any malicious*
' *Invective, so much the more provoking it is.*

Mr. Hamilton. These are Star Chamber Cases, and I was in hopes, that Practice had been dead with the Court.

Mr. Ch. Just. Mr. *Hamilton*, the Court have delivered their Opinion, and we expect you will use us with good Manners; you are not to be permitted to argue against the Opinion of the Court.

Mr. Hamilton. With Submission, I have seen the Practice in very great Courts, and never heard it deemed unmannerly to - - - - - -

Mr. Ch. Just. After the Court have declared their Opinion, it is not good Manners to insist upon a Point, in which you are over-ruled.

Mr. Hamilton. I will say no more at this Time; the Court I see is against us in this Point; and that I hope I may be allowed to say.

Mr. Ch. Just. Use the Court with good Manners, and you shall be allowed all the Liberty you can reasonably desire.

Mr. Hamilton. I thank your Honour. Then, Gentlemen of the Jury, it is to you we must now appeal, for Witness, to the Truth of the Facts we have offered, and are denied the Liberty to prove; and let it not seem strange, that I apply my self to you in this Manner, I am warranted so to do, both by Law and Reason. The Last supposes you to be summoned, *out of the Neighbourhood where the Fact is alleged to be committed;* and the Reason of your being taken out of the Neighbourhood is, *because you are supposed to have the best Knowledge of the fact that is to be tried.* And were you to find a Verdict against my client, you must take upon you to say, the Papers referred to in the Information, and which we acknowledge we printed and published, are *false, scandalous and seditious:* but of this I can have no Apprehension. You are Citizens of *New-York;* you are really what the Law supposes you to be, *honest and lawful Men;* and, according to my Brief, the Facts which we offer to prove were not committed in a Corner; they are notoriously known to be true; and therefore in your Justice lies our Safety. And as we are denied the Liberty of giving Evidence, to prove the Truth of what we have published, I will beg Leave to lay it down as a standing Rule in such Casess, *That the suppressing of Evidence ought always to be taken for the strongest Evidence;* and I hope it will have that Weight with you. But since we are not admitted to examine our Witnesses, I will endeavor to shorten the Dispute with Mr. Attorney, and to that End, I desire he would favor us with some Standard Definition of a Libel, by which it may be certainly known, whether a Writing be a Libel, yea or not.

Mr. Attorney. The Books, I think, have given a very full definition of a Libel; they say it is *in a strict Sense taken for a malicious Defamation, expressed either in Printing or Writing, and tending either to blacken the Memory of one who is dead, or the Reputation of one who is alive, and to expose him to publick Hatred, Contempt or Ridicule.* § ? But it is said, *That in a larger*

---

1 Hawk. Chap. LXXIII. § 1 & seq.

JOHN PETER ZENGER

Sense the Notion of a Libel may be applied to any Defamation whatsoever, expressed either by Signs or Pictures, as by fixing up a Gallows against a Man's Door, or by painting him in a shameful and ignominious Manner. § 3. And since the chief Cause for which the Law so severely punishes all Offences of this Nature, is the direct Tendency of them to a Breach of Publick Peace, by provoking the Parties injured, their Friends and Families to Acts of Revenge, which it would be impossible to restrain by the severest Laws, were there no Redress from Publick Justice for Injuries of this kind, which of all others are most sensibly felt; and since the plain Meaning of such Scandal, as is expressed by Signs or Pictures, is as obvious to common Sense, and as easily understood by every common Capacity, and altogether as provoking as that which is expressed by Writing or Printing, why should it not be equally criminal? § 4. And from the same Ground it seemeth also clearly to follow, That such Scandal as is expressed in a scoffing and ironical Manner, makes a Writing as properly a Libel, as that which is expressed in direct Terms; as where a Writing, in a taunting Manner reckoning up several Acts of public Charity done by one, says You will not play the Jew, nor the Hypocrite, *and so goes on in a Strain of Ridicule to insinuate, that what he did was owing to his Vainglory; or where a Writing, pretending to recommend to one the Characters of several great Men for his Imitation, instead of taking Notice of what they are generally esteemed famous for, pitched on such Qualities only which their Enemies charge them with the Want of, as by proposing such a one to be imitated for his Courage, who is known to be a great Statesman, but no Soldier, and an-*

other to be imitated for his Learning, who is known to be a great General, but no Scholar, &c., which Kind of Writing is as well understood to mean only to upbraid the Parties with the Want of these Qualities, as if it had directly and expressly done so.

Mr. Hamilton. Ay, Mr. Attorney; but what certain Standard Rule have the Books laid down, by which we can certainly know, whether the Words or the Signs are malicious? Whether they are defamatory? Whether they tend to the Breach of the Peace, and are a sufficient Ground to provoke a Man, his Family, or Friends to Acts of Revenge, especially those of the ironical sort of Words? And what Rule have you to know when I write ironically? I think it would be hard, when I say, *such a Man is a very worthy honest Gentleman, and of fine Understanding,* that therefore I meant *he was a Knave or a fool.*

Mr. Attorney. I think the Books are very full; it is said in 1 *Hawk, p.* 193. just now read, *That such Scandal as is expressed in a scoffing and ironical Manner, makes a Writing as properly a Libel, as that which is expressed in direct Terms; as where a Writing, in a taunt*-ing *Manner says, reckoning up several Acts of Charity done by one, says,* you will not play the Jew or the Hypocrite, *and so goes on to insinuate, that what he did was owing to his Vain-Glory, &c. Which kind of Writing is as well understood to mean only to upbraid the Parties with the Want of these Qualities, as if it had directly and expressly done so.* I think nothing can be plainer or more full than these Words.

Mr. Hamilton. I agree the Words are very plain and I shall not scruple to allow (when we are agreed that the Words are *false and scandalous, and were spoken in an ironical and scoffing Manner, &c.*) that they are really *libellous;* but here still occurs the Uncertainty, which makes the Difficulty to know, what Words are *scandalous* and what not; for you say, they may be *scandalous, true* or *false;* besides, how shall we know whether the Words were spoke in a *scoffing and ironical Manner*, or seriously? Or how can you know whether the Man did not think as he wrote? For by your Rule, if he did, it is no *Irony*, and consequently no *Libel.* But under Favour, Mr. Attorney, I think the same Book, and the same Section will shew us the only Rule by which all these Things are to be known. The Words are these; *which Kind of Writing is as well* UNDERSTOOD *to mean only to upbraid the Parties with the Want of these Qualities, as if they had directly and expressly done so.* Here it is plain, the Words are *scandalous, scoffing and ironical*, only as they are UNDERSTOOD. I know no Rule laid down in the Books but this, I mean, as the Words are *understood.*

Mr. Ch. Just. Mr. *Hamilton*, do you think it so hard to know, when Words are ironical, or spoke in a scoffing Manner?

Mr. Hamilton. I own it may be known; but I insist, the only Rule to know is, as I do or can *understand* them; I have no other Rule to go by, but as I *understand* them.

Mr. Ch. Just. That is certain. All Words are libellous, or not, as they are *understood.* Those who are to judge of the Words, must judge whether they *are scandalous or ironical, tend to the Breach of the Peace*, or are *seditious:* There can be no Doubt of it.

JOHN PETER ZENGER

Mr. Hamilton. I thank your Honour; I am glad to find the Court of this Opinion. Then it follows that those twelve Men must *understand* the Words in the Information to be *scandalous*, that is to say *false*; for I think it is not pretended they are of the *ironical* Sort; and when they understand the Words to be so, they will say we are guilty of Publishing a *false Libel*, and not otherwise.

Mr. Ch. Just. No, Mr. *Hamilton* the Jury may find that *Zenger* printed and published those Papers, and leave it to the Court to judge whether they are libellous; you know this is very common; it is in the Nature of a special Verdict, where the Jury leave the Matter of Law to the Court.

Mr. Hamilton. I know, may it please Your Honour, the Jury may do so; but I do likewise know, they may do otherwise. I know they have the Right beyond all Dispute, to determine both the Law and the Fact, and where they do not doubt of the Law, they ought to do so. This of leaving it to the Judgment of the Court, *whether the Words are libellous or not*, in Effect renders Juries useless (to say no worse) in many Cases; but this I shall have Occasion to speak to by and by; and I will with the Court's Leave proceed to examine the Inconveniences that must inevitably arise from the Doctrines Mr. Attorney has laid down; and I observe, in support of this Prosecution, he has frequently repeated the Words taken from the Case of *Libel, famosus*, in 5 *Co.* This is indeed the leading case, and to which almost all the other Cases upon the Subject of Libels do refer; and I must insist upon saying, That according as this Case

JOHN PETER ZENGER

seems to be understood by the [Court] and Mr. Attorney, it is not Law at this Day : For thou' I own it to be base and unworthy to scandalize any Man, yet I think it is even villanous to scandalize a Person of publick Character, and I will go so far into Mr. Attorney's Doctrine as to agree, that if the faults, Mistakes, nay even the Vices of such a Person be private and personal, and don't affect the Peace of the Publick, or the Liberty or Property of our Neighbour, it is unmanly and unmannerly to expose them either by Word or Writing. But when a Ruler of the People brings his personal Failings, but much more his Vices, into his Administration, and the People find themselves affected by them, either in their Liberties or Properties, that will alter the Case mightily, and all the high Things that are said in Favour of Rulers, and of Dignities, and upon the side of Power, will not be able to stop People's Mouths when they feel themselves oppressed, I mean in a free Government. It is true in Times past it was a crime to speak Truth, and in that terrible Court of Star Chamber, many worthy and brave Men suffered for so doing ; and yet even in that Court, and in those bad Times, a great and good Man durst say, what I hope will not be taken amiss of me to say in this Place, *to wit, The Practice of informations for Libels is a Sword in the Hands of a wicked King, and an arrant Coward, to cut down and destroy the innocent ; the one cannot, because of his high Station, and the other dares not, because of his want of Courage, revenge himself in another Manner.*

Mr. Attorney. Pray Mr. *Hamilton*, have a Care

what you say, don't go too far neither, I don't like those Liberties.

Mr. Hamilton. Sure, Mr. Attorney, you won't make any Applications; all Men agree that we are governed by the best of Kings, and I cannot see the Meaning of Mr. Attorney's Caution; my well known Principles, and the Sense I have of the Blessings we enjoy under His present Majesty, makes it impossible for me to err, and I hope, even to be suspected, in that Point of Duty to my King. May it please Your Honour, I was saying, That notwithstanding all the Duty and Reverence claimed by Mr. Attorney to Men in Authority, they are not exempt from observing the Rules of Common Justice, even in their private or public Capacities; the Laws of our Mother Country know no Exemption. It is true, Men in Power are harder to be come at for Wrongs they do, either to a private Person, or to the Publick; especially a Governor in the Plantations, where they insist upon an Exemption from answering Complaints of any Kind in their own Government. We are indeed told, and it is true they are obliged to answer a Suit in the King's Courts at *Westminster*, for a Wrong done to any Person here: But do we not know how impracticable this is to most Men among us, to leave their Families (who depend upon their Labour and Care for their Livelihood) and carry Evidences to *Britain*, and at a great, nay, a far greater Expense than almost any of us are able to bear, only to prosecute a Governour for an Injury done here. But when the Oppression is general, there is no Remedy even that Way, no, our Constitution has (blessed be God) given us an Opportunity, if not to have such Wrongs redressed, yet by our Prudence and Resolution we may in a great Measure prevent the committing of such Wrongs, by making a Governour sensible that it is to his interest to be just to those under his Care; for such is the Sense that Men in General (I mean Freemen) have of common Justice, that when they come to know, that a chief Magistrate abuses the Power with which he is trusted, for the good of the People, and is attempting to turn that very Power against the Innocent, whether of high or low degree, I say, Mankind in general seldom fail to interpose, and as far as they can, prevent the Destruction of their fellow Subjects. And has it not often been seen (and I hope it will always be seen) that when the Representatives of a free People are by just Representations or Remonstrances, made sensible of the Sufferings of their Fellow-Subjects, by the Abuse of Power in the Hands of a Governour, they have declared (and loudly too) that they were not obliged by any Law to support a Governour who goes about to destroy a Province or Colony, or their Priviledges, which by His Majesty he was appointed, and by the Law he is bound to protect and encourage. But I pray it may be considered of what Use is this mighty Priviledge, if every Man that suffers must be silent? And if a Man must be taken up as a Libeller, for telling his Sufferings to his Neighbour? I know it may be answer'd, *Have you not a Legislature? Have you not a House of Representatives, to whom you may complain?* And to this I answer, we have. But

JOHN PETER ZENGER

what then? Is an Assembly to be troubled with
every Injury done by a Governour? Or are they
to hear of nothing but what those in the Administration will please to tell them? Or what Sort of a
Tryal must a Man have? And how is he to be
remedied; especially if the Case were, as I have
known it to happen in *America* in my Time; That
a Governour who has Places (I will not ⌈say⌋ Pensions, for I believe they seldom give that to another
which they can take to themselves) to bestow, and
can or will keep the same Assembly (after he has
modeled them so as to get a Majority of the House
in his Interest) for near *twice Seven Years* together?
I pray, what Redress is to be expected for an honest
Man, who makes his Complaint against a Governour
to an Assembly who may properly enough be said,
to be made by the same Governour against whom
the Complaint is made? The Thing answers it self.
No, it is natural, it is a Priviledge, I will go farther, it is a Right which all Freemen claim, and are
entitled to complain when they are hurt; they have
a Right publickly to remonstrate the Abuses of
Power, in the strongest Terms, to put their Neighbours upon their Guard, against the Craft or open
Violence of Men in Authority, and to assert with
Courage the Sense they have of the Blessings of
Liberty, the Value they put upon it, and their Resolution at all Hazards to preserve it, as one of the
greatest Blessings Heaven can bestow. And when a
House of Assembly composed of honest Freemen
sees the general Bent of the Peoples Inclinations,
That is it which must and will (I'm sure it ought

to) weigh with a Legislature, in Spite of all the Craft, Caressing and Cajolling, made use of by a Governour, to divert them from hearkening to the Voice of their Country. As we all very well understand the true Reason, why Gentlemen take so much Pains and make such great Interest to be appointed Governours, so is the Design of their Appointment not less manifest. We know his Majesty's gracious Intentions to his Subjects; he desires no more than that his People in the Plantations should be kept up to their Duty and Allegiance to the crown of *Great Britain*, that Peace may be preserved amongst them, and Justice impartially administered; that we may he [sic] governed so as to render us useful to our Mother Country, by encouraging us to make and raise such Commodities as may be useful to *Great Britain*. But will any one say, that all or any of these good Ends are to be effected, by a Governour's setting his People together by the Ears, and by the Assistance of one Part of the People to plague and plunder the other? The Commission which Governours bear, while they execute the Powers given them, according to the Intent of the Royal Grantor, expressed in their Commissions, requires and deserves very great Reverence and Submission; but when a Governour departs from the Duty enjoined him by his Sovereign, and acts as if he was less accountable than the Royal Hand that gave him all that Power and Honour which he is possessed of; this sets People upon examining and enquiring into the Power, Authority and Duty of such a Magistrate, and to compare those with his Conduct, and just as far as they find he exceeds the Bounds of his Authority, or falls short in doing impartial Justice to the People under his Administration, so far they very often, in return, come short in their Duty to such a Governour. For Power alone will not make a Man beloved, and I have heard it observed, That the Man who was neither good nor wise before his being made a Governour, never mended upon his Preferment, but has been generally observed to be worse; For Men who are not endued with Wisdom and Virtue, can only be kept in Bounds by the Law; and by how much the further they think themselves out of the Reach of the Law, by so much the more wicked and cruel Men are. I wish there were no Instances of the Kind at this Day. And wherever this happens to be the Case of a Governour, unhappy are the People under his Administration, and in the End he will find himself so too; for the People will neither love him nor support him. I make no Doubt but there are those here, who are zealously concerned for the Success of this Prosecution, and yet I hope they are not many, and even some of those, I am perswaded (when they consider what Length such Prosecutions may be carried, and how deeply the Liberties of the People may be affected by such Means) will not all abide by their present Sentiments; I say, *Not All:* For the Man who from an Intimacy and Acquaintance with a Governour has conceived a personal Regard for him, the Man who has felt none of the Strokes of his Power, the Man who believes that a Governour has a Regard for him and confides in him, it is natural for such Men to wish well to the Affairs of such a Governour; and as they may be Men of Honour and Generosity, may, and no Doubt will, wish him Success, so far as the Rights and the Priviledges of their Fellow Citizens are not affected. But as Men of Honour, I can apprehend nothing from them; they will never exceed that Point. There are others who are under stronger Obligations, and those are such, as are in some Sort engaged in Support of a Governour's Cause, by their own or their Relations Dependance on his Favour, for some Post or Preferment; such Men have what is commonly called Duty and Gratitude, to influence their Inclinations, and oblige them to go to his Lengths. I know Men's Interests are very near to them, and they will do much, rather than foregoe the Favour of a Governour, and a Livelihood at the same Time; but I can with very just Grounds hope, even from those Men, whom I will suppose to be Men of Honour and Conscience too, that when they see, the Liberty of their Country is in Danger, either by their Concurrence, or even by their Silence, they will like *Englishmen*, and like themselves, freely make a Sacrifice of any Preferment or Favour rather than be accessory to destroying the Liberties of their Country, and entailing Slavery upon their Posterity. There are indeed another set of Men, of whom I have no Hopes, I mean such, who lay aside all other Considerations, and are ready to joyn with Power in any Shapes, and with any Man or Sort of Men, by whose Means or Interest they may be assisted to gratify their Malice and Envy against those whom they have been pleased to hate; and that have no other Reason, but because they are Men of Abilities and Integrity, or at least are possessed of some valuable Qualities far superior to their own. But as Envy is the Sin of the Devil, and therefore very hard, if at all, to be repented of, I will believe there are but few of this detestable and worthless Sort of Men, nor will their Opinions or Inclinations have any Influence upon this Tryal. But to proceed; I beg Leave to insist, That the Right of complaining or remonstrating is natural; And the Restraint upon this natural Right is the Law only, and that those Restraints can only extend to what is *false*; For as it is Truth alone which can excuse or justify any Man for complaining of a bad Administration, I as frankly agree, that nothing ought to excuse a Man who raises a false Charge or Accusation, even against a private Person, and that no manner of Allowance ought to be made to him who does so against a publick Magistrate. *Truth* ought to govern the whole Affair of Libels, and yet the Party accused runs Risque enough even then; for if he fails of proving every Tittle of what he has wrote, and to the Satisfaction of the Court and Jury too, he may find to his Cost, that when the Prosecution is set on Foot by Men in Power, it seldom wants Friends to Favour it. And from thence (it is said) has arisen the great Diversity of Opinions among Judges, about what words were or were not scandalous or libellous. I believe it will be granted, that there is not greater Uncertainty in any Part of the Law, than about Words of Scandal; it would be mispending of the Court's Time to mention the Cases; they may be said to be numberless; and therefore the uttermost Care ought to be taken in following Precedents; and the Times when the Judgments were given, which are quoted for Authorities in the Case of Libels, are much to be regarded. I think it will be agreed, That ever since the Time of the Star Chamber, where the most arbitrary and destructive Judgments and Opinions were given, that ever an *Englishman* heard of, at least in his own Country: I say, Prosecutions for Libels since the Time of that arbitrary Court, and until the glorious Revolution, have generally been set on Foot at the Instance of the Crown or its Ministers; and it is no small Reproach to the Law, that these Prosecutions were too often and too much countenanced by the Judges, who held their Places at Pleasure, (a disagreeable Tenure to any Officer, but a dangerous one in the Case of a Judge.) To say more to this Point may not be proper. And yet I cannot think it unwarrantable, to shew the unhappy Influence that a Sovereign has sometimes had, not only upon Judges, but even upon Parliaments themselves.

It has already been shewn, how the Judges differed in their Opinions about the Nature of a Libel, in the Case of the seven Bishops. There you see three Judges of one Opinion, that is, of a wrong Opinion, in the Judgment of the best Men in *England*, and one Judge of a right Opinion. How unhappy might it have been for all of us at this Day, if that Jury had understood the Words in that Information as the Court did? Or if they had left it to the Court, to judge whether the Petition of the

Bishops was or was not a Libel? No they took upon them, to their immortal Honour! to determine both *Law* and *Fact*, and to *understand* the Petition of the Bishops *to be no Libel, that is, to contain no falshood nor Sedition*, and therefore found them *Not Guilty*. And remarkable is the Case of Sir *Samuel Barnardiston*, who was fined 10,000*L.* for Writing a Letter, in which, it may be said, none saw any Scandal or Falshood but the Court and Jury; for that Judgment was afterwards looked upon as a cruel and detestable Judgment, and therefore was reversed by Parliament. Many more Instances might be given of the Complaisance of Court-Judges, about those Times and before; but I will mention only one Case more, and that is the Case of Sir *Edward Hales*, who tho' a *Roman Catholick*, was by King *James* II. preferred to be a Colonel of his Army, notwithstanding the Statute of 25 *Cha.* 2*d. Chap.* 2. by which it is provided, *That every one that accepts of an Office, Civil or Military, &c. shall take the Oaths, subscribe the Declaration, and take the Sacrament, within three Months, &c. otherwise he is disabled to hold such Office, and the Grant for the same to be null and void, and the Party to forfeit 500l.* Sir *Edward Hales* did not take the Oaths and Sacrament, and was prosecuted for the 500*l.* for exercising the Office of a Colonel by the Space of three Months, without conforming as in the Act is directed. Sir *Edward* pleads, *That the King by His Letters Patents did dispence with his taking the Oaths and Sacrament, and subscribing the Declaration, and had pardoned the forfeiture of 500l.* And whether the King's Dispensation was good, against the said Act of Parliament? was the Question. I shall mention no more of this Case, than to shew how in the Reign of an arbitrary Prince, where Judges held their Seats at Pleasure, their Determinations have not always been such as to make Precedents of, but the Contrary; and so it happened in this Case where it was solemnly judged, *That, notwithstanding this Act of Parliament, made in the strongest Terms, for Preservation of the Protestant Religion, That yet the King had, by his Royal Prerogative, a Power to dispence with that Law;* and Sir *Edward Hales* was acquitted by the Judges accordingly. So the King's Dispensing Power, being by the Judges set up above the Act of Parliament, this Law, which the People looked upon as their chief Security against Popery and Arbitrary Power, was by this Judgment rendered altogether ineffectual. But this Judgment is sufficiently exposed by Sir *Edward Atkins*, late one of the Judges of the Court of Common Pleas in his *Enquiry into the King's Power of dispensing with poenal Statutes;* where it is shewn, *Who it was that first invented Dispensations; how they came into* England; *what ill Use has been made of them there; and all this principally owing to the Countenance given them by the Judges.* He says of the Dispensing Power,* *The Pope was the Inventor of it; our Kings have borrowed it from them; and the Judges have from Time to Time nursed and dressed it up, and given it countenance; and it is still upon the Growth, and encroaching, 'till it has almost subverted all Law, and made Regal Power absolute if not*

Sir *Edward Atkins* Enquiry into the Power of Dispensing with poenal Statutes.

* Postscript to the *Enquiry, pag.* 51.

dissolute. This seems not only to shew how far Judges have been influenced by Power, and how little Cases of this Sort, where the Prerogative has been in Question in former Reigns, are to be relied upon for Law : But I think it plainly shews too, that a Man may use a greater Freedom with the Power of His Sovereign and the Judges in *Great Britain,* than it seems he may with the Power of a Governour in the Plantations, who is but a Fellow-Subject. Are these Words with which we are charged, like these ? Do Mr. *Zenger's* Papers contain any such Freedom with his Governour or His Council, as Sir *Edward Atkins* has taken, with the Regal Power and the Judges in *England ?* And yet I never heard of any Information brought against him for these Freedoms.

If then upon the whole there is so great an Uncertainty among Judges (learned and great Men) in Matters of this Kind; If Power has had so great an Influence on Judges; how cautious ought we to be in determining by their Judgments, especially in the Plantations, and in the Case of Libels ? There is Heresy in Law, as well as in Religion, and both have changed very much; and we well know that it is not two Centuries ago that a Man would have been burnt as an Heretick, for owning such Opinions in Matters of Religion as are publickly wrote and printed at this Day. They were fallible Men, it seems, and we take the Liberty not only to differ from them in religious Opinion, but to condemn them and their Opinions too; and I must presume, that in taking these Freedoms in thinking and speaking about Matters of Faith and Religion, we are in the right: For, tho' it is said there are very great Liberties of this Kind taken in *Newe York*, yet I have heard of no Information prefered by Mr. Attorney for any Offences of this Sort. From which I think it is pretty clear, That in *New-York* a Man may make very free with his God, but he must take special Care what he says of his Governour. It is agreed upon by all Men that this is a Reign of Liberty, and while Men keep within the Bounds of Truth, I hope they may with Safety both speak and write their Sentiments of the Conduct of Men in Power, I me[a]n of that Part of their Conduct only, which affects the Liberty or Property of the People under their Administration; were this to be denied, then the next Step may make them Slaves. For what Notions can be entertained of Slavery, beyond that of suffering the greatest Injuries and Oppressions, without the Liberty of complaining; or if they do, to be destroyed, Body and Estate, for so doing?

It is said and insisted upon by Mr. Attorney, *That Government is a sacred Thing; That it is to be supported and reverenced; It is Government that protects our Persons and Estates; That prevents Treasons, Murders, Robberies, Riots, and all the Train of Evils that overturns Kingdoms and States, and ruins particular Persons; and if those in the Administration, especially the Supream Magistrate, must have all their Conduct censured by private Men, Government cannot subsist.* This is called *a Licentiousness not to be tollerated.* It is said, *That it brings the Rulers of the People into Contempt, and their Authority not to be regarded, and so in*

the End the Laws cannot be put in Execution. These
I say, and such as these, are the general Topicks in-
sisted upon by Men in Power, and their Advocates.
But I wish it might be considered at the same Time,
How often it has happened, that the Abuse of Power
has been the primary Cause of these Evils, and that
it was the Injustice and Oppression of these great
Men, which has commonly brought them into Contempt with the People. The Craft and Art of such
Men is great, and who, that is the least acquainted
with History or Law, can be ignorant of the specious
Pretences, which have often been made use of by
Men in Power, to introduce arbitrary Rule, and destroy the Liberties of a free People. I will give two
Instances; and as they are Authorities not to be denied, nor can be misunderstood, I presume they will
be sufficient.

The *first* is the Statute of 3*d.* of *Hen.* 7. *Cap.* I.

The Preamble of the Statute will prove all and
more than I have alledged. It begins, ' *The King*
' *Our Sovereign Lord remembereth how by unlawful*
' *Maintenances, giving of Liveries, Signs and Tokens,*
' *&c. untrue Demeanings of Sheriffs in making of Pan-*
' *nels, and other untrue Returns, by taking of Money, by*
' *Injuries, by great Riots and unlawful Assemblies; the*
' *Policy and good Rule of this Realm is almost subdued;*
' *and for the not punishing these Inconveniences, and by*
' *Occasion of the Premises, little or nothing may be found*
' *by Inquiry, &c. to the Increase of Murders, &c. and*
' *unsureties of all Men living, and Losses of their Lands*
' *and Goods.'* Here is a fine and specious Pretence
for introducing the Remedy, as it is called, which

is provided by this Act; *that is;* instead of being lawfully accused by 24 good and lawful Men of the Neighbourhood, and afterwards tried by 12 like lawful Men, here is a Power given to the Lord Chancellor, Lord Treasurer, the Keeper of the King's privy Seal, or two of them, calling to them a Bishop, a temporal Lord, and other great Men mentioned in the Act, (who, it is to be observed, were all to be Dependants on the Court) to receive Information against any Person for any of the Misbehaviours recited in that Act, and by their Discretion to examine, and to punish them according to their demerit.

The second Statute I proposed to mention, is the 11*th* of the same King, *Chap. 3d.* the Preamble of which Act has the like fair Pretences as the former; *for the King calling to his Remembrance the good Laws made against the receiving of Liveries, &c. unlawful Extortions, Maintenances, Embracery, &c. unlawful Games, &c. and many other great Enormitys, and Offences committed against many good Statutes, to the Displeasure of Almighty God, which,* the Act says, *could not, nor yet can, be conveniently punished by the due Order of the Law, except it were first found by 12 Men, &c. which, for the Causes aforesaid, will not find nor yet present the Truth.* And therefore the same Statute directs, *that the Justices of Assize, and Justices of the Peace, shall, upon Information for the King before them made, have full Power, by their Discretion, to hear and determine all such Offences.* Here are two Statutes that are allowed to have given the deepest Wound to the Liberties of the People of *England* of any that

JOHN PETER ZENGER

I remember to have been made, unless it may be said, that the Statute made in the Time of *Henry 8th,* by which his Proclamations were to have the Effect of Laws, might in its Consequence be worse. And yet we see the plausible Pretences found out by the great Men to procure these Acts. And it may justly be said, That by those Pretences the People of *England* were cheated or aw'd into Delivering up their antient and sacred Right of Tryals by Grand and Petit Juries. I hope to be excused for this Expression, seeing my Lord *Coke* calls it *an unjust and strange Act, that tended in its Execution to the great Displeasure of Almighty God, and the utter Subversion of the common Law.*

These, I think, make out what I alledged, and are flagrant Instances of the Influence of Men in Power, even upon the Representatives of a whole Kingdom. From all which I hope it will be agreed, that it is a Duty which all good Men owe to their Country, to guard against the unhappy Influence of ill Men when intrusted with Power, and especially against their Creatures and Dependants, who, as they are generally more necessitous, are surely more covetous and cruel. But it is worthy of Observation, that tho' the Spirit of Liberty was born down and oppressed in *England* at that Time, yet it was not lost; for the Parliament laid hold of the first Opportunity to free the Subject from the many insufferable Oppressions and Outrages committed upon their Persons and Estates by Colour of these Acts, the last of which being deemed the most grievous,

4. *Inst.*

was repealed in the first Year of *Hen.* 8*th.* Tho'
it is to be observed, that *Hen.* 7*th,* and his Creatures
reap'd such great Advantages by the grievous Oppressions and Exactions, *grinding the Faces of the
poor Subjects,* as my Lord *Coke* says, by Colour of
this Statute by information only, that a Repeal of
this Act could never be obtained during the Life of
that Prince. The other Statute being the favourite
Law for Supporting arbitrary Power, was continued
much longer. The Execution of it was by the great
Men of the Realm; and how they executed it, the
Sense of the Kingdom, expressed in the 17*th* of
Charles 1*st.* (by which the Court of Star Chamber,
the Soil where Informations grew rankest) will best
declare. In that Statute *Magna Charta,* and the
other Statutes made in the Time of *Edw.* 3*d.* which,
I think, are no less than five, are particularly enumerated as Acts, by which the Liberties and Priviledges of the People of *England* were secured to
them, against such oppressive Courts as the Star-
Chamber and others of the like Jurisdiction. And
the Reason assigned for their pulling down the Star-
Chamber, is, *That the Proceedings, Censures and Decrees of the Court of Star Chamber, even tho' the great
Men of the Realm, nay and a Bishop too* (holy Man)
*were Judges, had by Experience been found to be an in-
tolerable Burthen to the Subject, and the Means to introduce an arbitrary Power and Government.* And
therefore that Court was taken away, with all the
other Courts in that Statute mentioned, having like
Jurisdiction.

I don't mention this Statute, as if by the taking

away the Court of Star Chamber, the Remedy for many of the Abuses or Offences censured there, was likewise taken away; no, I only intend by it to shew that the People of *England* saw clearly the Danger of trusting their Liberties and Properties to be tried, even by the greatest Men in the Kingdom, without the Judgment of a Jury of their Equals. They had felt the terrible effects, of leaving it to the Judgment of these great Men to say what was *scandalous and seditious, false or ironical.* And if the Parliament of *England* thought this Power of judging was too great to be trusted to Men of the first Rank in the Kingdom, without the Aid of a Jury, how sacred soever their Characters might be, and therefore restored to the People their original Right of tryal by Juries, I hope to be excused for insisting, that by the Judgment of a Parliament, from whence no Appeal lies, the Jury are the proper Judges, of what is *false* at least, if not of what is *scandalous and seditious.* This is an Authority not to be denied, it is as plain as it is great, and to say, that this Act indeed did restore to the People Tryals by Juries, which was not the Practice of the Star Chamber, but that did not give the Jurors any new Authority, or any Right to try Matters of Law, I say this Objection will not avail; for I must insist, that where Matter of Law is complicated with Matter of Fact, the Jury have a Right to determine both. As for Instance; upon Indictment for Murder, the Jury may, and almost constantly do, take upon them to judge whether the Evidence will amount to Murder or Manslaughter, and find accordingly; and I

must say I cannot see, why in our Case the Jury
have not at least as good a Right to say, whether
our News Papers are a Libel or no Libel, as another
Jury has to say, whether killing of a Man is Murder or Manslaughter. The Right of the Jury, to
find such a Verdict as they in their Conscience do
think is agreeable to their Evidence, is supported
by the Authority of *Bushel's* Case, in *Vaghan's Reports, pag.* 135. beyond any Doubt. For, in the
Argument of that Case, the Chief Justice who delivered the Opinion of the Court, lays it down for
Law, *That in all General Issues, as upon* Non Cul. *in*
Trespass, Non Tort. Nul Disseizin *in Assize,* &c.
*tho' it is Matter of Law, whether the Defendant is a
Trespasser, a Disseizer. &c. in the particular Cases in
Issue, yet the Jury find not (as in a special Verdict) the
Fact of every Case, leaving the Law to the Court; but
find for the Plaintiff or Defendant upon the Issue to be
tried, wherein they resolve both Law and Fact complicately.* It appears by the same Case, that tho' the
discreet and lawful Assistance of the Judge, by Way
of Advice, to the Jury, may be useful; yet that Advice or Direction ought always to be *upon Supposi-
tion, and not positive, and upon Coersion.* The Reason
given in the same Book is, *Because the Judge (as
Judge) cannot know what the Evidence is which the
Jury have,* that is, *he can only know the Evidence given
in Court; but the Evidence which the Jury have, may
be of their own Knowledge, as they are returned of the
Neighbourhood. They may also know from their own
Knowledge, that what is sworn in Court is not true; and*

Vaughan's Rep. p. 150. *Pag.* 144. *pag.* 147.

they may know the Witnesses to be stigmatized, to which the Court may be strangers. But what is to my Purpose, is, that suppose that the Court did really know all the Evidence which the Jury know, yet in that Case it is agreed, *That the Judge and Jury may differ in the Result of their Evidence as well as two Judges may,* which often happens. And in *pag.* 148 the Judge subjoins the Reason, why it is no Crime for a Jury to differ in Opinion from the Court, where he says, *That a Man cannot see with another's Eye, nor hear by another's Ear; no more can a Man conclude or infer the Thing by another's Understanding or Reasoning.* From all which (I insist) it is very plain, *That the Jury are by Law at Liberty (without any affront to the Judgment of the Court) to find both the Law and the Fact, in our Case,* as they did in the Case I am speaking to, which I will beg Leave just to mention, and it was this. Mr. *Penn* and *Mead* being Quakers, and having met in a peaceable Manner, after being shut out of their Meeting House, preached in *Grace Church Street* in *London,* to the People of their own Perswasion, and for this they were indicted; and it was said, *That they with other Persons, to the Number of 300. unlawfully and tumultuously assembled, to the Disturbance of the Peace, &c.* To which they pleaded *Not Guilty.* And the Petit Jury being sworn to try the Issue between the King and the Prisoners, that is, whether they were Guilty, according to the Form of the Indictment? Here there was no Dispute but they were assembled together, to the Number mentioned in the Indictment; But *Whether that Meeting together was riotously, tumultuously, and to the Disturb-*

ance of the Peace? was the Question. And the Court told the Jury it was, and ordered the Jury to find it so ; *For* (said the Court) *the Meeting was the Matter of Fact, and that is confessed, and we tell you it is unlawful, for it is against the Statute ; and the Meeting being unlawful, it follows of Course that it was tumultuous, and to the Disturbance of the Peace.* But the Jury did not think fit to take the Courts Word for it, for they could neither find *Riot, Tumult,* or any Thing tending to the *Breach of the Peace* committed at that Meeting; and they acquitted Mr. *Penn* and *Mead.* In doing of which they took upon them to judge both the *Law* and the *Fact,* at which the Court (being themselves true Courtiers) were so much offended, that they fined the Jury 40 Marks a piece, and committed them till paid. But Mr. *Bushel,* who valued the Right of a Juryman and the Liberty of his Country more than his own, refused to pay the Fine, and was resolved, (tho' at a great Expence and trouble too) to bring, and did bring, his *Habeas Corpus,* to be relieved from his Fine and Imprisonment, and he was released accordingly ; and this being the Judgment in his Case, it is established for Law, *That the Judges, how great soever they be, have no Right to Fine, imprison, or punish a Jury, for not finding a Verdict according to the Direction of the Court.* And this I hope is sufficient to prove, That Jurymen are to see with their own Eyes, to hear with their own ears, and to make use of their own Consciences and Understandings, in judging of the Lives, Liberties or Estates of their fellow Subjects. And so I have done with this Point.

JOHN PETER ZENGER

This is the second Informotion for Libelling of a Governour that I have known in *America*. And the first, tho' it may look like a Romance, yet as it is true, I will beg Leave to mention it. Governor *Nicholson*, who happened to be offended with one [of] his Clergy, met him one Day upon the Road, and as was usual with him (under the Protection of his Commission) used the poor Parson with the worst of Language, threatened to cut off his Ears, slit his Nose, and at last to shoot him through the Head. The Parson being a reverend Man, continued all this Time uncovered in the Heat of the Sun, until he found an Opportunity to fly for it; and coming to a Neighbours House felt himself very ill of a Fever, and immediately writes for a doctor; and that his Physician might the better judge of his Distemper, he acquainted him with the Usage he had received; concluding, that the Governor was certainly mad, for that no Man in his Senses would have behaved in that manner. The Doctor unhappily shews the Parson's Letter; the Governour came to hear of it; and so an Information was preferred against the poor Man for saying *he believed the Governour was mad*; and it was laid in the Information to be *false, scandalous*, and *wicked, and wrote with Intent to move Sedition among the People, and bring His Excellency into Contempt*. But by an Order from the late Queen *Anne*, there was a Stop put to that Prosecution, with sundry others set on foot by the same Governour, against Gentlemen of the greatest Worth and Honour in that Government.

And may not I be allowed, after all this, to say,

JOHN PETER ZENGER

That by a little Countenance, almost any Thing which a Man writes, may, with the Help of that useful Term of Art, called an *Innuendo*, be construed to be a Libel, according to Mr. Attorney's Definition of it, That *whether the Words are spoken of a Person of a publick Character, or of a private Man, whether dead or Living, good or bad, true or false* all make a Libel; for according to Mr. Attorney, *after a Man hears a Writing read, or reads and repeats it, or laughs at it, they are all punishable.* It is true, Mr. Attorney is so good as to allow, *after the Party knows it to be a Libel,* but he is not so kind as to take the Man's Word for it.

Here were several Cases put to shew, That tho' what a Man writes of a Governour was true, proper and necessary, yet according to the foregoing Doctrine it might be construed to be a libel: But Mr. *Hamilton* after the Tryal was over, being informed, That some of the Cases he had put had really happened in the Government, he declared he had never heard of any such; and as he meant no personal Reflections, he was sorry he had mentioned them, and therefore they are omitted here.

Mr. Hamilton. If a Libel is understood in the large and unlimited Sense urged by Mr. Attorney, there is scarce a Writing I know that may not be called a Libel, or scarce any Person safe from being called to an Account as a Libeller: For *Moses*, meek as he was, Libelled *Cain*; and who is it that has not

116

libelled the Devil? For according to Mr. Attorney, it is no Justification to say one has a bad Name. *Echard* has libelled our good King *William; Burnet* has libelled among many others King *Charles* and King *James*; and *Rapin* has libelled them all. How must a Man speak or write, or what must he hear, read, or sing? Or when must he laugh, so as to be secure from being taken up as a Libeller? I sincerely believe, that were some Persons to go thro' the Streets of *New-York* now-a-days, and read a Part of the Bible, if it was not known to be such, Mr. Attorney, with the Help of his *Innuendo's*, would easily turn it into a Libel. As, for instance, *Is* IX. 16. *The Leaders of the People cause them to err, and they that are led by them are destroyed.* But should Mr. Attorney go about to make this a Libel, he would treat it thus; *The Leaders of the People* [innuendo, the Governour and Council of *New-York*] *cause them* [innuendo, the People of this Province] *to err, and they* [the people of this Province meaning] *that are led by them* [the Governour and Council meaning] *are destroyed* [innuendo, are deceived into the Loss of their Liberty] which is the worst Kind of Destruction. Or if some Persons should publickly repeat, in a Manner not pleasing to his Betters, the 10*th* and 11*th* Verses of the LVIth. *Chap.* of the same Book, there Mr. Attorney would have a large Field to display his Skill, in the artful Application of his *Innuendo's*. The Words are, *His Watchmen are all blind, they are ignorant, &c. Yea, they are greedy Dogs, that can never have enough.* But to make them a Libel, there is according to Mr. Attorney's Doctrine, no more wanting but the Aid of his Skill, in the right adapting his *Innuendo's*. As for Instance ; *His Watchmen* [*innuendo*, the Governour's Council and Assembly] *are blind, they are ignorant* [*innuendo*, will not see the dangerous Designs of His Excellency] *Yea, they* [the Governour and Council meaning] *are greedy Dogs, which can never have enough* [*innuendo*, enough of Riches and Power.] Such an Instance as this is seems only fit to be laugh'd at ; but I may appeal to Mr. Attorney himself, whether these are not at least equally proper to be applied to His Excellency and His Ministers, as some of the Inferences and *Innuendo's* in his Information against my Client. Then if Mr. Attorney is at Liberty to come into Court, and file an Information in the King's Name, without Leave, who is secure, whom he is pleased to prosecute as a Libeller ? And as the Crown Law is contended for in bad Times, there is no Remedy for the greatest Oppression of this Sort, even tho the Party prosecuted is aquitted with Honour. And give me Leave to say, as great Men as any in *Britain*, have boldly asserted, That the Mode of Prosecuting by Information (when a Grand Jury will not find *Billa vera*) is a national Grievance, and greatly inconsistent with that Freedom, which the Subjects of *England* enjoy in most other Cases. But if we are so unhappy as not to be able to ward off this Stroke of Power directly, yet let us take Care not to be cheated out of our Liberties, by Forms and Appearances ; let us always be sure that the Charge in the Information is made out clearly even beyond a Doubt ; for tho Matters in the Information may be called *Form* upon Tryal, yet they may be, and often have been found to be *Matters of Substance* upon giving judgment.

Gentlemen: The Danger is great, in Proportion to the Mischief that may happen, through our too great Credulity. A proper Confidence in a Court is commendable; but as the Verdict (whatever it is) will be yours, you ought to refer no Part of your Duty to the Discretion of other Persons. If you should be of Opinion, that there is no Falsehood in Mr. *Zenger's* Papers, you will, nay (pardon me for the Expression) you ought to say so; because you don't know whether others (I mean the Court) may be of that Opinion. It is your Right to do so, and there is much depending upon your Resolution, as well as upon your Integrity.

The loss of liberty to a generous Mind, is worse than Death; and yet we know there have been those in all Ages, who for the sake of Preferment, or some imaginary Honour, have freely lent a helping Hand, to oppress, nay to destroy their Country. This brings to my Mind that saying of the immortal *Brutus*, when he looked upon the Creatures of *Cæsar*, who were very great Men, but by no Means good Men. " *You* Romans *said* Brutus, *if yet I may call you so, consider* " *what you are doing; remember that you are assisting* " Cæsar *to forge those very Chains, which one Day he* " *will make your selves wear.*" This is what every Man (that values Freedom) ought to consider: He should act by Judgment and not by Affection or Self-Interest; for, where those prevail, No Ties of either Country or Kindred are regarded, as upon the other Hand, the Man, who loves his Country, prefers it's

Liberty to all other Considerations, well knowing that without Liberty, life is a Misery.

A famous Instance of this is found in the History of another brave *Roman* of the same Name, I mean *Lucius Junius Brutus*, whose story is well known and therefore I shall mention no more of it, than only to shew the Value he put upon the Freedom of his Country. After this great Man, with his Fellow Citizens whom he had engag'd in the Cause, had banish'd *Tarquin* the Proud, the last King of *Rome*, from a Throne which he ascended by inhuman Murders and possess'd by the most dreadful Tyranny and Proscriptions, and had by this Means, amass'd incredible Riches, even sufficient to bribe to his Interest, many of the young Nobility of *Rome*, to assist him in recovering the Crown; but the Plot being discover'd, the principal Conspirators were apprehended, among whom were two of the Sons of *Junius Brutus*. It was absolutely necessary that some should be made Examples of, to deter others from attempting the restoring of *Tarquin* and destroying the Liberty of *Rome*. And to effect this it was, that *Lucius Junius Brutus*, one of the Consuls of *Rome*, in the Presence of the *Roman* People, sat Judge and condemned his own Sons, as Traitors to their Country: And to give the last Proof of his exalted Virtue, and his Love of Liberty: He with a Firmness of Mind (only becoming so great a Man) caus'd their Heads to be struck off in his own Presence; and when he observ'd that his rigid Virtue, occasion'd a sort of Horror among the People, it is observ'd he only said, " *My Fellow-* " *Citizens, do not think that this Proceeds from any Want*

" *of natural Affection: No, The Death of the Sons of*
" Brutus *can affect* Brutus *only ; but the loss of Liberty*
" *will affect my Country.*" Thus highly was Liberty
esteem'd in those Days that a Father could sacrifice
his Sons to save his Country. But why do I go to
Heathen *Rome,* to bring Instances of the Love of
Liberty, the best Blood of *Britain* has been shed in
the Cause of Liberty ; and the Freedom we enjoy at
this Day, may be said to be (in great measure) owing to the glorious Stand the famous *Hamden,* and
others of our Countrymen, made against the arbitrary Demands, and illegal Impositions, of the Times
in which they lived ; Who rather than give up the
Rights of *Englishmen,* and submit to pay an illegal
Tax of no more, I think, than 3 Shillings, resolv'd
to undergo, and for their Liberty of their Country
did undergo the greatest Extremities, in that arbitrary
and terrible Court of Star Chamber, to whose arbitrary Proceedings, (it being compos'd of the Principal Men of the Realm, and calculated to support
arbitrary Government) no Bounds or Limits could be
set, nor could any other Hand remove the Evil but
a Parliament.

Power may justly be compared to a great River,
while kept within its due Bounds, is both Beautiful
and Useful ; but when it overflows it's Banks, it is
then too impetuous to be stemm'd, it bears down all
before it, and brings Destruction and Desolation
wherever it comes. If then this is the Nature of
Power, let us at least do our Duty, and like wise
Men (who value Freedom) use our utmost care to
support Liberty, the only Bulwark against lawless

Power, which in all Ages has sacrificed to its wild Lust and boundless Ambition, the Blood of the best Men that ever liv'd.

I hope to be pardon'd Sir for my Zeal upon this Occasion; it is an old and wise Caution, *That when our Neighbours House is on Fire, we ought to take Care of our own.* For tho' Blessed be God, I live in a Government where Liberty is well understood, and freely enjoy'd; yet Experience has shewn us all (I'm sure it has to me) that a bad Precedent in one Government, is soon set up for an Authority in another; and therefore I cannot but think it mine, and every Honest Man's Duty, that (while we pay all due Obedience to Men in Authority) we ought at the same Time to be upon our Guard against Power, wherever we apprehend that it may affect ourselves or our Fellow-Subjects.

I am truely very unequal to such an Undertaking on many Accounts. And you see I labour under the Weight of many Years, and am born down with great Infirmities of Body; yet Old and Weak as I am, I should think it my Duty, if required, to go to the utmost Part of the Land, where my Service could be of any Use in assisting to quench the Flame of Prosecutions upon Informations, set on Foot by the Government, to deprive a People of the Right of Remonstrating (and complaining too) of the arbitrary Attempts of Men in Power. Men who injure and oppress the People under their Administration provoke them to cry out and complain; and then make that very Complaint the Foundation for new Oppressions and Prosecutions. I wish I could say there were no Instances of this Kind. But to conclude; the Question before the Court and you, Gentlemen of the Jury, is not of small nor private Concern, it is not the Cause of a poor Printer, nor of *New-York* alone, which you are now trying: No! It may in its Consequence, affect every Freeman that lives under a British Government on the main of *America*. It is the best Cause. It is the Cause of Liberty; and I make no Doubt but your upright Conduct, this Day, will not only entitle you to the Love and Esteem of your Fellow-Citizens; but every Man who prefers Freedom to a Life of Slavery will bless and honour You, as Men who have baffled the Attempt of Tyranny; and by an impartial and uncorrupt Verdict, have laid a noble Foundation for securing to ourselves, our Posterity, and our Neighbours, That, to which Nature and the Laws of our Country have given us a Right,— —The Liberty— — — —both of exposing and opposing arbitrary Power (in these Parts of the World, at least) by speaking and writing Truth.

Here Mr. Attorney observ'd, that Mr. Hamilton had gone very much out of the Way, and had made himself and the People very merry: But that he had been citing Cases, not at all to the Purpose; he said, there was no such Cause as Mr. Bushel's or Sir Edward Hales before the Court; and he could not find out what the Court or Jury had to do with Dispensations, Riots or unlawful Assemblies: All that the Jury had to consider of was Mrs. (sic) Zenger's Printing and Publishing two scandalous Libels, which very highly reflected on his Excellency and the principal Men concern'd in the Administration of this Government, which is confess'd. That is, the Printing and Publishing of the Journals set forth in the Information is confess'd. And concluded that as Mr. Hamilton *had confess'd the Printing and there could be no doubt but they were scandalous Papers, highly reflecting upon his Excellency, and the principal Magistrates in the Province. And therefore he made no Doubt but the Jury would find the Defendant Guilty, and would refer to the Court for their Direction.*

Mr. Ch. Just. Gentlemen of the Jury. The great pains Mr. *Hamilton* has taken, to shew how little Regard Juries are to Pay to the Opinion of the Judges; and his insisting so much upon the Conduct of some Judges in Tryals of this kind; is done, no doubt, with a Design that you should take but very little Notice, of what I might say upon this Occasion. I shall therefore only observe to you that, as the Facts or Words in the Information are confessed: The only Thing that can come in Question before you is, whether the Words as set forth in the Information, make a Lybel. And that is a Matter of Law, no Doubt, and which you may leave to the Court. But I shall trouble you no further with any Thing more of my own, but read to you the Words of a learned and upright Judge* in a Case of the like Nature.

'*To say that corrupt Officers are appointed to ad-*
'*minister Affairs, is certainly a Reflection on the Gov-*
'*ernment. If People should not be called to account for*

*Ch. J. *Holt* in *Tutchin's* Case.

possessing the People with an ill Opinion of the Gov-
' ernment, no Government can subsist. For it is very
' necessary for all Governments that the People should
' have a good Opinion of it. And nothing can be worse
' to any Government, than to endeavour to procure Ani-
' mosities; as to the Management of it, this has always
' been look'd upon as a Crime, and no Government can
' be safe without it be punished.

' Now you are to consider, whether these Words I
' have read to you, do not tend to beget an ill Opinion of
' the Administration of the Government? To tell us,
' that those that are employed know nothing of the Mat-
' ter, and those that do know are not employed. Men are
' not adapted to Offices, but Offices, to Men out of a par-
' ticular Regard to their Interest, and not to their Fitness
' for the Places; this is the Purport of these Papers.

Mr. Hamilton I humbly beg Your Honours
Pardon; I am very much mis-apprehended, if you
suppose what I said was so designed.

Sir, you know; I made an Apology for the Freedom I found myself under a Necessity of using on
this Occasion. I said, there was Nothing personal
designed; it arose from the Nature of our Defence.

The Jury withdrew and in a small Time returned and being asked by the Clerk whether they
were agreed of their Verdict, and whether *John
Peter Zenger* was guilty of Printing and Publishing
the Libels in the Information mentioned? They
answered by *Thomas Hunt*, their Foreman, *Not
Guilty*, Upon which there were three Huzzas in the
Hall which was crowded with People, and the next
Day I was discharged from my Imprisonment."

JOHN PETER ZENGER

The cheers of the crowd annoyed the court and the Chief Justice attempted a rebuke, but Captain Norris, son-in-law of Lewis Morris, replied boldly, saying, " Cheers were customary on such occasions, and especially on the occasion of the trial of the Bishop of London."

The verdict of the jury might have been foreseen when the Chief Justice allowed himself to be drawn into an argument with Hamilton. De Lancey was then a young man without much experience in his profession, and was no match for Hamilton, who was near the close of a long and brilliant career, while his age and manner were as convincing to the jury as his eloquence.

A dinner was given to Hamilton in the evening at the Black Horse Tavern. This famous old inn was then situated in Smith street (now William). In 1750 it was in Queen street (now Pearl street.) Zenger says, " Above forty of the Citizens entertained Mr. *Hamilton* at the black Horse that Day at Dinner, to express their Acknowledgment of his Generosity on this Occasion, and at his Departure next Day he was saluted with the great guns of several Ships in the Harbour, as a publick Testimony of the glorious Defense he made in the Cause of Liberty in this Province."

At a meeting of the Common Council held on September 16, 1735, it was ordered that Hamilton be presented with the Freedom of the Corporation. A committee appointed for the purpose brought in later an appropriate resolution, and also reported, *" that sundry of the Members of this Corporation and*

JOHN PETER ZENGER

Gentlemen of this City have voluntarily Contributed suf-
ficient for a Gold Box of five Ounces and a half Inclos-
ing the Seal of said Freedom; Upon the Lid of which, we
are of Opinion should be engraved the Arms of the City
of New-York."

In addition to the arms of the city the cover bore
the following motto, "DEMERSÆ LEGES-TIMEFACTA
LIBERTAS-HAEC TANDEM EMERGUNT," and on the
inside of the cover, "NON NUMMIS,-VIRTUTE PAR-
ATUR," and part of Tully's wish, "ITA CUIQUE EVENI-
AT, UT DE REPUBLICA MERUIT."

The box and the resolution were taken to Philadelphia by Alderman Stephen Bayard and by him
presented to Hamilton, " who gratefully accepted it."

There was great interest taken in the trial
throughout the country and the papers in Boston
and Philadelphia published full accounts of the proceedings. The first edition entitled " A brief Narrative of the Cafe and Tryal of *John Peter Zenger,*
Printer of the *New-York weekly Journal,*" was published by Zenger in 1736. It was scattered broad-
cast and many copies were sent to London. It is a
folio of forty pages and now very rare. It was edited
by James Alexander, as appears by the following letter from Andrew Hamilton :

" I have at last Sent you my Draught of Mr. Zenger's tryall. When I first wrote you I intended to revise it by my Notes but being interrupted with Business I neglected and at last being in hopes that you
was not like to obtain Mr. Chambers's and Mr. Atty.'s
Argument, your design of publication was over and so
it lay over until our Assembly broke up ye last of Feb-

ruary. Since then we have had Court every day and rather than give you ye trouble of writing again I have Sent it ill done as it is. I have had no time to read it over but once since it was finished. I wrote it by half sheets and copied it as fast as I wrote. The meaning of all this is to beg of you to alter and Correct it agreeable to your own Mind."

There were four editions of the trial published in London in 1738, one edition in Boston, one in Lancaster, Pennsylvania, and it was republished in 1770 in New York when McDougal was tried.

Zenger was made public printer in 1737 as a reward for his troubles, and in 1738 was appointed to the same office in New Jersey. He was naturalized in New Jersey in 1738.

In the fourth volume of the Colonial Documents of the State of New York it is stated on page 1042 that "He was a printer by trade; in arrears to a small amount as collector of taxes in the city, and the Assembly had refused to allow him to discharge the small debt by doing public printing enough to cover it"—a lively instance of ingratitude for the services he had rendered. His absence from the City, however, could not have been very prolonged, for he continued printing the "Journal" until his death, which occurred on July 28, 1746. His obituary was published as follows in the "Evening Post" of August 4, 1746.

"On Monday Evening last, departed this Life, Mr. *John Peter Zenger* Printer, in the 49 Year of his Age; He has left a Wife and six Children behind, he was a loving Husband, and a tender Father, and his Death is much lamented by his Family and Relations."

He is said to have been buried in Trinity Church-yard. The record of the descendants of the Zenger family shows none in the male line. Nothing is known of Johannes, the brother of the printer, and his sister Anna Catharina, who was married September 16, 1727, to Frederick Becker, and died without issue. John, son of the printer by his first wife, married in 1741 Anneke Lynssen, but it does not appear that he left any children who came to maturity. Pieter, son of the second marriage, married October 26, 1751, Brachy Montange of Harlem, but there is no record of any children of this marriage. Elizabeth, born 1726, one of the daughters of the printer's second marriage, married July 6, 1745, John George Kook, a weaver, and left descendants. She died in 1817. Another daughter, Catherine, born 1738, died September 16, 1836, at the advanced age of ninety-eight; she married Matthias Lane, born 1736, died August 14, 1801, and they also left descendants. The Lanes lived in Camden, New Jersey, and are buried there in the Evergreen Cemetery.

Thomas, in his "History of Printing," says, "One of his [Zenger's] daughters was mistress of a tavern in New York in 1758," but which one it was does not appear. There were three other children of John Peter Zenger by his second marriage, who apparently died young or unmarried.

His wife published the "Journal" from the time of her husband's death until December, 1748, when it was taken over by John Zenger, the son of the first marriage. He continued it until 1751, when the publication ceased entirely.

As to the legal and practical result of the trial it is interesting to review briefly the origin and development of the law of libel. When the art of printing was invented, the press immediately became subjected to a severe censorship, a power assumed first by the church and later by the state. This authority was exercised by the Star Chamber during the reign of Elizabeth, and when that body was done away with in 1641, Parliament exercised the right with almost the same degree of severity. Under the Licensing Act of 1662, the control of the press was taken charge of by the Crown. This Act, limited to three years, was, on its expiration, renewed until 1679, and in 1685 it was renewed again for seven years more. But political censorship finally ceased in 1695, when the House of Commons failed to renew the Act by means of which the right was exercised.

After the censorship was thus done away with, the only restraints upon the right to freedom of discussion were those imposed by the law of libel, which became enforceable by the judgments of courts founded on the verdict of juries, but these restraints were practically as despotic as the edicts of the Star Chamber, since the rights and duties of judges and juries remained unsettled. For, though the law of the country entitled a defendant to a trial by jury, yet as the judges were allowed to pass upon both the facts and the law, the result was a practical denial of the right of trial. This state of affairs continued until 1791, when the Libel Act of Fox passed the Commons, establishing the principle that in cases of libel the jury were to be the judges of both the law and the fact, and by this means the judicial tyranny which succeeded the censorship was done away with forever.

The trial of Zenger first established in North America the principle that in prosecution for libel the jury were the judges of both the law and the facts. The liberty of the press was secure from assault and the people became equipped with the most powerful weapon for successfully combating arbitrary power, the right of freely criticizing the conduct of public men, more than fifty years before the celebrated trial of " Junius " gave the same privilege to the people of England.

By degrees the Province of New York resumed its state of former quiet. Cosby died in March, 1736, and was succeeded by George Clarke, a man of more liberal mind. But the old conditions were changed, the result of the trial had imbued the people with a new spirit ; henceforth they were united in the struggle against governmental oppression, and as Gouverneur Morris has well said : " The trial of Zenger in 1735 was the germ of American freedom, the morning star of that liberty which subsequently revolutionized America."

FACSIMILE OF ZENGER'S POWER-OF-ATTORNEY TO JAMES ALEXANDER AND WILLIAM SMITH, TO ACT AS HIS ATTORNEY.

At a Supream Court of Judicature held for the province of New York at the City Hall of the City of New York on Wednesday the 16 Day of April 1735

Present —   The hon'ble James DeLancey Esq'r Chief Justice
The hon'ble Fred.k Phillipse Esq Second Justice

James Alexander Esq'r and William Smith Attorney of this court having performed (notwithstanding they were forewarned by the court of their displeasure if they should do it) to sign and having actually signed and put into court Exceptions in the Names of John Peter Zenger thereby denying the legality of the Judges their Commissions &c'a in the usual form, and the being of this Supream Court: It is therefore ordered that for the said Contempt the said James Alexander and William Smith be excluded from any farther practice in this Court and that their names be struck out of the Role of Attorneys of this court

Jn Chu
James Lyne & Cur

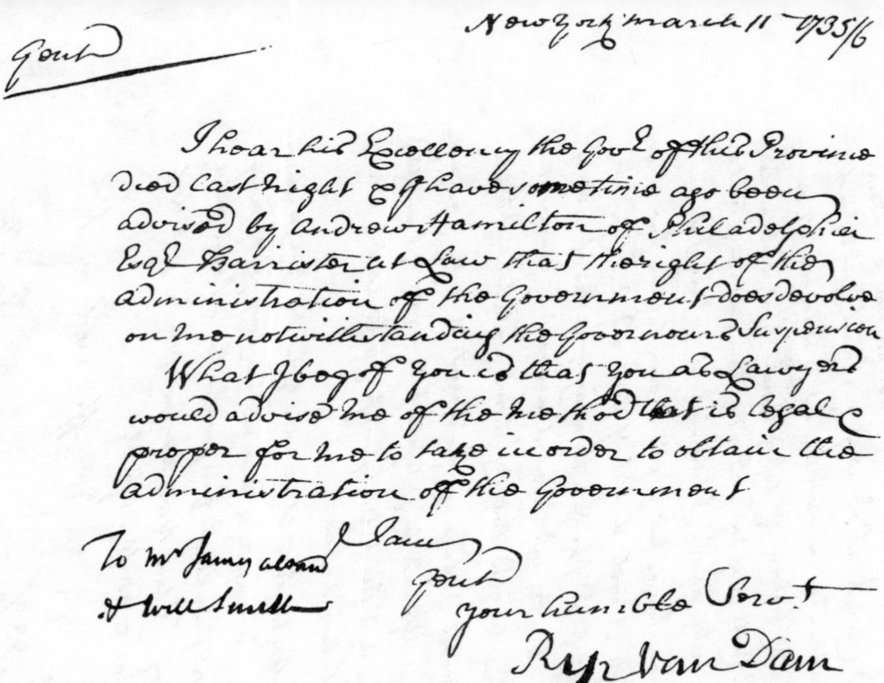

New York march 11 1735/6

Gent

I hear his Excellency the Gov.r of this Province dyed last night & I have some time ago been advised by Andrew Hamilton of Philadelphia Esq.r Barrister at Law that the right of the administration of the Government does devolve on me notwithstanding the Governours Suspension

What I beg of you is that you as Lawyers would advise me of the method that is legal & proper for me to take in order to obtain the administration of the Government

To Mr James Alexand.r & Will Smith

I am
Gent
your humble Serv.t
Rip van Dam

FACSIMILE OF LETTER FROM RIP VAN DAM TO JAMES ALEXANDER AND WILLIAM SMITH, SEEKING THEIR ADVICE WITH REGARD TO THE GOVERNORSHIP.

Sr Jr

I have at last Sent you my Draught of Mr Zenger's tryall which I first wrote yours I intended to revise it by my Nott but being interrupted with Business I neglected and at last being in hopes as you was not like to obtain Mr Chambers and Mr attny's argument your design of publication was over and so it lay over tile our assembly broke up yt Last of February Since which we have had Courts every day and rather than give you ye trouble of writing again I have Sent it ill done as it is — I have had no time to read it over but our find it was finish I wrote it by half sheets and Cud Copid it as fast as I wrote the meaning of all this is to beg of you to alter and Correct it agreeable to your own mind I would be glad that Capt Norris would take ye trouble to Correct ye Language for it wants it much You must add ye Afferend to ye flatt tryall I am obliged to Send it as farr as Burlyton after ye post not being able to get thro it sooner

Be So good as to let me know by the next post what you think Mr Hamilton is doing and how I may get my mony notwithstanding all his faire promisses that day I Left you at Amboy I have never heard from him Since be so good as to advise me yrself

yr affed and huble St

A: Hamilton

Mar 16 1735/6

FACSIMILE OF LETTER FROM ANDREW HAMILTON TO JAMES ALEXANDER, ACCOMPANYING NOTES OF THE TRIAL.

May 6, 1787

Give me leave thus to acknowledge the undeserved favours you were pleased to confer on me last Night, as yet I am in no Capacity of making any other Returns but Thanks, accept them, not only from my self but Family; the Service is (I am sure) great for that compleated my Deliverance, if your more important Affairs can admit, I shall beg leave to be admitted to your Presence this Evening, then to assure you that while I live I shall ever be your more faithful &

your honours much obliged

and most humble servt

Jno Zenger

BIBLIOGRAPHY
OF THE
ISSUES OF THE
ZENGER PRESS
1725–1751

EXPLANATION OF ABBREVIATIONS

The capital letters (as below) following each title indicate the Public Libraries (and in a few cases private collections) which contain the several items:

B. M.	British Museum.
B. P. L.	Boston Public Library.
C. E. N.	Charles Eliot Norton, Cambridge, Mass.
C. H. S.	Connecticut Historical Society, Hartford, Conn.
E. D. C.	E. Dwight Church, New York.
H. S. P.	Historical Society of Pennsylvania.
H. U.	Harvard University.
L.	New York Public Library, Lenox Collection.
L. C. P.	Library Company of Philadelphia.
N. J. H. S.	New Jersey Hi·torical Society.
N. J. S. L.	New Jersey State Library.
N. Y. H. S.	New York Historical Society.
N. Y. S. L.	New York State Library.
W. N.	William Nelson, Paterson, N. J.
Ed.	Editor.

No effort has been made to locate all known copies.

BIBLIOGRAPHY

WILLIAM BRADFORD AND JOHN PETER ZENGER

1725

 LAGTE/Van Eenige Leeden der/NEDER-DUYTSE HERVORMDE KERK,/Woonnede op *Raretans*, &c., in de Provincie van / *NIEU-JERSEY*, in *NOORD-AMERICA*,/ Onder de Kroon van *Groot-Brittanje*./Over het GEDRAG, Aldaar en Elders, / VAN / Do. *THEODORUS JACOBUS FRILING-HUISEN*,/Met syn Kerken-Raaden./TEN/ ANTWOORD/Op hunne/*Ban-Dreygende Daag-Brieven*, &c./ AAN/Alle *Liefhebbers der Waarheyd*, ter ondersoek, voorgesteld, /Hoe Die Gegrond zyn, of Niet./MET een/*Noodige Voor-Reeden*, tot opheldering van de *Klagte*./Uytgegeven Door/*De Gevolmagtigden der gemelde Leeden*./[Small square printer's ornament.] / Te *Nieu-York*, Gedrukt by *William Bradford* en *J. Peter Zenger*. 1725./

4to, 86 leaves.

Collation : Title, 1 page; blank, 1 page ; "Verklaaring," 4 pages ; "Voor de Vitgeevers Van deze Klagte," 3 pages "Op de Klagte zelf," 1 page ; "Voor-Reeden," etc., pages [i]–xvi; text, beginning "Eerste Daagbrief," pages 1–144; Errata, middle of page 144–146.   L.

JOHN PETER ZENGER

1726

DE AANBIDDELYKE/WEGEN GODS/in zyne/*Souveraine Bestieringe*,/Besonder over/DE/MACHTEN deser WEER-ELD, / Verklaart en toegepast / IN / DRIE PREDICATIEN,/

137

JOHN PETER ZENGER

DOOR/*PETRUS VAN DRIESSEN*, V. D. M./Te NIEUW-
ALBANIA. / [Printer's ornament.] / Te NIEUW - YORK,/
Gedrukt by *J. PIETER ZENGER*, MDCCXXVI.

4to, 46 leaves.

Collation : Title, 1 page, printed in black and red ; "Immobilis ad Immobile Numen," etc., 5 lines, printed in red, 1 page ; "Opdragt," 8 pages ;
text, pages [1]–79 ; blank, page [80] ; Errata, page [81] ; blank, page [82].
                                                                    L.

THE ADORABLE / WAYS of GOD / In His / *Sovereign
Government*,/Particularly over/THE/POWERS of this WORLD,
/Explained and Applied/IN/THREE SERMONS./By *PETRUS
VAN DRIESSEN*, V. D. M. / At *NEW-ALBANY*. / NEW-
YORK :/Printed by *John Peter Zenger*, MDCCXXVI.

4to, 43 leaves.

Collation : Title, 1 page ; "Immobilis ad Immobile Numen," 1 page ;
Dedication "To his Excellency William Burnet," 7 pages ; blank, 1 page ;
text, pages [1]–75 ; blank, page [76]. Pages 54, 65, 70, 71 and 72 misnum-
bered 56, 59, 58, 57 and 60. Pages 68 and 69 not numbered.   L.

TSAMENSHRAAK,/Tusschen/*Impetus*, *Legatus* en *Temper-
atus*.

4to, 12 leaves.

Collation : Text, pages 3–24.   H. S. P.
The only copy traced lacks the title-leaf. The above is at the top of page 3.

THE/ INTEREST/ OF THE / COUNTRY/In Laying/
DUTIES :/OR/A DISCOURSE, Shewing how/Duties on some
Sorts of Mer-/chandize may make the Pro-/vince of New-York
richer than/it would be without them./Sold by J. Peter Zenger,
near the City-/Hall in New-York.   Price 6.d./

8vo, 18 leaves.

Collation : Title, page [1]; blank, page [2]; text, pages 3–35; blank,
page [36].   ED.

SAMENSPRAAK /Over de / KLAGHTE / DER / RARI-
TANDERS ;/So in't Gemeen, als wel in't Beson-/der, wegens het
gene in die ter/neder gestelt isten Laste/VAN/CORNELIUS
van SANTVOORD,/Predikant op Staten-Eilant./Meteen/Na-

138

schrift tot Vrede./[Printer's ornament.]/TE NIEUW-YORK,/
Gedrukt by J. Peter Zenger, 1726./

8vo, 107 leaves.

Collation : Title, 1 page ; blank, 1 page ; " Bericht aan der Leeser," 2
pages ; text, pages 1–194 ; " Naschrift tot Vrede," pages i–xiv ; Errata, 1 page;
blank, 1 page.   W. N.

VERDEEDIGING/VAN/D. BERNARDUS FREEMAN,/
WEGENS/HET gene hem voornaamlyk ten Laste/gelegt word
in zeeker BOEK,/GENAAMT KLAGTE, &c./[Printer's ornament.]/Te NIEUW-YORK,/Gedrukt by *J. Peter Zenger*,
in 't Jaar,/MDCCXXVI./

8vo.

Collation : Title and text, pages 1–125 ; [1].
Not seen.   Title furnished by Mr. Wilberforce Eames.

1727

THE/CHARGE/Given by The/CHIEF JUSTICE/OF
THE/*Province* of NEW-YORK,/TO THE/GRAND JURY/
OF/The CITY Of NEW-YORK,/In March Term, 1726–7./
Printed at the Request of the said Grand Jury./*New-York*, Printed
and sold by *John Peter Zenger*, 1727. (pr. 6d.)/

4to, 10 leaves.

Collation : Title, page [1] ; blank, page [2] ; text, pages [3]–19 ;
blank, page [20].   H. S. P.

(1)/To the HONOURABLE/ADOLPH PHILIPSE, Esq;/As it
is a noble and brave thing to defend ones country against the usur-/
pations [etc.].

Folio, 1 leaf.

Collation : Text, pages 1 and 2.   L.

SIR,/IN my Former I frankly informed you in what Manner
your Adver-/saries [etc.].

4to, 2 leaves.

Collation : No separate title-page. Text, pages [1]–[3] ; page [4] blank.
Signed at bottom of page [3], " I am your's &c."   L.
A second letter to Adolph Philipse.

JOHN PETER ZENGER

1728

Willem Christoffel Berkenmeyers/Bedienaars des Heyligen Euan-
geliums van de/*Nederduytsche* Gemeente/TE/*Nieuw-York, Albanie*
on daar ontrent,/Insgelyks/der Parochye der *Palatynen* by *Quassayk,*/
DE ONVERANDERDE A. C. *TOEGEDAAN,* / GER-
TOUWE/HERDER-en WACHTER-/STEM/Ana de Hoog-
en Neder-Duitsche Lutheriaanen/in dese Gewesten,/eenstemmig
te zyn vertoont/met *twee Brieven* en andere Redenen *Luther-
scher Theologanten.*/AANGAANDE/'t *Van Dierensche* Beroep,/EN
/De *Henkelsche* Bevestiging./Te *Nieuw-York,* by *J. Peter Zenger,*
A.C. MDCCXXVIII.

4to, 90 leaves.

Collation: Title, 1 page; "I Timoth. IV., 1, 2 " [etc.], 1 page; blank, 1
page; "Opdracht " [etc.], 1 page; text, pages 1–150, with numerous errors
in the pagination; Postscript, 12 pages; " Druck Feilen," 10 lines, 1 page; blank,
1 page.   H. U.

1729

REMARKS/UPON/ A DISCOURSE/INTITULED / AN
OVERTURE/Presented to the REVEREND SYNOD/of Dissenting MINISTERS sitting/in Philadelphia, in the Month of Sep-/
tember, 1728./In a Letter to the Author./By a Member of the said
SYNOD./[Jonathan Dickinson.]/Printed by J. Peter Zenger,
in Smith-Street,/in New York, 1729./

8vo, 16 leaves.

Collation: Title, p. [1]; blank, p. [2]; text, pages 3–32.   B. P. L.

EEN TROUWHERTIG/VERTOOG/VAN/*Een waare
Rechtveerdige,*/IN TEGENSTELLINGE VAN/*Een Godloose Son-
daar.*/Voorgestelt IN/*Twee Predikatien,*/Over I *Pet.* IV. 18./
Door *Do. Theodorus Jacobus Frilinghuisen,* Predi-/kant der Gereform-
eerde Gemeentens op de/RARITAN./Uit gegeeven volgens de
Vermaaning van den/Propheet *Jesaias,* Cap. III. 10, 11./*Segget den
Rechtveerdigen dat het* (hem) *wel gaan/sal dat sy de Vrucht haarer
Werken sullen eeten.*/*Wee den Godloosen, het sal* (hem) *quaalyk gaan,
want/de Vergeldinge syner handen sal hem geschieden.*/ Nieuw-York,
Gedrukt voor *S. Gerritsen,* en *J. D.*/*Puy,* by *John Peter Zenger,*
MDCXXIX./

8vo, 30 leaves.

Collation : Title, page [1]; verses, beginning : "O ! Snood verkeerd

BIBLIOGRAPHY

Geslacht van ons Nieuw Nederland", page [2], text, beginning "Een Trou-
whertig Vertoog;" pages [3]–59; Errata, page [60].
The imprint has the date 1629 instead of 1729. **L.**

1730

DE/HEERLYKHEIT der GENADE/VAN DEN/EENI-
GEN *en* DRIE-EENIGEN / VERBONDS-GOD:/Volgens de
Gronden/VAN DEN / HEIDELBERGSCHEN / CATECHIS-
MUS,/TOT/Vorderinge en Opbouw in Gods-Keniffe/en waare
Heiligmaakinge,/VOOR/*Het Euangelische Verbonds-Volk verklaart, be-*
/*vestigd en toegepast, met Vraagen en Antwoorden.*/DOOR/PETRUS
VAN DRIESSEN, *V.D.M./te Nieuw-Albanien/* [Printer's orna-
ment.] Gedrukt te *Nieuw-Jork*, by *J. Peter Zenger,*/MDCCXXX./

8vo, 235 leaves.

Collation : Title, 1 page; blank, 1 page; "Verklaaring", 2 pages, dated
at end "Nieuw-York, den 24 Junii, Anno 1730." and signed "G. D. Bois"
and "Henricus Boel."; verses "Op het eerste Deel de Heerlykheit der Genade,"
2 pages, signed at end "Jacob Goelet."; "Opdracht Aan de Bloejende
Gemeinte te Nieuw Albanien", pages [i]–xx, dated at end "Albany den 26 Sept.,
1729," and signed "Petrus Van Driessen."; text, pages [1]–444. Page 194 is
wrongly numbered 94; 319 is 219 and 355 is 323. **N. Y. H. S.**

KORTE SCHETS/En ONTWERP van de voorname/
Grond-Regelen/DER/LEERSTUKKEN/VAN DE/*Hervormde
Nederduytsche*/KERK./Kort en beknoptelyk 'tsamen gesteld/tot on-
derwys en leering van de Jeugt, als der aankommende Leedemaaten./
DOOR/PETRUS VAS, Dienaar Jesu Christi,/in de Gemeinte tot
KINGSTON. / *Den tweeden Druk.*/ [Printer's ornament.]/ Ge-
drukt te *Nieuw-York*, by *J. Pieter Zenger*/MDCCXXX./

12mo.

The only copy traced is imperfect, consisting of title, 1 page; blank, 1 page
prefatory poem, 1 page, the leaf containing page [4] being pasted down upon
the marbled paper cover of a copy of Venema's "Arithmetica." Remainder of
book is lacking. **N. Y. S. L.**

Berkenmeyer (W. C.).   Consilium in Arena, oder Mitleidens
volle Antwort auf das Bitt-Schreiben der Hoch-Teutsch-Luthrischen
Gemeinde im Camp.   Nieuw York.

4to.

Not seen.   Title taken from Sabin, Vol. II, p. 94, No. 4886.   This was
written by Berkenmeyer and as Zenger printed one of his books in 1728 and John
Zenger another in 1749, it is very probable that Zenger printed this one also.

JOHN PETER ZENGER

ARITHMETICA/OF/Cyffer-Konst,/Volgens de Munten Maten en/Gewigten, te NIEU-YORK,/gebruykelyk/Als Mede/ Een kort ontwerp van de/ALGEBRA,/Opgestelt door/PIETER VENEMA,/*Mr.* in de Mathesis en Schryf-Konst/[Printer's or- nament]/NIEU-YORK,/Gedruckt voor *Jacob Goelet*,by de/Oude- Slip, by *J. Peter Zenger*,/MDCCXXX./

12mo, 63 leaves.

Collation: Title, 1 page; blank, 1 page; preface, 2 pages; errata, 1 page; blank, 1 page; text, pages 1–120.　　　　　N. Y. S. L., N. Y. H. S.

Letter to a Parishioner, which J. Mott Pretended to answer in a Pamphlet entitled The Great Work of Christ's Spirit, &c. New- York; Printed by John Peter Zenger. 1730?

sm. 8vo.

Not seen. Title taken from Sabin, Vol. X, p. 262, No. 40421. Probably by Samuel Johnson.

1731

Necessarius/THE continuance of an able and Godly/Minister very needful to a Peopl:./A/SERMON/Preached at the Funeral of the Reve-/rend Mr. JOHN DAVENPORT,/late Pastor of the Church in Stam/ford; who died on Fryday Febr. 5,/1730–1, in the 62 Year of his Age,/and 36 of his Ministry: And was/decently in- terred on Munday folow-/ing./By the Rev. SAMUEL COOKE, Pastor of the/Church of Christ in Stratfield./2 Reg. ii 12. My Father, my Father! the Chariot of/Israel, and the Horsemen thereof./ Printed by J. P. Zenger in New-York, 1731./

8vo, 32 leaves.

Collation: Pages 1 and 2 lacking in the only copy examined, perhaps a half- title; title, page [3]; blank, page [4]; text, pages [5]–62, Pages 63–64 lack- ing in the copy examined, probably blank.　　　　　N. Y. H. S.

[Two rows of printer's ornaments.]　GEORGE the second, by the Grace of God, of *Great Brittain*,/*France* and *Ireland*, King, Defender of the Faith, &c./To all to whom/these Presents shall come, Greeting.

Folio, 4 leaves.

Collation: No separate title-page. Text pages [1]–8. Dated at end "at Fort George in the City of New-York, the eighth day of June, in the fourth year of our Reign, Annoq; Domini, One Thousand seven Hundred and Thirty-one,'' and signed ''Clarke.'' Following the document proper is an extract from the original Letters Patent, 9 lines, with heading, 2 lines.   N. Y. H. S.

Patent granting to Thomas Hanly, Nathan St. John and others, four tracts of land known as the Oblong, situated on the partition line between New York and Connecticut. '' To Zenger for 200 copies of our patent with paper £4, 7,0.'' *Accounts of the Equivalent Land Co.*, p. 5.

1732

A/True and Just/VINDICATION/OF/Mr *Alexander Campbell*,/FROM/The several Aspersions cast upon him, and that/Load of undeserved Calumny and Reproach, he at/present lyes under./ In a Letter directed, *To* Edmund, *Lord Bishop/of* LONDON./ *NEW-YORK*:/Printĕd by *John Peter Zenger,* MDCCXXXII./

12mo, printed in fours.

Collation: Title, p. [1]; blank, p. [2]; text, pp. [3]–14; blank, pages [15–16]. Dated at end ''New-York, July 30, 1732.'' and signed ''Alex. Campbell.''   L.

A/SUPPLEMENT/TO THE/VINDICATION/OF/Mr. *Alex. Campbell:*/WHEREIN/All the Objections made to the said Vindica-/tion are answered, particularly, those in a/late Paper, called, *Mr Noxons Observa-/tions &c.*/[Row of printer's ornaments.]/*New-York,*/Printed by *J. Peter Zenger*, in/*Smith-Street.*/

12mo, printed in fours.

Collation: Title, page [1]; blank, page [2]; text, pages [3]–35; blank, page [36]. Dated at end (page 35), ''New-York, August 15, 1732.'' and signed ''Alex. Campbell.''   L.

Mr. *NOXON'S*/OBSERVATIONS/UPON/Parson *Campbell's* Vindication./

[Colophon :] NEW-YORK, Printed by *John Peter Zenger,* M DCC XXXII./

Folio, 1 leaf.

Collation: Text, 1 page; blank, 1 page. The above heading at top, extending across the page; text below, in two columns, beginning: ''I Resolve (as you have done in | the 12th Page of your Vindication) | [etc.]''   L.

[Two rows of printer's ornaments.] *Maxima libertatis custodia est, ut magna Imperia diurturna/non sint, & temporis modus imponatur quibus juris imponi/non potest.* Mammerc. *apud* Liv./

JOHN PETER ZENGER

[Colophon:] *NEW-YORK*, printed by *John Peter Zenger*, M DCC XXXII./

Folio, 1 leaf.

Collation: Text, pages [1] and [2]. The above heading is at top of page [1] extending across the page. The text is in two columns and begins: "If ever we shall lose our Liberties in | Great Britain [etc.]" Signed at end, above the colophon, "M. B."   L.

[Two rows of printers ornaments.] *Nullum tempus, ulla praescriptio occurit veritati.* Tertul./*Lex est sanctio recta, jubens honesta, prohibens contraria.* Cicero.

Folio, 2 leaves.

Collation: No separate title-page. Text, beginning: "Men are subject to Errors, and it is the Work of the Best and | Wisest" etc., signed "Yonr humble Servant. | John Sydney." pages [1] and [4]; pages 2 and 3 are blank. [4].
The above is the description of the only copy known. It is evidently a proof and it was probably the intention to issue the sheet as a single leaf, printed on both sides.

[One row of printer's ornaments.]/*Vincit amor patriæ,* Virg./

Folio, 1 leaf.

Collation: Text, pages [1] and [2]. The row of printer's ornaments extends across the page. Text is in two columns, the above heading being at top of the first column of page [1]. Text begins "Some Gentlemen, who are other- | wise Men of Sense, [etc.]" Signed at end, "Andrew Fletcher."   L.
Advising annual elections to the Assembly.

[Three rows of printer's ornaments.]/O Liberty, thou Goddess heavenly bright!/Profuse of Bliss, and pregnant with Delight!/Eternal Pleasures in thy Presence Reign,/And smiling Plenty leads thy wanton Train./Eas'd of its Load, Subjection grows more light,/And Poverty looks chearful in thy Sight./Thou mak'st the gloomy Face of Nature gay,/Giv'st Beauty to the Sun, and Pleasure to the Day./ 'Tis Liberty that crowns *Brittania's* Isle,/And makes her barren Rocks and her bleak Moun-/tains smile./*Addison.*/

Folio, 2 leaves.

Collation: No separate title-page. Text, pages [1]-3; page [4] blank. The above verses quoted from Addison, printed in large type at top of page [1]; text in long lines beginning:
"There is nothing in which the Generality of Mankind are so much | mistaken, as when they talk of Government [etc.]" Signed at end, "Portius."
On the necessity of frequent elections.   L.

144

BIBLIOGRAPHY

A LETTER/From a Gentleman in in the COUNTRY/to his Friend in TOWN./

Folio, 1 leaf.

Collation: Text, page [1], page [2] blank. Heading as above at top. Text, printed in long lines, signed, at bottom, "Robt. Dissolution."

On Cosby's first Assembly.   L., N. Y. S. L.

[One row of printer's ornaments.]/*To F—H—Esq;*/

Folio, 2 leaves.

Collation: No separate title-page. Text, pages [1]-4. Printed in two columns, the above heading in small type at the top of the first column of page [1]. Text begins: " I am very much oblig'd to you/for your sincere Wishes, and do/[etc.]"   L.

Addressed to Francis Harison, apparently, and in defence of Alexander Campbell.

(1)/*To the Reverend Mr.* Vesey *and his two/Subalterns, viz.* Tom Pert *the Beotian,/and Clumsy* Ralph *the Cimmerian.*/

Folio, 2 leaves

Collation: No separate title-page. Text, pages 1-4. The above heading is at top of page 1. The text is in long lines and begins : " It is somewhat surprizing that Gentlemen who pretend to Learning/and Discretion," [etc.] L.

1733

[Four rows of printer's ornaments.]/To the Author of those Intelligencers/printed at *Dublin,* to which is pre-/fix'd the following Motto,/*Omne vafer vitium ridenti* Flaccus *amico/Tangit, & admissus circum præcordia ludit./Persius./*Being a Defence of the Plantations against the/virulent Aspersions of that Writer, and such/as copy after him./[One row of printer's ornaments.]/

[Colophon:] NEW-YORK, Printed and Sold By *J. Peter* Zenger. 1733./

Folio, 5 leaves.

Collation: No separate title-page. Text pages 1-10. Heading as above at top of page 1. Signed at end "Roscommon."   L.

THE/ARGUMENTS/OF THE/Council for the Defen-dant,/In Support of/A Plea to the JURISDICTION,/Pleaded to a Bill filed in a Course of EQUITY,/At the SUIT of/The

145

JOHN PETER ZENGER

ATTORNEY GENERAL,Complainant,/AGAINST/RIP VÁN DAM, Defendant,/IN THE/Supream Court of/NEW-YORK./ (Printers' Ornament) *NEW-YORK:*/Printed by *JOHN PETER ZENGER*, M,DCC,XXXIII./

Folio, 27 leaves.

Collation: Title, 1 page; blank, 1 page; text, pages 1–51, with Errata, 5 lines at bottom of page 51; page [52] blank. L.

The latest date of any of the documents included seems to be April 9, 1733. This portion was probably published during the summer.

[One row of printer's ornaments.] The Proceedings of *Rip Van Dam*, Esq; in order/for obtaining Equal Justice of His Excellency/*William Cosby*, Esq;/[Colophon at bottom of p. 63:]/*New York* : Printed and Sold by *John Peter Zenger*, where also/is to be sold, *The Argument of* Van Dam's *Couucil in Support of/his Plea to the Jurisdiction of the Supream Court of* New-York./

MDCCXXXIII./

Folio, 6 leaves

Collation: No separate title-page. Text, pages 53–63; page 64 blank. Heading in large type as above at top of page 53. Text begins, "My Plea being over-ruled, as by the Minutes of Court and Ar-/guments" [etc]. Signed at end "Rip Van Dam." L.

The latest document included is dated October 22. This piece was advertised in the *New York Weekly Journal*, No. 5, Dec. 3, 1733, as follows :

"There is now printing and will shortly be published, and to be sold by the Printer of this Paper, *The Proceedings of* Rip Van Dam *Esq*; *in order for* obtaining equal Justice of His Excellency William Cosby, *Esq*; by which it seemeth that said *Van Dam* conceives an Attack has been made in this Province on *the Priviledge of* JURIES *in the Case where it is of greatest Value, to* witt, *between* THE KING and HIS SUBJECTS, or rather, GOVERNOUR and PEOPLE : it contains three Sheets, price 9d."

Eleutherius Enervatus;/OR/An Answer to a Pamphlet, Intitu-/led, The divine Right of Presbyte-/rian Ordination, &c., argued./ Done by way of Dialogue/BETWEEN/Eusebius and Eleutherius, together with/two Letters upon this Subject, some/Time agoe sent to the supposed Auther/of that Pamphlet./Isai. 65. 2.5. I have spread out my Hands all the Day/unto a rebellious People, which walketh in a way that/was not good, after their own Thoughts, which say stand/ by thy self, come not near to me, for I am holier than thou./These are

BIBLIOGRAPHY

a smoke in my Nose; a Fire that Burneth all the/Day./NEW-YORK
/Printed by J. Peter Zenger,/MDCCXXXIII./

8vo, 58 leaves.

Collation: Title, page [1]; blank, page [2]; text, pages 3–115; blank
page [116].   B. P. L.

[Two rows of printer's ornaments.]/Farther proceedings concerning the Case of *Rip*/*Van Dam*, Esqr. at the Suit of the Attor-
ney/General being for the Use of his Excellency/Coll. *Cosby* Governour of this Province, in/the Equity Side of the *Exchequer*./

Folio, 2 leaves.

Collation: No separate title-page.   Text pages 65–[68], page 68 being
wrongly numbered 80.   Heading, as above, in large type at top of page 65.
Text begins "Some People have been pleased to blame me for not accepting of the
/Accommodation [etc]" Signed at bottom of page [68] "Rip Van Dam."   L.
   As one document included is dated "19th Day of January, 1733–4" this
was printed, probably in January, or in February at the latest.

A/LETTER/From a Gentleman in New-York, to his/Friend
in London./
   [Colophon:] America : Printed in the Year 1733./

4to, 2 leaves.

Collation: No separate title-page. Text, pages 1–3, blank, p. [4]. Signed
at end "Sir,/Your most Humble Servant,/P. P."   N.Y.S.L.
   A criticism of Cosby for taking a present from the Assembly.

A/LETTER/FROM/*A Minister of the Church*/OF/ENG-
LAND/TO HIS/*Dissenting Parishioners.* / CONTAINING / A
brief Answer to the most material Objec-/tions against the Establish'd Church that/are to be found in De Laune's Plea, The/Ans-
wer to the Bishop of Derry, The plain/Reasons for separating, &c.
and others./ Together with plain Reasons for Confor-/mity to
the Church of *England.*/1 Kings 18, 21. *How long halt ye between
two Opinions.*/1 Cor. 14, 40. *Let all Things be done decently and in*
(or ac-/cording to) *Order.*/1 Pet. 2, 13. *Be subject to every Ordinance of Man for the/Lord's Sake.*/ *New-York*, Printed by *John
Peter Zenger*, 1733./

12mo, printed in fours ; 16 leaves.

Collation : Title, page [1]; blank, page [2]; text, pages 3–31; blank,
page [32].   N. Y. S. L.
Probably by Samuel Johnson, D.D.

147

JOHN PETER ZENGER

A PROTESTATION. [1733]

Folio, 3 leaves.

Collation: No separate title-page. Text, pages 1–5; blank, page [6].
Above heading at top of page 1. Dated at end "this Twenty-sixth Day of
March, . . . 1733," and signed "Alex. Campbell." Signature of Notary
and postscript, 17 lines, at end.   L.

Protestation of Alexander Campbell against his examination on charges preferred to the Bishop of London.

The Opinion and Argument of the Chief Justice of the Province of New-York.

A first edition of this piece must have been printed, but no copy has been
found.

(1)/The Opinion and Argument of the/Chief Justice of the
Province of *New-*/*York,* concerning the Jurisdiction of the/supream
Court of the said Province,/*to determine Causes in a Course of Equity.*/
The Second Edition Corrected and Amended./To his Excellency *WIL-
LIAM COSBY*, Esq;/[etc.].

[Colophon:] NEW-YORK, Printed and sold by *John Peter
Zenger*, in Smith Street, 1733./

Folio, 8 leaves.

Collation: No separate title-page. Text, pages 1–15; page [16] blank.
Heading, as above, at top of page 1. Colophon, as above, at bottom of page
15. Text is signed at end "Lewis Morris."   L.

(2)/The Opinion and Argument of the/Chief Justice of the
Province of *New-*/*York,* concerning the Jurisdiction of the/supream
Court of the said Province,/*to determine Causes in a Course of Equity.*/
—*The Second Edition Corrected.*/To his Excellency *WILLIAM
COSBY*, Esq;/[etc.].

[Colophon:] NEW-YORK, Printed and Sold by *J. Peter
Zenger.* 1733./

Folio, 8 leaves.

Collation: No separate title-page. Text, pages [1]–15; blank, page [16].
Page [1] is wrongly numbered 2. Heading, as above, at top of page [1].
Text is signed at end "Lewis Morris." Below the signature is a list of errata,
six lines (where the edition is corrected: "for second read third.") and colophon, as above.   L.

THE/VINDICATION./OF/*James Alexander,*/One of His
Majesty's Council for the Province of *New-York,*/AND OF/

148

BIBLIOGRAPHY

William Smith,/Attorney at Law,/From the Matters charged and suggested against/them in two Pamphlets lately published./THE ONE/A Paper addressed to the Mayor, Aldermen and Commonalty of/the City of *New-York*, by the Honourable *Francis Harrison*, Esq ;/one of His Majestys Council, for the Province of *New-York*./ THE OTHER/A Report of the Committee of His Majesty's Council, to whom it/was referred to examine and make Inquiry touching a Letter found/in the House of Mr. *Alexander*, in *New-York* on Fryday the 1*st* of/*February, 1732–3 in order to make the fullest Discovery concerning the*/*Author of the same.*/ *To which is added*/A/SUPPLEMENT/CONTAINING/A brief Account of the Case of *William Trusdell*, Plaintiff,/AGAINST/the Honourable *Francis Harison*, Esq; Defendant,/For Arresting and Imprisoning the Plaintiff and keeping him 9 Weeks in Prison, at/the Suit of *Joseph Weldon*, without the Assent, Consent, or Knowledge of the/same *Joseph Weldon.*/Which Cause was tried in the Supream Court of *New-York*, on the 19*th* of *April,*/1734. wherein the Jury found for the Plaintiff *Trusdell* l.150. Damages, and/Costs of Suit./Printed by *John Peter Zenger*, and to be sold by him at his House in *Broad Street*, near/the upper End of the long Bridge, in *New-York*, 1733. Price 1*s.*/

Folio, 11 leaves.

Collation: Title, 1 page; Errata, 1 page; text, pages [1]–15; Supplement, pages, 16–20.　　　　　　　　　　　　　　　　　　　　　L.

Advertised in the *New York Weekly Journal*, No. 27, dated May 6, 1734, as " This Day is published The Vindication of *James Alexander*,'' etc.

THE/New-York Weekly Journal./Containing the freshest Advices, Foreign, and Domestick./ [/Colophon :] NEW-YORK : Printed and Sold by *John Peter Zenger* : By whom Subscriptions/for this Paper are taken in at three Shillings *per* Quarter./

Nine numbers. From No. 1, dated October 5 (a misprint for November 5), 1733, to No. 9, dated December 31, 1733. Each number consists of four pages.

1734

[Two rows of printer's ornaments.]/Some Observations on the Charge given/by the Honourable *James DeLancey,*/Esq; Chief Justice of the Province of/*NEW-YORK*, to the Grand Jury, the/15*th* Day of *January,* 1733·/

JOHN PETER ZENGER

[Colophon:] NEW-YORK./Printed and sold by *J. Peter Zenger*, Price 1*s.* 1733–4./

Folio, 9 leaves.

Collation: No separate title-page. Text, pages 1–18; page 8 being wrongly numbered 6. Heading, as above, at top of page 1; Colophon, as above, at bottom of page 18. Not signed.   **L.**

This piece was advertised in the *New York Weekly Journal*, No. 20, March 18, 1733–4, as follows:

"THere are Printed and Sold, by the Publisher hereof some Observations on the Charge given by the Honorable *James De Lancey*, Esqr., Chief Justice of the Province of *New York*, to the grand Jury, on the 15th Day of *January* 1733, Price, 1s."

The above advertisement was repeated in Nos. 21 and 22, March 25 and April 1, 1734.

A Song made upon the Election of/new Magistrates for this City./To the tune of, To you fair Ladies now/on land/

Folio, 1 leaf.

Collation: Text, 1 page, blank, 1 page. Two songs printed in two columns, above heading being at top of first column. The second song begins near the bottom of the first column and continues, filling the second. It has the heading, "A Song made upon the foregoing/Occasion." Text and headings printed from italic types of two different founts.

L.; N. Y. S. L.; B. M.

[Two rows of printer's ornaments.]/*King's County, the* 12*th of September*, 1734./Mr. *Zenger*;/I Received two Days ago a Letter from some of my Brother Trades-Men in/the City, [etc.]

Folio, 2 leaves.

Collation: No separate title-page. Text, pages 1–3; page [4] blank. The above is the beginning of a letter, 7 lines, besides superscription and subscription, signed "Timothy Wheelwright." Following this, filling the remainder of page 1, all of page 2, and 7 lines (besides superscription) on page 3, is a second letter dated "New York, the 8th of September, 1734.", addressed to "Brother Chip;" and signed "John Chisel." Following this, on page 3, is a third letter, also addressed to "Brother Chip;" but signed "Timothy Wheelwright." It is undated.   **L.**

— — *Ridentem dicere verum*/*Quid vetat?* — — —/

Narrow folio, 1 leaf, being one-half of an ordinary folio leaf.

Collation: Text, 1 page; blank, 1 page. Forty lines of verse beginning:

"In antient Days a Bestial Train
In Council met upon the Plain:"

BIBLIOGRAPHY

printed in Roman type, the heading, as above, being in large black-faced italics.

L.

Satirical verses directed against Francis Harison, apparently.

[Two rows of printer's ornaments.]/*DAMON* and *ALEXIS*./ A/PASTORAL./[One row of printer's ornaments]. *Deus nobis haec Otia fecit.* Virg. [One row of printer's ornaments].

4to, 2 leaves.

Collation: No separate title-page. Text, pages [1] 4. Above heading is at the top of page [1].

L.

A Copy of a Letter from James Jackson/of Goshen, in Orange County, in the/Province of New York, to his Friend/in Ireland./

Folio, 2 leaves.

Collation: Text, pp. 1–4.

The only copy seen has the following endorsement in the handwriting of James Alexander : " 1734–Aprile 13th. James Jackson brought me this, on reading of it I asked him who wrote it for him for it was very well wrote, he told me he had wrote the Substance of it himself, but it was Mr. P. had corrected it and put it in good form for him. I asked him who printed it, he said Zenger. I asked him the use he proposed by it, he said their Court was going to Sit, and he was threatened to be indicted, and he thought but to have his case publick for his Justification. I asked him if he had not been with Mr. Harrison upon this Matter, he said not till this Morning that he carried him a Coppy of it.

[Two rows of printer's ornaments.]/Heads of Articles of Com-plaint, made by *Rip Van*/*Dam*, Esq ; on *Thursday* the 30*th* of *May*, 1734,/to the Committee of Grievances, appointed by/the General Assembly for the Province of *New-*/*York*; reduced to Writing by order of the said/Committee ; who also ordered, that a Copy there-/of be served on the Chairman, and Mr Justice/*Phillipse.*/

Folio, 2 leaves.

Collation: No separate title-page. Text, pages 69–71; page [72] blank. Heading, as above, is at top of page 69. Signed at end "Rip Van Dam." L.

THE/New-York Weekly Journal./Containing the freshest Advices, Foreign, and Domestick./

[Colophon] NEW-YORK : Printed and Sold by *John Peter Zenger* : By whom Subscriptions/for this Paper are taken at three Shillings *per* Quarter ; and Advertisements at three/Shillings the first Week, and one Shilling every Week after :/

151

JOHN PETER ZENGER

Fifty-one numbers. From No. 10, dated January 7, 1733, to No. 60, dated December 30, 1734. No number was issued for Nov. 18. Each number consists of four pages, except No. 21, March 25, which has six pages, and No. 27, May 6, which has two pages only.

1735

A/SERMON/Preach'd before the/Commission/OF THE/ SYNOD,/AT/PHILADELPHIA./ April 20th, 1735./ By E. PEMBERTON,/Pastor of the Presbyterian Church in the/City of New-York./NEW-YORK,/Printed by John Peter Zenger, 1735./

8vo, 11 leaves.

Collation: Title, p. [1]. blank, p. [2]; "To the Reverend Commission of the Synod." [etc.], pages 3–4; text, pages 5–21.   B. P. L.

THE/ESPOUSALS/OR/A Passionate Perswasive to a Mar-/ riage with the Lamb of God,/WHEREIN/The Sinners Misery/ AND / The Redeemers Glory/ is Unvailed in/A Sermon upon *Gen.* 24 49. Preach'd/at *N. Brunswyck, June* the 22d, 1735./By *Gil-bert Tennent*, A.M./And Minister of the Gospel there./*Qui Christum neiset, nil est si cetera discit/Qui Christum discit, sat est si cetera nescit.*/ NEW-YORK,/Printed by J. Peter Zenger, 1735./

8vo, 34 leaves.

Collation: Title, page [1]; blank, page [2]; "Courteous Reader," page 3; text, pages 4–66; "Advertisement," page 67; Errata, page [68]. H.S.P.

THE/Danger of forgetting GOD,/describ'd./AND/The Duty of Considering our Ways/explain'd./IN A/SERMON/ON Psalm L. 22/Preach'd at *New-York,* March 1735./By GILBERT TEN-NENT A.M./and Minister of the Gospel at *New-Brun-/swick* in *New-Jersey.*/NEW-YORK./Printed by *John Peter Zenger,* 1735./.

12mo, printed in fours; 16 leaves, the last blank.

Collation: Title, page [1]; "Courteous Reader," page [2]; text, pages 3–30.   H. S. P.

This piece was advertised in the *New York Weekly Journal,* No. 111, dated December 22, 1735, and in several later numbers, as follows :

" JUST published, and to be sold by the Printer hereof, a Sermon preached in *New-York,* last *March,* by the Rev. Mr. *Gilbert Tennent* of *New Bruns-wick.*"

THE/CHARTER/OF THE/ CITY/OF/NEW-YORK;/ Printed by Order of the Mayor, Recor-/der, Aldermen and Com-

BIBLIOGRAPHY

monalty of/the City aforesaid./TO WHICH IS ANNEXED,/ The Act of the General Assembly Confirming the/same [One row of printer's ornaments.]/NEW-YORK,/Printed by *John Peter Zenger*. 1735./

Folio, 26 leaves.

Collation: Title, page [1]; blank, page [2]; text, pages 3–52. Pages 12 and 13 are wrongly numbered 10 and 11.   L., N. Y. H. S.

Advertised in the *New York Weekly Journal*, No. 98, dated September 23, 1735, as follows :

"New York, Sept. 19.—This Day was published, and to be sold by the Printer hereof, THE/CHARTER/OF THE/CITY of NEW-YORK/Containing 13 Sheets, price 3s."

Advertised, also, in several later numbers.

[Three rows of printer's ornaments.]/The Complaint of *James Alexander* and/*William Smith* to the Committee of/the General Assembly of the Colony/of *New-York, &c.*/

Folio, 10 leaves

Collation: No separate title-page. Text, pages 1–19; page [20] blank. Heading, as above, is at the top of page 1. The affidavit at end is dated December 27, 1735.   L.

THE/New-York Weekly Journal./Containing the freshest Advices, Foreign, and Domestick./

[Colophon] NEW-YORK : Printed and Sold by *John Peter Zenger* : By whom Subscriptions/for this Paper are taken at three Shillings *per* Quarter ; and Advertisements at three/Shillings the first Week, and one Shilling every Week after./

Fifty-two numbers. From No. 61, dated January 6, 1734, to No. 112, dated December 29, 1735. Each number consists of four pages, except No. 99, which has two pages only.

1736

THE/VANITY/OF/Human Institutions/IN THE/Worship of God./A/SERMON/Preached at Newark, June 2, 1736. To/which are added, some little Enlarge-/ments./By Jonathan Dickinson, M.A./Minister of the Gospel at Elizabeth/Town, in New-Jersey./[*Quotation from* Gal. iv. 9]/New-York, Printed by John Peter Zenger, 1736./

12mo

Collation: Title, 1 page; blank, 1 page; "To the Presbyterian/Congregation at Newark in New-Jersey," pages i–vi; text, pages 1–32; "Errata," ten lines, a slip. /

JOHN PETER ZENGER

Not seen. Title furnished by Mr. Wilberforce Eames, from a copy formerly owned by Mrs. Daniel Van Pelt of Astoria, Long Island.

[One row of printer's ornaments.] / *New-York, March* 24, 1735, 6. / WHEREAS on the 13*th* day of this Instant *March,* / *James Alexander*, Esq; one of his Majesty's Council/[etc.].

Folio, 1 leaf.

Collation: Text, 1 page; blank, 1 page. Printed in large type and in long lines, beginning as above. Signed at end "James Alexander."   L.

SIR; *New-York, April* 26*th*, 1736. / WHEREAS on the 10*th* Day of *March* last, immediately u-/pon the Death of His Excellency *William Cosby*, Esq; [etc].

Folio, 1 leaf.

Collation: Text, 1 page; blank, 1 page. Printed in long lines, beginning as above. Signed at end "Your humble Servant." The Lenox copy is signed in ink below "Rip Van Dam."   L.

[Three rows of printer's ornaments.] / To All to whom these Presents shall/come or may any Way concern; / *RIP VAN DAM* sendeth greeting./

Folio, 3 leaves

Collation: No separate title-page. Text, pages 69–73; page [74] blank. Heading as above is at top of page 69. Signed at end "Rip Van Dam."   L.

Advertised in the *New York Weekly Journal*, No. 125, dated March 29, 1736, as follows :

By Order of Rip Van Dam Esq, LAST Week was published His the said *Van Dam's* Protestation, Shewing the Steps he has taken in offering his Claim of Right to the Administration of this Government on the decease of Governour Cosby. To be sold by John Peter Zenger. Price 6d.

A LETTER/To one of the Members of the late General/Assembly,/

[Colophon :] Printed by *John Peter Zenger*, 1736./

Folio, 1 leaf.

Collation: No separate title-page. Text, 2 pages. The above heading is at the top of page [1], extending across the page. Text in double columns, signed at end " I am/Sir, Your very humble Servant,/— — —./"   L

[Two rows of printer's ornaments.] Copy of a Letter from *Rip Van Dam/Esq*; to the several Members of that/General Assembly of *New-York*, that/stood adjourned to the last *Tuesday*/of *March*, 1736.

Folio, 2 leaves.

BIBLIOGRAPHY

Collation : No separate title-page. Text, pages 1–4. Page 2 is wrongly numbered 11 and page 4 is wrongly numbered 13. **L.**

Advertised in the *New York Weekly Journal*, No. 130, dated May, 3, 1736, as follows :

"LAst week was published, by Order of *Rip Van Dam*, Esq, *a Coppy of his Letter, to the Several Members of the General Assembly that stood adjourned to the Last Tuesday of March 1726.* sent with a Copy of his Protestation.

Last Week was also published, by Order of the said Members, *The Declaration of a Majority of the Members of the said General Assembly met at the City Hall of* New-York, *on the* 29th *of* April, 1736, *with their Reasons, why they thought it not safe to act, upon the Foot of a late Adjournment by* George Clarke, Esq; &c.

Both the said Papers are printed together, and to be sold by the Printer hereof, *price* 4*d.*"

[Two rows of printer's ornaments.]/His Majesty's Royal/ COMMISSION/TO/*WILLIAM COSBY*; Esq,/For the Government of the Province of/NEW-YORK./[One row of printer's ornaments.]

[Colophon:] Printed by *John Peter Zenger*, Printer to the King's M∿st Excellent Majesty,/for the Province of *New-York.* M,DCC,XXXVI./

Folio, 4 leaves.

Collation: No separate title-page. Text, pages 1–8. Heading as above, filling the upper half of page 1. Above the colophon, printed in large type is found the legend:

"By Order of the Honourable Rip Van Dam, Esq;/Eldest Councillor, and Commander in Chief of/the Province of New-York./ **L.**

(1) [Three rows of printer's ornaments.] A brief Narrative of the Case and Try-/al of *John Peter Zenger*, Printer of the/*New-York weekly Journal.*/ [One row of ornaments.] As There was but one Printer in the Province of *New-York*, [etc.].

[Colophon:] *New-York*, Printed and sold by *John Peter Zenger.* MDCCXXXVI./

Folio, 20 leaves.

Collation: No separate title-page. Text, pages 1–[40], pages 15 to 40 being wrongly numbered 17 to 42. With 2 lines of errata at end, above colophon. **L.**

Advertised in the *New York Weekly Journal*, No. 98, dated September 23, 1735, as follows :

"There is now in the Press, and will be publish-/ed with all imaginable Speed, *A brief Narative of/the Case and Tryal of* John Peter Zenger, *Printer of/the* New-York weekly Journal.—Containing a/brief Account of the Proceed-

JOHN PETER ZENGER

ings against him, and/of his Tryal, for Printing his Journals No. 13 &/23, both before and during his 9 Months Impri-/sonment on that Pretence./"

Also advertised in the *Journal*, No. 137, dated June 21, 1736, and in other numbers, as follows :

" *Just published,*/

A brief Narrative of the Case and Try-/al of *John Peter Zenger*, Printer of the/ *New-York weekly Journal*./ To be sold by the Printer hereof./ April 12, 1736./"

City of New-York, Sept. 28, 1736./A WORD IN SEASON./ *Fellow Citizens.*/

[Colophon :] *Printed by* J. Peter Zenger./

Folio, 1 leaf.

Collation: Text, 2 pages.   N.Y.S.L.; B.M.

OBSERVATIONS/On the REASONS given by Mr. *Ha-/milton's* Advisers, for his Detaining the/Seals of the Province of *New-Jersie*, after/the Demand made of them by *Lewis*/*Morris*, **Esq**; President of the Council/and Commander in Chief of the Pro-/vince of New-Jersie./In a LETTER to a FRIEND./

Folio, 6 leaves.

Collation: No separate title-page. Text, pages 1–11; blank, page [12].
N.J.S.L.

WAARSCHOUWING/Tegens Zeker Boekje, genaamt/ VADERLIK GESCHENK, &c./DOOR/JACOBTENCATE/ Waar in de Dweperyen en Vrygeestery van Ten / Cate en de befaamde Antoinette de Bourignon Dui-/delyk ontdekt worden, ten dienste der klein-/weetende misleide Zielen, en Bestieringe der/ Regtzinnigen./Opgesteltt door/De Predikanten van Groningen./ [Printer's Ornament]/voor heen te Groningen by Jurijen Spandaw, nu gedrukt./TE NEW-YORK door J. Peter Zenger.
MDCCXXXVI./

4to, 17 leaves.

Collation. Title, 1 page; "Uitgegeven volgens Kerten ordere," 1 page; text, pages 1–28; "Herders Kouwt Tusschen Vaarmond en Veederyk," pages 24–32. Title furnished by Mr. Wilberforce Eames.

THE/New-York Weekly Journal./Containing the freshest Ad-vices, Foreign, and Domestick.

[Colophon :] NEW-YORK : Printed and Sold by *John Peter*

BIBLIOGRAPHY

Zenger : By whom Subscriptions/for this Paper are taken at three Shillings *per* Quarter; and Advertisements at three/Shillings the first Week, and one Shilling every Week after :/

Fifty-two numbers. From No. 113, dated January 5, 1735, to No. 164, dated December 27, 1736. Each number consists of four pages.

1737

[Two rows of printer's ornaments.] A Journal of the Votes and Proceed-/ings of the General Assembly of His/Majesty's Colony of *New-York*, in/*America*./

Folio, 54 leaves.

Collation: No separate title-page. Text, pages 1–107. Page 57 is omitted in the pagination and page 106 is repeated. Pages 57 to 105 are therefore wrongly numbered 58 to 106. Made up of 24 numbers, each a separate publication, as follows:

[No. 1]. Pages 1–5 (page 6 blank).
No. 2   "   7–8
No. 3   "   9–12
No 4   "   13–22
No. 5   "   23–25 (page [26] blank).
No 6   "   27–29   "   [30]   "
No. 7   "   31–33   "   [34]   "
No. 8   "   35–39   "   [40]   "
No. 9   "   41–43   "   [44]   "
No. 10   "   45–47   "   [48]   "
No. 11   "   49–52
No 12   "   53–55   "   [56]   "
No. 13   Pages 58–59 (page 57 omitted in the pagination.)
No. 14   "   60–62 (page 63 blank).
No 15   "   64–68   "   69   "
No. 16   "   70–71
No 17 (wrongly numbered 16) Pages 72–77.
No. 18 Pages 78–81
No 19   "   82–85
No. 20   "   86–89
No. 21   "   90–92 (page 93 blank).
No. 22   "   94–97
No. 23   "   98–101
No. 24   "   102–107 (with page 106 repeated).

Each number contains, at end, the following notice:

"By Virtue of an Order of the General Assembly I do appoint John Peter Zenger to print these Votes, and that no other Person do presume to Print the same," Signed "Lewis Morris, junr., Speaker."

The date of the first meeting reported in No. 1, is June 15, 1737, and of the last, reported in No. 24, Dec. 16, 1737.   L., N.Y.H.S.

JOHN PETER ZENGER

There is also in the Lenox volume an earlier issue of No. 2, a single leaf only, page 6 (verso blank), printed from the same types as the first page (7) of the later No. 2.

[One row of printer's ornaments.] The SPEECH of the Honourable/*George Clark*, Esq; Lieut. Governor and/Commander in Chief of the Province/of *New-York*, &c./

[Colophon:] *By Virtue of an Order of the General Assembly I do appoint* John Peter Zenger/*to print these Votes.*/Lewis Morris, *junr. Speaker.*/

Folio, 1 leaf.

Collation : Text, 2 pages. The Address of the General Assembly on page [1] is signed "Lewis Morris, Jun., Speaker' and is dated "Die Jovis, 16 Junii, 1737." The Speech is signed at end " George Clark."   L.

[Two rows of printer's ornaments.] The SPEECH of the Honourable/*George Clarke*, Esq; Lieut. Governor/and Commander in Chief of the Pro-/vince of *New York*, &c./

[Colophon:] *By Virtue of an Order of the General Assembly I do appoint* John Peter Zenger/*to print this Speech, and that no other Person do presume to print the same.*/Lewis Morris, *junr. Speaker.*/

Folio, 1 leaf.

Collation : Text, pages (1) and 2. Heading as above, text in long lines signed at end "Geo. Clarke." and dated "September 2, 1737."   L.

[One row of printer's ornaments.] To the Honourable GEORGE CLARKE,/Esq; Lieut. Governour and Commander in/Chief of the Province of *New-York*, &c./*The Humble Address of the General Assembly of the Colony of*/New-York,/

[Colophon:] *By Virtue of an Order of the General Assembly I do appoint* John Peter Zenger/*to print this Address, and that no other Person do presume to print the same.*/Lewis Morris, *junr. Speaker.*/

Folio, 3 leaves.

Collation: No separate title-page. Text, pages 1–6. In long lines beginning " May it please Your Honour,"   L.

A/DEFENCE/OF A/SERMON/Preached at Newark, June 2 1736./entituled, the Vanity of human Instituti-/ons in the Worship of God, against the/Exceptions of Mr. John Beach, in a/Letter to him./By JONATHAN DICKINSON, M.A./Minister of

BIBLIOGRAPHY

the Gospel, at Elizabeth-/Town in New-Jersey./1 Joh. ii.19. They went from us ; but/they were not of us : For if they had been of/ us they would no Doubt have continued with us./Jam. 1.6. He that wavereth is like a Wave/of the Sea driven with the Wind and tossed./New-York, Printed by J. Peter Zenger./

12mo, printed in fours; 52 leaves

Collation: Title, page [1]; blank, page [2]; text, pages 3–104.

C. H. S.

THE/New-York Weekly Journal./Containing the freshest Ad-vices, Foreign, and Domestick./

[Colophon :] NEW-YORK : Printed and Sold by *John Peter Zenger* : By whom Subscriptions/for this Paper are taken at three Shillings *per* Quarter; and Advertisements at three/Shillings the first Week, and one Shilling every Week after./

Fifty-two numbers. From No. 165, dated January 10, 1736, to No. 216, dated December 26, 1737. Each number consists of four pages.

1738

(1)/[Two rows of printer's ornaments.] A Journal of the Votes and Proceed-/ings of the General Assembly of His Majesty's Col-ony of *New-York*,/in *America*./

Folio, 18 leaves.

Collation: No separate title-page. Text, pages 1–[36]. Page 23 repeated and pages 24 to 36 are wrongly numbered 23 to 35. Made up of seven num-bers, each a separate publication, as follows:

No. 1	Pages	1–4
No. 2	"	5–8
No. 3	"	9–12
No. 4	"	13–15 (page 16 blank).
No. 5	"	17–18
No. 6	"	19–25 (page 23 being repeated in the pagination).
No. 7	"	26–35

Each number contains, generally at the end, the same notice or license as the Votes of 1737.

The date of the earliest session reported is April 4, 1738; and the latest is Sept. 20, 1738.

N. Y. H. S.

KETEN/Der/Geddelyke Waarheden,/DIE/Men geloven en betrachten moet/OM/Salig te worden,/In haar natuurlyk verband

JOHN PETER ZENGER

kortlyk/same gaschakelt; DOOR/GERARD. HAEGHOORT,/ predikant te Second-River./Door order van den Kerkenraed inge-woert in/de Gemmeente van Second-River./Te Nieuw-York,/ Gedrukt by J. Peter Zenger, 1738./

12mo, printed in fours; 22 leaves.

Collation: Title, 1 page; blank, 1 page; "Vooreeden" pages i–iv; "Op de Keten der Goddelyke Waarheden," page [5]; blank, page [vi]; text, pages 1–36.   N. J. H. S.

Anno Regni/GEORGII/SECUNDI/REGIS/*Magnæ Britan-niæ, Franciæ & Hiberniæ*,/UNDECIMO/[Acts and Laws Passed]/ At a General Assembly begun and holden/at *New-York*, the *Fif-teenth* Day of *June,/Anno Domini*, 1737. In the *Eleventh/Year* of the Reign of our Sovereign Lord/GEORGE *the second*, by the Grace of/God, of *Great Britain, France* and *Ire-/land*, KING, Defender of the Faith, &c. [Two rows of printer's ornaments]/ NEW-YORK,/Printed by *John Peter Zenger*, MDCCXXXVIII./

Folio, 52 leaves.

Collation: Title, 1 page; blank, 1 page; text, pages 1–100; Table, 1 page; blank, 1 page. Page 28 is wrongly numbered 82.   N. Y. H. S.

[Three rows of printer's ornaments.]/The VOTES and Pro-ceedings of the/General Assembly of the Province/of *New-Jersey*, which began the 27*th*/of *October*, 1738./

Folio, 37 leaves.

Collation: No separate title-page. Text, pages 1–70, with the "Treasurer's Report," 4 pages, inserted between pages 63 and 64. Pages 33, 36, 37, 40, 60, 61, 62, 63 and 64 are wrongly numbered 32, 33, 36, 39, 55, 54, 58, 56 and 46. Made up of four numbers, each a separate publication, as follows :

No. [1]	Pages	1–10
No. 2	"	11–16
No. 3	"	17–56
No. 4	"	57–70

The "Treasurer's Report" four pages, unnumbered, is inserted between pages 63 and 64, in No. 4. Nos. [1], 2, and 3 have at end :
"*By Virtue of an Order of the House, I do appoint* John Peter Zenger *to print/these Votes. Joseph Bonnel, Speaker*."   L.

The SPEECH of His Excellency LEWIS MORRIS, Esq ;/ Captain General and Governour in Chief in and over His Ma-/

BIBLIOGRAPHY

jesty's Province of *Nova Cæsarea*, or *New-Jersey* and the Terri-/
tories thereon depending in *America*, and Vice Admiral in the/same,
&c./

[Colophon:] Printed by *John Peter Zenger*, 1738.

Folio, 2 leaves.

Collation: No separate title-page. Text, pp. [1-4].   N. J. S. L.

THE/New-York Weekly Journal./Containing the freshest
Advices, Foreign and Domestick.

[Colophon:] New York, Printed by *John Peter Zenger*, where
Advertisements are taken in./

Fifty-two numbers were probably printed. Of No. 217, which should
have been dated January 2, no copy has been traced. The last number of the
year was No. 263, dated December 25, 1738. Each number, so far as seen
consists of four pages, except No. 259, dated November 27, 1738, which has
six pages. There are numerous errors in numbers and dates.

1739

INTERCESSION Every Christian's Duty. A Sermon
preach'd by the Rev. George Whitefield, A.B. of Pembrock College, Oxford. New-York, Reprinted by *John Peter Zenger*, and
sold by Jacob Goelet. 1739.

Not seen. Advertised in the *New York Weekly Journal*, No. 317, dated
January 7, 1739 [1740].

The Danger of Schisms and Contentions, with respect to the
Ministry and Ordinance of the Gospel, represented in a Sermon.
[By Jonathan Dickinson.] New York, 1739.

12mo.

Not seen. Title taken from Sabin, Vol. V, page 412, No. 20062. Probably
printed by Zenger.

A SHORT/DIRECTION/FOR AN/Unregenerate Sin-
ner,/Shewing how he may come to/CHRIST./Written in *Dutch*
by a Lover of the/Truth, and Translated into *English*/by a Well-
Wisher to all Men./NEW-YORK,/Reprinted by *John Peter Zenger*, 1739./

8vo, 12 leaves.

Collation: Title, page [1]; blank, page [2]; text, pages 3-24. H. S. P.

JOHN PETER ZENGER

TO His Excellency LEWIS MORRIS,/Esq; Captain, Gen-/eral and Gover-/nour in Chief, in and over his Ma-/jesty's Pro-/vince of *Nova-Cæsarea or/New-Jersey*, and Territories thereon/de-/pending in *America*, and Vice Admiral in the same, *&c.*/The hum-/ble Address of His Majesty's Council of the Province/aforesaid./
    [Colophon :] Printed by *John Peter Zenger*, *Jan.* 4. 1738–9,/

Folio, 2 leaves.

Collation: No separate title-page; text, 4 pages.   N. J. S. L.

TO His Excellency LEWIS MORRIS, Esq; Captain, Gen-/eral and Gover-/nour in Chief, in and over His Ma-/jesty's Pro-/vince of *Nova Cæsarea or/New-Jersey*, and Territories thereon/de-/pending in *America*, and Vice Ad-/miral in the same, *&c.*/THE/humble Address of the Representatives of the Province of/*Nova Cæsarea*, or *New-Jersey*, met in General Assembly./
    [Colophon:] *By Virtue of an Order of the House, I do appoint* John Peter Zenger *to print/this Address* Joseph Bonnel, Spr./

Folio, 2 leaves.

Collation: No separate title-page; text, 3 pages; blank, 1 page.
N. J. S. L.

THE/New-York Weekly Journal./Containing the freshest Advices, Foreign, and Domestick.
    [Colophon:] New York, Printed by *John Peter Zenger*, where Advertisements are taken in./

Fifty-two numbers. From No. 264, dated January 1, 1738, to No. 315, dated December 24, 1739. Each number probably consists of four pages.

1740

THE/QUERISTS,/The Rev. Mr. *Whitefield's*/ANSWER,/The Rev. Mr *Garden's*/LETTERS, *&c.*/[Printer's ornament.]/*NEW YORK*, Printed by *J. P. Zenger*, 1740./

    [Second title page :] THE / QUERISTS, / OR / An EX-/TRACT of sundry Passages/taken out of Mr *Whitefield's* prin-/ted Sermons, Journals and Let-/ters :/TOGETHER WITH/Some SCRUPLES propos'd in proper/*QUERIES* raised on each Remark./*By some Church-Members of the Presbyterian Persuasion.*/2

162

BIBLIOGRAPHY

Tim i. 13. *Hold fast the Form of sound words.*—/Turpe est doctori cum culpa redarguit ipsum. / *NEW-YORK.* / Printed in the Year M,DCC,XL./

12mo, printed in fours; 80 leaves.

Collation: First title as above, page [i]; blank, page [ii]; second title as above, page [iii]; "To the Readers," pages iv–12; "The Address of several Persons of the Presbyterian Persuasion," pages 13–58 ; "A Letter from the Rev. Mr. Whitefield," pages 59–71; "Six Letters to the Reverend Mr. G. Whitefield," pages 72–151; "A Short Trip to Rome," pages 152–160.   C. E. N.

VOORBIDDING een ieder Christen's Plicht, vertoont in een PREDICATIE door GEORGE WHITEFIELD, A.B. &c. Gedrukt en te koop by J. Peter Zenger, en Jacobus Goelet.

Not seen. Advertised in the *New York Weekly Journal*, No. 325, dated March 3, 1739.

Een Geestelyk Lied, Bequaam on Gesongen te werden in alle Godvruchtige Vergaderingen, ofte Particuleere 't Samenkomsten.

Not seen. Advertised in the *New York Weekly Journal*, No. 366, dated December 8, 1740.

A/Short History/OF A/Long Journey,/IT being some Account of the Life/of IOSIAH QUINBY, un-/till he came to enter into the/48*th* Year of his Age, with Re-/marks and Reflections upon his/own past Actions./ [Printer's ornament] / *NEW-YORK* Printed by *John Peter Zenger* 1740./

12mo, printed in fours; 32 leaves, the last blank.

Collation: Title, page [1]; blank, p. [2]; "To the Reader," pages 3–10; text, pages 11–61; blank, page 62. Signed at bottom of page 10, "Josiah Quinby," and at end, "Your Friend and Well Wisher, Josiah Quinby." L.

EEN KORTE/ HANDLEIDING / VOOR EEN / ON-WEDERGEBOREN/SONDAAR, / OM TOT /CHRISTUS/ TE KOOMEN/Opgestelt door een Liefhebber der Waarheid./ [Printer's ornament.]/NIEUW-YORK, Gedrukt by *J. Peter Zenger*, 1740.

12mo, printed in fours; 12 leaves.

Collation: Title, page [1]; blank, pages [2]; text, pages 3–23; blank, page [24].   H. S. P.

JOHN PETER ZENGER

THE/New-York Weekly Journal./Containing the freshest
Advices, Foreign, and Domestick./
[Colophon:] New York, Printed by *John Peter Zenger*, where
Advertisements are taken in./

53 numbers. From No. 316, dated January 1, 1739, to No. 369, dated
December 29, 1740. Each number probably consists of four pages.

1741

Nederduitsche Almanacke Voor 1742.

Not seen. Advertised in the *New York Weekly Journal*, No. 415, dated
November 9, 1741. It is very doubtful that this was printed by Zenger.

Copy of a Letter from Capt. Peter Lawrence, to Andrew Arch-
dickne, Esq; dated off Carthagena, March 20, 1741.

Not seen. Advertised in the *New York Weekly Journal*, No. 389, dated
May 18, 1741. Doubtfully ascribed to Zenger's press.

A Spiritual Journey Temporaliz'd or an Alegorical Description
of the Work of Grace in Man.

Not seen. Advertised in the *New York Weekly Journal*, No. 420, dated
December 14, 1741, as follows :
"Just Publish'd and to be Sold by the Printer hereof, A Spiritual Journey
Temporaliz'd, or an Alegorical Discription of the Work of Grace in Man.

> A Verse may find him who a Sermon flies,
> And turn delight into a Sacrifice.
>
> HERBERT."

THE/New-York Weekly Journal./Containing the freshest
Advices, Foreign, and Domestick./
[Colophon:] New York, Printed by *John Peter Zenger*, where
Advertisements are taken in./

52 numbers. From No. 370, dated January 5, 1740, to No. 422, dated
December 28, 1741. Each number probably consists of four pages

1742

Sermons by Alexander Garden.

12mo.

The only copy traced is imperfect, lacking the first leaf and one or more
leaves at end. The collation of this copy is : Text (apparently of the Sermon
"Take Heed How Ye Hear"), pages 3–32; title; "*Regeneration* and *the Tes-*

BIBLIOGRAPHY

timony of the SPIRIT./Being the Substance of/Two SERMONS/Lately preached in the Parish Church of *St. Phi-/lip, Charles-Town,* in SOUTH CAROLINA./ *Occasioned by some erroneous Notions of certain Men who call/themselves Methodists.*/ By ALEXANDER GARDEN, M. A. Rector of the/said Parish./ [Printer's ornament]. *NEW-YORK.*/ Printed by *John Peter Zenger,* 1742." page [1]; blank, page [2]; text, pages 1-72, ending imperfectly with the catchword "God." L.C.P.

This book was advertised in the *New York Weekly Journal,* No. 451, dated July 19, 1742, as follows:

" *To be published this Week.*

TAKE HEED HOW YE HEAR, A SERMON on *Luke* viii. 18. And, *Regeneration,* and *the Testimony of the Spirit.* Both by ALEXANDER GARDEN, M.A., Rector of *St. Philips, Charles Town, S. Carolina.*

It was advertised also in the next number, No. 452, dated July 26, 1742, as follows:

"TAKE HEED HOW YE HEAR, A SERMON on *Luke* viii. 18. And *Regeneration,* and *the Testimony of the Spirit.* With a Preface, containing some Remarks on Mr. *Whitefield's* Journal. By *Alexander Garden,* M.A., Rector of *St. Philips, Charles Town, S. Carolina.* Printed By *John Peter Zenger,* 1742."

S*S Een leersaam ondersoek der Waarheid meest in betrekkinge to de selfs Verlocheninge, voorgestelt in een 'Tsaamenspraak tusschen Leerlievende en Waarheidlievende : Gedruckt by J: Peter Zenger, en te koop by Jacob Goelet na by de Oude Slip in New York.

Not seen. Advertised in the *New York Weekly Journal,* No. 452, dated July 26, 1742.

THE/New-York Weekly Journal./Containing the freshest Advices, Foreign, and Domestick./

[Colophon:] New York, Printed by *John Peter Zenger,* where Advertisements are taken in./

52 numbers. From No. 432, dated January 4, 1741, to No. 475, dated December 27, 1742. Each number consists of four pages. There are several errors in numbering.

1743

Nederduitsche Almanack voor, 1743.

Not seen. Title taken from Mr. Hildeburn's notes. Advertised, also, in the *New York Weekly Journal,* No. 470, dated November 22, 1742, as follows:

" Just published and Sold by the Printer hereof.

Dutch & English }
ALMANACKS } for the year 1743-44."

It seems very doubtful, however, that these were *printed* by Zenger

JOHN PETER ZENGER

THE/New-York Weekly Journal./Containing the freshest
Advices, Foreign, and Domestick./
[Colophon:] New York, Printed by *John Peter Zenger*, where
Advertisements are taken in./

52 numbers. From No. 476, dated January 3, 1742, to No. 527, dated
December 26, 1743. Each number consists of four pages.

1744

THE/New-York Weekly Journal./Containing the freshest Ad-
vices, Foreign, and Domestick./
[Colophon :] New York, Printed by *John Peter Zenger*, where
Advertisements are taken in./

Probably 53 numbers. From No. 528, dated January 2, 1743, to No. 581,
dated December 31, 1744. Each number probably consists of four pages.

1745

Advertisement,/*Perth-Amboy, September* 17, 1745./WHEREAS
sundry of the Purchasors at/*Romopock*, have neglected to come to
the Trustees/of the Council of Proprietors at *Perth-Amboy* [etc.].

4to, 1 leaf.

Collation: Text, 1 page; blank, 1 page. Signed at end, "Laur. Smyth,
Clerk."   N. Y. H. S.
Addressed to the delinquent purchasers of Romopock lands. Appears also
in No. 628 of the *New York Weekly Journal* dated September 30, 1745.

THE/New-York Weekly Journal./Containing the freshest Ad-
vices, Foreign, and Domestick.
[Colophon :] New York, Printed by *John Peter Zenger*, where
Advertisements are taken in./

Probably 52 numbers. The first issue seems to have been No. 582 for
January 7, and the last No. 630 for December 30. Either there were errors
made in numbering or three issues were omitted between No. 620, dated September 30 and No. 628, dated December 26.

———

CATHARINE ZENGER AND JOHN ZENGER, JR.

1746

A/Brief VINDICATION/OF/THE Purchassors / Against

BIBLIOGRAPHY

the PROPRITORS,/IN/A Christian Manner./[Printer's orna-
ment] NEW-YORK./Printed, by *J. Zenger*, jun. 1745-6/

12mo, printed in fours.

Collation : Title, page [i]; blank, page [ii]; "The Preface. To the
Reader." pages iii–vi ; " A Song of Praise to God," etc., pages vii–xi ; text,
pages 1–32 ; "Ejaculation I." [etc.] pages 33–37. Signed at bottom of page
32, "Griffin Jenkins." The catchword at page 33 is "Ejaculation V." (should
be II.), and the catchwords on pages 34 and 35 are both "Ejaculation VI." That
on page 34 should be III. and that on page 35 should be IV.   E. D. C.

Nathan's Almanac for 1747.

Not seen. Title taken from Haven's list.

THE/New-York Weekly Journal./Containing the freshest Ad-
vices, Foreign, and Domestick./
[Colophon:] NEW-YORK : Printed by the Widow Catharine
Zenger, where Advertisements are taken in./

Probably 52 numbers. The first issue seems to have been No. 631, for
January 6, and the last No. 680, for December 29. If no issues were omitted
there must have been several errors in the numbering. Each number probably
consists of four pages.

1747

An ANSWER to the Council of Proprietor's two/Publications;
Sett forth at Perth-Amboy the 25th/of March 1746, and the 25th
of March 1747. As/also some Observations on Mr. Nevil's Speech
to the/House of Assembly, in Relation to a Petition presented/to
the House of Assembly, met at Trentown in the/Province of New-
Jersey, in May, 1746./
[Colophon:] NEW-YORK :/Printed and Sold by the Widow
Catherine Zenger, at the/Printing-Office in Stone-Street, 1747,/

Folio, 7 leaves.

Collation: No separate title-page. Text, pages 1–13; page [14] blank.
                                                                    L.

Nathan's Almanac for 1748.

Not seen. Title taken from Haven's list.

THE/New-York Weekly Journal./Containing the freshest Advices, Foreign, and Domestick./
[Colophon:] NEW-YORK : Printed by the Widow Cathrine

JOHN PETER ZENGER

Zenger at the Printing-Office in Stone-Street,/where Advertisements are taken in, and all Persons may be supplied with this Paper./

Probably 52 numbers. The first issue seems to have been No. 681, for January 5, and the last No. 732 for December 28. Each number probably consists of four pages.

1748

AN/Almanack,/FOR/The Year of Christian Account,/1749,/ Being the first after LEAP-YEAR/*Wherein is Contained*,/The Lunations, Eclipses, and Judgment of the/Weather, Planets Motions, and Mutual Aspects and/Time of Sun and Moon's rising and setting, the rising/southing and setting of the Seven Stars, and several/ other remarkable Stars, length of Days, a Tide-Table/Fairs, Courts, Observable Days, &c./ Fitted to the Vertex of the City of *Perth Amboy*/in *New-Jersey*, but may without sensible Error serve/serve the adjacent Provinces from *Newfoundland*/to *South Carolina*./By JOHN NATHAN, Philomath/NEW-YORK/Printed and Sold by the *Widow Catharine Zenger*, at the/Printing Office in Stone Street./

Small 8vo.

Collation: Title and text, pages 1–24.   E. D. C.

THE/New-York Weekly Journal./Containing the freshest Advices, Foreign, and Domestick./

[Colophon:] NEW-YORK: Printed by the Widow Catharine Zenger at the Printing-Office in Stone-Street,/where Advertisements are taken in, and all Persons may be supplied with this Paper./

Probably 52 numbers. The first issue seems to have been No. 733, for January 4, and the last No. 784, for December 26. Each number probably consists of four pages.

1749

Wilhelm Christopher Berkenmyers/ Geheime unt offentliche ANSPRACHE/ samt einer SCHLUS-REDE, / AN / HEREN / *Johann Christopher Hartwick*,/MIT ET'LICHEN/Zur ERLAUTERUNG, und zur ENTDECKUNG/des *Criptoherrn Huthianisme*, dienenden Anmer-/kungen nach der Vorschrift unsrer *Nieu-Yorksen* K.O. p. ii./*Cap.* 11. art· 6./Zum DRUCK klaar gemacht./ Da von die Schlus-Rede vorlaufen aus gegeben/ist das in *theerbosh*, gegebene offentliche/ Ergernis, am Tage des HERREN, *d.* 5./

BIBLIOGRAPHY

Februarii, 1748–9. *Christ-vernunftig* beurthei-/len zu konnen./ [Printer's ornament.]/Gedruckt zu *Neiu-York*, by *Johann Zenger*, M DCCXLIX./

4to, printed in twos; 58 leaves.

Collation: Title, 1 page; blank, 1 page; text, pages 1–114, with the following errors in pagination: 69 is 65, 70 is 66, 91 is 29. At end is this notice: "Van Pagina 27 Litra H. is gedruckt by my/Henry De Foreest." H.U.

THE/New-York Weekly Journal./Containing the freshest Advices, Foreign, and Domestick./

[Colophon:] NEW-YORK, Printed by JOHN ZENGER, in Stone Street near Fort George:/where ADVERTISEMENTS are taken in at a moderate Rate./

Probably 52 numbers. The first issue was No. 785, dated January 2, 1749, and the last was probably No. 836 for December 26. Each number probably consists of four pages, except No. 786, dated January 9, and No. 798, dated April 3, which consist of six pages.

THE/New-York Weekly Journal./Containing the freshest Advices, Foreign and Domestick./

[Colophon:] NEW-YORK, Printed by JOHN ZENGER, in Stone Street near Fort George:/where ADVERTISEMENTS are taken in at a moderate Rate./

Probably 52 numbers. The first issue was No. 837, dated January 2, and the last was probably No. 1006, for December 31. The issues seem to have been correctly numbered up to 888, dated October 29. The issues for November 5, 12 and 19 have not been traced; that for November 26 is No. 1001. This error is continued

1751

THE   (Royal)   WEEKLY/
New-York   (Arms)   Journal/
Containing the freshest Advices, Foreign and Domestick./

[Colophon:] NEW-YORK: Printed and Sold by John Zenger, at the PRINITNG-OFFICE,/in Stone-Street, near Fort GEORGE, where Persons may be supp'lyd with this/Paper at 10s. a YEAR. And where Advertisements are taken in./

The last year of the *Journal*. Just how many issues were printed cannot now be traced. The first issue seems to have been No. 1007 for January 7, 1750. The latest issue now known is No. 1017 (misprinted 0117), dated March 18, 1750. Hildeburn says that John Zenger the younger died "some time before July, 1751, when his presses and type were sold by auction."

KLAGTE
Van Eenige Leeden der
NEDERDUYTSE HERVORMDE KERK,
Woonende op *Raretans*, &c., in de Provincie van
NIEU-JERSEI, in *NOORD-AMERICA*,
Onder de Kroon van *Groot-Brittanie*.
Over het GEDRAG, Althar en Elders,
VAN
Do. *THEODORUS JACOBUS FRILINGHUISEN*,
Met syn Kerken-Raaden.
TEN
ANTWOORD
Op hunne
Ban-Dreygende Daag-Brieven, &c.

AAN
Alle *Liefhebbers der Waarheid*, ter onderfoek, voorgefteld,
Hoe Die Gegrond zyn, of Niet.

MET een
Noodige Voor-Reeden, tot opheldering van de *Klagte*.
Uytgegeven Door
De Gevolmagtigden der gemelde Leeden.

Te Nieu-York, Gedrukt by *William Bradford* en *J. Peter Zenger*, 1725.

THE

Charter

OF THE

CITY

OF

NEW-YORK;

Printed by Order of the Mayor, Recorder, Aldermen and Commonalty of the City aforesaid.

TO WHICH IS ANNEXED,

The Act of the General Assembly Confirming the same.

NEW-YORK,
Printed by *John Peter Zenger*. 1735.

LITERAL REPRINT
OF THE
FIRST EDITION
OF THE
CASE AND TRIAL

A brief Narrative of the Case and Try-al of *John Peter Zenger*, Printer of the *New-York weekly Journal*.

AS There was but one Printer in the Province of *New-York*, that printed a publick News Paper, I was in Hopes, if I undertook to publish another, I might make it worth my while; and I soon found my Hopes were not ground-less: My first Paper was printed, *Nov.* 5th, 1733. and I continued printing and publishing of them, I thought to the Satisfaction of every Body, till the *January* following: when the Chief Justice was pleased to animadvert upon the Doctrine of Libels, in a long Charge given in that Term to the Grand Jury, and afterwards on the third *Tuesday* of *October*, 1734. was again pleased to charge the Grand Jury in the following Words.

' *Gentlemen*; I shall conclude with reading a Paragraph
' or two out of the same Book, concerning Libels; they are
' arrived to that Height, that they call loudly for your
' Animadversion; it is high Time to put a Stop to them; for
' at the rate Things are now carried on, when all Order and
' Government is endeavoured to be trampled on; Reflections
' are cast upon Persons of all Degrees, must not these
' Things end in Sedition, if not timely prevented? Lenity,
' you have seen will not avail, it becomes you then to en-
' quire after the Offenders, that we may in a due Course of
' Law be enabled to punish them. If you, *Gentlemen*, do
' not interpose, consider whether the ill Consequences that

' may arife from any Difturbances of the publick Peace, may
' not in part, lye at your Door?

' *Hawkins*, in his Chapter of Libels, confiders three
' Points, 1*st*. *What shall be said to be a Libel*. 2*dly*. *Who are*
' *lyable to be punished for it*. 3*dly*. *In what Manner they are*
' *to be punished*. Under the 1*st*. *he says*, §. 7. *Nor can there*
' *be any Doubt, but that a Writing which defames a private*
' *Person only, is as much a Libel as that which defames Per-*
' *sons intrusted in a publick Capacity, in as much as it manifestly*
' *tends to create ill Blood, and to cause a Disturbance of the*
' *publick Peace; however it is certain, that it is a very high*
' *Aggravation of a Libel, that it tends to scandalize the Gov-*
' *ernment, by reflecting on those who are entrusted with the*
' *Administration of publick Affairs, which does not only en-*
' *danger the publick Peace, as all other Libels do, by stirring*
' *up the Parties, immediately concerned in it, to Acts of Re-*
' *venge, but also has a direct Tendency to breed in the People*
' *a Dislike of their Governours, and incline them to Faction*
' *and Sedition*, As to the 2*d*. Point he fays. § 10 *It is cer-*
' *tain, not only he who composes or procures another to compose*
' *it but also that he who publishes, or procures another to pub-*
' *lish it, are in Danger of being punished for it; and it is said*
' *not to be material whether he who disperses a Libel, knew*
' *any Thing of the Contents or Effects of it or not; for nothing*
' *could be more easy than to publish the most virulent Papers*
' *with the greatest Security, if the concealing the Purport of*
' *them from an illiterate Publisher, would make him safe in*
' *the dispersing them: Also, it has been said, that if he who*
' *hath either read a Libel himself, or hath heard it read by an-*
' *other, do afterwards maliciously read or report any Part*
' *of it in the Presence of others, or lend or shew it to another,*
' *he is guilty of an unlawful Publication of it. Also it hath*
' *been holden, that the Copying of a Libel shall be a conclusive*
' *Evidence of the Publication of it, unless the Party can prove,*
' *that he delivered it to a Magistrate to examine it, in which*
' *Case the Act* subfequent *is said to explain the Intention* pre-
' cedent. *But it seems to be the better Opinion, that he who*

' *firft writes a Libel, dictated by another, is thereby guilty of*
' *Making of it, and confequently punifhable for the bare Writ-*
' *ing ; for it was no Libel till it was reduced to Writing.*

' Thefe, *Gentlemen*, are fome of the Offences which are to
' make Part of your Enquiries ; and if any other fhould arife
' in the Cqurfe of your Proceedings, in which you are at
' a Lofs, or conceive any Doubts, upon your Application
' here, We will affift and direct you.

The Grand Jury not indicting me as was expected, the
Gentlemen of the Council proceeded to take my Journals
into Confideration, and fent the following Meffage to the
general Affembly.

' *Die Jovis*, 3 *ho.* P. M. 17*th of* October, 1734.

' A Meffage from the Council by *Philip Cortlandt*, in
' thefe Words, *to wit*,
' That Board having had feveral of *Zenger's New-York*
' *weekly Journals*, laid before them, and other fcurrilous
' Papers, tending to alienate the Affections of the People of
' this Province from His Majefty's Government, to raife
' Seditions and Tumults among the People of this Province,
' and to fill their Minds with a Contempt of His Majefty's
' Government : And confidering the pernicious Confe-
' quences that may attend fuch growing Evils, if not fpeedi-
' ly and effectually put a Stop to. And conceiving that the
' moft likely Method to put a Stop to fuch bold and feditious
' Practices, to maintain the Dignity of his Majefty's Govern-
' ment, and to preferve the Peace thereof, would be by a
' Conference between a Committee of this Board, and a
' Committee of the Affembly ; it is therefore ordered, That
' the Gentlemen of this Board, NOW ASSEMBLED, or
' any feven of them, be a Committee, to join a Committee
' of the Houfe of Reprefentatives, in order to confer to-
' gether, and to examine and enquire into the faid Papers,
' and the Authors and Writers thereof.
' Which Meffage being read.

JOHN PETER ZENGER

' *Ordered*, That the Members of this Houſe, or any
' fourteen of them, do meet a Committee of the Council, at
' the Time and Place therein mentioned.

' *Die Veneris*, 9 *ho.* 18 *October*, 1734.

' Mr. *Garretſon* from the Committee of this Houſe re-
' ported, That they laſt Night met the Committee of the
' Council, on the ſubject Matter of their Meſſage of yeſter-
' day to this Houſe; and that after ſeveral Preliminaries be-
' tween the ſaid Committees, the Gentlemen of the Council
' reduced to Writing, what they requeſted of this Houſe,
' and delivered the ſame to the Chairman, who delivered it
' in at the Table, and being read, is in the Words following.

At a Committee of the Council held the 17*th* of *October*,
1734.

PRESENT.

Mr. *Clarke.*	Mr. *Livingſton.*	Mr. *Courtland.*
Mr. *Hariſon.*	Mr. *Kennedy.*	Mr. *Lane.*
Dr. *Colden.*	Mr. Chief Juſtice.	Mr. *Horſmanden.*

' *Gentlemen*;
' The Matters we requeſt your Concurrence in, are,
' That *Zenger's* Papers, No. 7. 47. 48. 49. which were read,
' and which we now deliver, be burnt by the Hands of the
' common Hangman, as containing in them many Things
' derogatory of the Dignity of His Majeſty's Government,
' reflecting upon the Legiſlature, upon the moſt conſiderable
' Perſons, in the moſt Diſtinguiſhed Stations in the Province,
' and tending to raiſe Seditions and Tumults among the
' People thereof.

' That you concur with us in the Addreſſing the Gover-
' nour, to iſſue His Proclamation, with a Promiſe of Reward
' for the Diſcovery of the Authors or Writers of theſe Sedi-
' tious Libels.

' That you concur with us in an Order for Proſecuting
' the Printer thereof.

' That you concur with us in an Order to the Magif-
' trates, to exert themfelves in the Execution of their Of-
' fices, in order to preferve the publick Peace of the Pro-
' vince.

> ' *By Order of the Committee.*
>> *Fred. Morris,* Cl. Con.

' Mr. *Garretfon* delivered likewife to the Houfe the fev-
' eral Papers referred to in the faid Requeft.

' *Ordered,* That the faid Papers be lodg'd with the Clerk
' of this Houfe, and that the Confideration thereof, and the
' faid Requeft, be referred till *Tuefday* next.

> ' *Die Martis,* 9 *ho.* A. M. 22 *October,* 1734.

' The Houfe according to Order proceeded to take into
' Confideration the Requeft of a Committee of Council, de-
' livered to a Committee of this Houfe, on the 16*th* inftant,
' as likewife of the feveral Papers therein referred to. And
' after feveral Debates upon the fubject Matters, it was OR-
' DERED THAT THE SAID PAPERS AND RE-
' QUEST LYE ON THE TABLE.'

The Council finding the General Affembly would not
do any Thing about it, they fent the following Meffage to
the Houfe.

> ' *Die Sabbati,* 9 *ho.* A. M. 2 *November,* 1734.

' A Meffage from the Council by Mr. *Livingfton,* de-
' firing this Houfe to return by him to that Board, the
' feveral feditious journals of *Zenger's* No. 7. 47. 48. 49.
' which were delivered by a Committee of that Board to a
' Committee of this Houfe, the 17*th* of *October* laft, together
' with the Propofals of the Committee of that Board, de-
' livered therewith to a Committee of this Houfe; and then
' withdrew.

On *Tuefday* the 5*th* of *November,* 1734. the *Quarter Sef-
fions* for the City of *New-York* began, when the Sheriff delivered to the Court AN ORDER, which was read in thefe
Words.

JOHN PETER ZENGER

' At a Council held at Fort *George*, in *New-York*, the 2*d*
' of *November*, 1734.

PRESENT,

His Excellency *William Cofby*, Capt. General and Governour in Chief, *&c.*

Mr. *Clark.*   Mr. *Livingfton.*   Mr. *Cortland.*
Mr. *Harifon.*   Mr. *Kennedy.*   Mr. *Lane.*
* Dr. *Colden.*   Mr. Chief Juftice.   Mr. *Horfmanden.*

' *Whereas by an Order of this Board, of this Day, fome of*
' John Peter Zenger's *Journals, entitled*, The New-York
' weekly Journal, containing the frefheft Advices, foreign and
' domeftick, No. 7. 47. 48. 49. *were ordered to be burnt by*
' *the Hands of the common Hangman, or Whipper, near the Pil-*
' *lory in this City, on* Wednefday *the* 6th *Inftant, between the*
' *Hours of Eleven and Twelve in the Forenoon, as containing in*
' *them many Things tending to Sedition and Faction, to bring*
' *His Majefty's Government into Contempt, and to difturb the*
' *Peace thereof, and containing in them likewife, not only Re-*
' *flections upon His Excellency the Governour in particular, the*
' *Legiflature in general, but alfo upon the moft confiderable Per-*
' *fons in the moft diftinguifhed Stations in this Province. It is*
' *therefore ordered, That the Mayor, and Magiftrates of this*
' *City, do attend at the Burning of the feveral Papers or Jour-*
' *nals aforefaid, Numbered as above mentioned.*

Fred. Morris, D. Cl. Con.

' To *Robert Lurting*, Efq; Mayor of the City of *New-*
' *York*, and the Reft of the Magiftrates for the faid
' City and County.

Upon reading of which ORDER, the Court forbad the
Entring thereof in their Books at that Time, and many of
them declared, that if it fhould be entred, they would have
their Proteft entered againft it.

---

* N.B. Doctor Colden *was that day, at* Efopus, 90
Miles from New-York, *tho' mentioned as prefent in Council.*

THE CASE AND TRIAL

On *Wednesday* the 6*th* of *November*, the Sherriff of *New-York* moved the Court of *Quarter Seſſions*, to comply with the ſaid Order, upon which one of the Aldermen offered a proteſt, which was read by the Clerk, and approved of by all the Aldermen, either expreſsly or by not objecting to it, and is as followeth.

' Whereas an ORDER has been ſerved on this Court, in theſe Words.

[The Order as above incerted.]

' And whereas this Court conceives, they are only to be
' commanded by the King's Mandatory Writs, authorized by
' Law, to which they conceive they have the Right of ſhew-
' ing Cauſe why they don't obey them, if they believe them
' improper to be obey'd, or by ORDERS, which have
' ſome known Laws to authorize them; and whereas this
' Court conceives THIS ORDER to be no Mandatory
' Writt warranted by Law, nor knows of no Law that author-
' izes the making the Order aforeſaid; ſo they think them-
' ſelves under no Obligation to obey it: Which Obedience,
' they think, would be in them, an opening a Door for ar-
' bitrary Commands, which, when once opened, they know
' not what Dangerous Conſequences may attend it. Wherefore
' this Court conceives it ſelf bound in Duty (for the Preſer-
' vation of the Rights of this Corporation, and as much as
' they can, the Liberty of the Preſs and the People of the
' Province, ſince an Aſſembly of the Province, and ſeveral
' Grand Juries, have refuſed to meddle with the Papers,
' when applied to by the Council) *to proteſt againſt the*
' ORDER *aforeſaid, and to forbid all the Members of this*
' *Corporation, to pay any Obedience to it*, until it be ſhewn to
' this Court, that the ſame is Authorized by ſome known
' Law, which they neither know nor believe that it is.'

Upon reading of which, it was required of the Honour-able *Francis Hariſon*, Recorder of this Corporation, and one of the Members of the Council, (preſent at making ſaid Order) to ſhew by what Law or Authority the ſaid ORDER was made; upon which he spoke in Support of it, and cited the Case of Doctor *Sacheverel's* Sermon, which was by the House of Lords ordered to be burnt by the Hands of the Hangman, and that the Mayor and Aldermen of *London* should attend the doing of it, to which one of the Aldermen answered to this Purpose; that he conceived the Case was no ways parallel, because Doctor *Sacheverel,* and his Sermon, were impeached by the House of Commons of *England,* which is the Grand Jury of the Nation, and Representative of the whole People of *England:* That this their Impeachment they prosecuted before the House of Lords, the greatest Court of Justice of *Britain,* and which beyond Memory of Man, has had Cognizance of Things of that Nature, that there *Sacheverel* had a fair Hearing in Defence of himself and of his Sermon. And after that fair Hearing, he and his Sermon were justly, fairly and legally condemened; that he had read the Case of Dr. *Sacheverel,* & thought he could charge his Memory, that the Judgment of the House of Lords in that Case was, That the Mayor and Sheriffs of *London* and *Middlesex,* only should attend the Burning of the Sermon, and not the Aldermen; and farther he remembred, that the Order upon that Judgment, was only directed to the Sheriffs of *London,* and not even to the Mayor, who did not attend the doing it; and farther said, that would Mr. Recorder shew, that the Governour and Council had such Authority as the House of Lords, and that the Papers ordered to be burnt were in like manner legally prosecuted and condemned, there the Case of Doctor *Sacheverel* might be to the Purpose; but without shewing that, it rather proved that a Censure ought not to be pronounced, till a fair Tryal by a Competent and legal Authority were first had. Mr. Recorder was desired to produce the Books from whence he cited his Authorities, that the Court might judge of them themselves, and was told, that if he could produce sufficient Authorities to warrant *this ORDER,* they would readily obey it, but otherwise not. Upon which he said, he did not carry his Books about with him. To which it was answered, he might fend for them, or order a Conſtable to fetch them. Upon which he aroſe, and at the lower End of the Table he mentioned, That Biſhop *Burnet's* Paſtoral Letter, was ordered by the Houſe of Lords, to be burnt by the High Bailiff of *Weſtminſter*; upon which he abruptly went away, without waiting for an Anſwer or promiſing to bring his Books, and did not return ſitting the Court.

After Mr. Recorder's Departure, it was moved that the *Proteſt* ſhould be entered; to which it was anſwered, That the *Proteſt* could not be entered without entering alſo the ORDER, and it was not fit to take any notice of IT, and therefore it was propoſed that no Notice ſhould be taken in their Books of either, which was unanimouſly agreed to by the Court.

The Sherriff then moved, that the Court would direct their Whipper to perform the ſaid ORDER; to which it was anſwered, That as he was the Officer of the Corporation, they would give no ſuch *Order*. Soon after which the Court adjourned, and did not attend the Burning of the Papers. Afterwards about Noon, the Sheriff after reading the Numbers of the ſeveral Papers which were ordered to be burnt, delivered them unto the Hands of his own Negroe, and ordered him to put them into the Fire which he did, at which Mr. Recorder, *Jeremiah Dunbar*, Eſq; and ſeveral of the Officers of the Garriſon attended.

On the Lord's Day the 17th *of November*, 1734. I was taken and impriſoned by Virtue of a Warrant in theſe Words.

'At a Council held at Fort *George* in *New-York*, the 2d Day of *November*, 1734.

PRESENT,

His Excellency *William Coſby*, Captain General and Governour in Chief, &c.

Mr. *Clarke*.	Mr. *Kennedy*.	Mr. *Lane*.
Mr. *Hariſon*.	Chief Juſtice.	Mr. *Horſmanden*.
Mr. *Livingſton*.	Mr. *Cortlandt*.	

JOHN PETER ZENGER

'It is ordered that the Sheriff for the City of *New-
'York*, do forthwith take and apprehend *John Peter Zenger*,
'for printing and publishing several Seditious Libels, dis-
'persed throughout his Journals or News Papers, entituled
'*The New-York Weekly Journal, containing the freshest Ad-
'vices, foreign and domestick;* as having in them many Things,
'tending to raise Factions and Tumults, among the People
'of this Province, inflaming their Minds with Contempt of
'His Majesty's Government, and greatly disturbing the Peace
'thereof, and upon his taking the said *John Peter Zenger, to
'commit him to the Prison or common Goal of the said City and
'County.*

Fred. Morris, D. Cl. Con.

And being by Virtue of that Warrant so imprisoned in
the Goal, I was for several Days denied the use of Pen, Ink
and paper, and the Liberty of Speech with any Persons. - -
- - Upon my Commitment, some Friends soon got a *Habeas
Corpus*, to bring me before the Chief Justice, in order to
my Discharge, or being bailed; on the Return whereof, on
Wednesday the 20*th* of *November*, my Council delivered Exceptions to the Return, and the Chief Justice ordered them
to be argued publickly at the City-Hall, on the *Saturday* following.

On *Saturday* the 23*d* of *November*, the said Exceptions
came to be argued, by *James Alexander* and *William Smith*,
of Council for me, and by Mr. Attorney General and
Mr. *Warrel*, of Council against me, in Presence of some
Hundreds of the Inhabitants; where my Council (saving the
Benefit of Exception to the illegality of the Warrant) insisted
that I might be admitted to reasonable Bail.   And to shew
that it was my Right to be so, they offered *Magna Charta*,
The Petition of Right, 3 Car. *The* Habeas Corpus *Act of* 31
Car. 2. which directs the Sum in which Bail is to be taken,
to be, '*according to the Quality of the Prisoner, and Nature
'of the Offence.*'   Also 2*d Hawkins*, Cap. 15 §. 5. in these
Words, '*But Justice must take Care, that under Pretence of*

' *demanding sufficient Security, they do not make so excessive a*
' *Demand, as in Effect amounts to a Denyal of Bail; for this is*
' *lookt on as a great Grievance, and is complained of as such,*
' *by* 1 W. *&* M. Sefs. 2d. *by which it is declared,* That excef-
' five Bail ought not to be required.' It was alfo fhewn
that the feven Bifhops, who in King *James* the IId's Time,
were charged with the like Crime that I ftood charged with,
were admitted to Bail on their own Recognizances, the Arch-
Bifhop in 200*l.* & each of the other fix in a 100*l.* apiece only.
Sundry other Authorities and Arguments were produced
and infifted on by my Council, to prove my Right to be admitted to moderate Bail, and to fuch Bail as was in my
Power to give; and fundry Parts of Hiftory they produced,
to fhew how much the requiring exceffive Bail had been
refented by Parliament. And in order to Enable the Court
to judge what Surety was in my Power to Give, I made Affidavit, *That (my Debts paid) I was not worth Forty Pounds,*
(*the Tools of my Trade and wearing Apparel excepted.*)

Some warm Expreffions (to fay no worfe of them) were
dropt on this Occafion fufficiently known and refented by
the Auditory, which for my Part I defire may be buried in
Oblivion : Upon the whole it was *Ordered that I might be*
admitted to Bail, my self in 400.l. *with two Sureties, each in*
200l. *and that I fhould be remanded till I Gave it.* And
as this was Ten Times more, than was in my Power to
counter-fecure any Perfon in giving Bail for me, I conceived
I could not afk any to become my Bail on thefe Terms ;
and therefore I returned to Goal, where I lay until *Tuesday*
the *28th of January,* 1734,5, being the laft Day of that
Term ; and the Grand Jury having found nothing againft
me, I Expected to have been difcharged from my Imprifonment : But my Hopes proved vain ; for the Attorney General then charged me by *Information,* for Printing and publifhing Parts, of my Journals No. 13. and 23. as being *false,*
scandalous, malicious and seditious.

To this Information my Council appeared, and offered
Exceptions, leaving a Blank for inferting the Judges Com-

miffions, which the Court were of opinion not to receive till
thofe Blanks were filled up. In the fucceeding Vacation
the Judges gave Copies of their Commiffions; and on *Tuefday* the 15th of *April* laft, the firft Day of the fucceeding
Term, my Council offered thefe Exceptions; which were as
follows.

The Attorney General, *v.* *John Peter Zenger.*	On Information for a Mifde- meanour.

' Exceptions humbly offered by *John Peter Zenger*, to the
' Honourable *James De Lancey*, Esq; to judge in this
' Caufe.

' The Defendant comes and prays Hearing of the Com-
' miffion, by Virtue of which the Honourable *James De
' Lancey*, Efq; claims the Power and Authority to judge in
' this Caufe, and it is read to him in thefe Words;
' GEORGE *the fecond, by the Groce of God, of* Great Brit-
' ain, France *and* Ireland, *King, Defender of the Faith*, &c.
' *To Our trufty and well beloved* James De Lancey, *Efq; We
' repofing fpecial Truft and Confidence in your Integrity, Abil-
' ity and Learning; have affigned, conftituted and appointed, and
' We do by thefe Prefents affign conftitute and appoint you the
' faid* James De Lancey, *to be Chief Juftice in and over Our
' Province of* New-York, *in* America, *in the Room of* Lewis
' Morris, *Efq; Giving and by thefe Prefents granting unto you,
' full Power and lawful Authority, to hear try and determine
' all Pleas whatfoever, civil, criminal and mixt, according to the
' Laws, Statutes and Cuftoms of Our Kingdom of* England, *and
' the Laws and Ufages, of Our faid Province of* New-York,
' *not being repugnant thereto, and Executions of all Judgments
' of the faid Court to award, and to make fuch Rules and Or-
' ders in the faid Court, as may be found convenient and ufeful,
' and as near as may be, agreeable to the Rules and Orders of
' Our Courts of King's Bench, Common Pleas and Exchequer in
' England. To have hold and enjoy the faid Office or Place*

THE CASE AND TRIAL

' of *Chief Juſtice, in and over Our ſaid Province, with all and*
' *ſingular the Rights, Privileges, Profits and Advantages, Sallar-*
' *ies, Fees and Perquiſites unto the ſaid Place belonging, or in*
' *any Ways appertaining, in as full and ample Manner as any*
' *Perſon heretofore Chief Juſtice of Our ſaid Province hath*
' *held and enjoyed, or of Right ought to have held and enjoyed*
' *the ſame, To you the ſaid* James De Lancey, *Eſq; for and*
' DURING OUR WILL AND PLEASURE. *In Teſ-*
' *timony whereof we have cauſed theſe Our Letters to be made*
' *Patent, and the great Seal of Our Province of* New-York *to*
' *be hereunto affixed. Witneſs Our truſty and well beloved*
' WILLIAM COSBY, *Eſq; Our Captain General and Gov-*
' *ernour in Chief of Our Provinces of* New-York, New-Jersey
' *and the Territories thereon depending in* America, *Vice-Ad-*
' *miral of the ſame, and Colonel in Our Army, at Fort* George,
' *in* New-York, *the Twenty-firſt day of* Auguſt, *in the ſeventh*
' *Year of Our Reign*, Annoq; Domini, 1733.

' Which being read and heard, the ſaid *John Peter Zenger*,
' by Proteſtation not confeſſing nor ſubmitting to the Power
' of any other Perſon to Judge in this Cauſe, doth except to
' the Power of the Honourable *James De Lancey*, Eſq;
' aforeſaid to judge in this Cauſe, by Virtue of the Commiſ-
' ſion aforeſaid, for theſe Reaſons, viz.

' 1st. For that the Authority of a Judge of the King's
' Bench, in that Part of *Great Britain* called *England*, by
' which the Cognizance of this Cauſe is claimed, is by the
' ſaid Commiſſion granted to the Honourable *James De*
' *Lancey*, Eſq; aforeſaid, only *during Pleaſure;* whereas that
' Authority (by a Statute in that Caſe made and provided,)
' ought to be granted *during good Behaviour.*

' 2d. For that by the ſaid Commiſſion, the Juriſdiction
' and Authority of a Juſtice of the Court of Common Pleas
' at *Weſtminſter* in that Part of *Great-Britain*, called *Eng-*
' *land*, is granted to the ſaid *James De Lancey*, Eſq; which
' Juriſdiction and Authority, cannot be granted to, and ex-
' erciſed by, any one of the Juſtices of the King's Bench.

' 3d. For that the Form of the ſaid Commiſſion, is not

' founded on nor warranted by the Common Law, nor any
' statute of *England*, nor of *Great-Britain*, nor any Act of
' Assembly of this Colony.

"*4th.* For that it appears by the Commission aforesaid,
' that the same is granted under the Seal of this Colony, by
' His Excellency *William Cosby*, Esq; Governour thereof; and
' it appears not, that the same was granted, neither was the
' same granted, by and with the Advice and Consent of His
' Majesty's Council of this Colony; without which Advice
' and Consent, His Excellency could not grant the same.

' Wherefore, and for many other Defects in the said
' Commission, this Defendant humbly hopes, that the Hon-
' ourable *James De Lancey* Esq; will not take Cognizance of
' this Cause, by Virtue of the Commission aforesaid.

Was signed, { *James Alexander.*
{ *William Smith.*

The Exceptions to the Commission of the Honourable
Frederick Philipse, Esq; were the same with the foregoing,
including therein his Commission, which is in these Words.

' GEORGE *the second, by the Grace of God, of* Great
' Britain, France *and* Ireland, *King Defender of the Faith,*
' &c. *To Our trusty and well beloved* Frederick Philipse, *Esq;*
' *Greeting: Whereas it is Our Care, that Justice be duely ad-*
' *ministered to Our Subjects within Our Province of* New-
' York, *and Territories thereon depending in* America; *and*
' *We reposing especial Confidence, in your Integrity, Ability and*
' *Learning, have assigned, constituted and appointed, and We*
' *do by these Presents assign, constitute and appoint you the said*
' Frederick Philipse, *to be second Justice, of Our Supream*
' *Court of Judicature of Our Province of* New-York, *in the*
' *Room of* James De Lancey, *Esq; Giving and granting unto*
' *you the said* Frederick Philipse, *full Power and Authority,*
' *with Our other Justices of Our said Supream Court, to hear, try*
' *and determine, all Pleas whatsoever, civil, criminal and mixt,*
' *according to the Laws, Statutes and Customs of Our Kingdom*
' *of* England, *and the Laws and Usages of Our said Province*

THE CASE AND TRIAL

' *of* New-York, *not being repugnant thereto, and Executions of*
' *all Judgments of the said Court to award, and to act and do*
' *all Things, which any of* Our Juftices of either Bench, or
' Baron of the Exchequer, in Our faid Kingdom of *Eng-*
' *land, may or ought to do* ; *and alfo to affift, in the making fuch*
' *Rules and Orders in Our faid Court, as fhall be for the Good*
' *and Benefit of Our faid Province* ; *and as near as conveniently*
' *may be, to the Rules and Orders of Our faid Courts in Our*
' *faid Kingdom of* England : *To have, hold and enjoy, the faid*
' *Office or Place of fecond Juftice of our faid Province of*
' New-York, *together with all and fingular the Rights, Priv-*
' *ileges, Salaries, Fees, Perquifites, Profits and Advantages*
' *thereto, now or at any Time heretofore belonging, or in any*
' *wife of Right appertaining* ; *unto you the faid* Frederick Phil-
' *ipfe, for and* during Our Pleafure. *In Teftimony whereof,*
' *We have caufed thefe our Letters to be made Patent, and*
' *the Great Seal of Our faid Province of* New-York *to be here-*
' *unto affixed. Witnefs Our trufty and well beloved* WIL-
' LIAM COSBY, *Efq; Our Captain General and Governour*
' *in Chief, of Our Provinces of* New-York, New-Jersey, *and*
' *Territories thereon depending in* America, *Vice Admiral of*
' *the fame, and Colonel in Our Army, &c,* at Fort George *in*
' New-York, *the Twenty-firft Day of* Auguft, *in the Seventh*
' *Year of Our Reign,* Annoq; Domini, 1733.

Fred. Morris, D. Secry.

Tuefday, the 15*th of April,* 1735.

Mr. *Alexander* offered the above Exceptions to the Court,
and prayed that they might be filed.   Upon this the Chief
Juftice faid to Mr. *Alexander* and Mr. *Smith,* That they
ought well to confider the Confequences of what they offered;
to which both anfwered, That they had well confidered what
they offered, and all the Confequences.   And Mr. *Smith*
added, that he was fo well fatisfied of *the Right of the Subject to take an Exception to the Commiffion of a Judge, if he
thought fuch Commiffion illegal,* - - - - that he durft venture
his Life upon *that Point.*   As to *the Validity of the Excep-*

tions then offered, he faid he took that to be a *fecond Point ;* but was ready to argue them both, if their Honours were pleafed to hear him. To which the Chief Juftice replied, That he would confider the Exceptions in the Morning; and ordered the Clerk to bring them to him.

Wednefday the 16th *April,* 1735.

The Chief Juftice delivered one of the Exceptions to the Clerk, and Juftice *Philipfe* the other, upon which Mr. *Smith* arofe and afked the Judges, whether their Honours would hear him upon thefe two points.* 1st. *That the Subject has a Right to take fuch Exceptions, if they judged the Commiffions illegal.* 2dly. *That the Exceptions tendred were legal and valid.* To which the Chief Juftice faid, that they would neither hear nor allow the Exceptions; *for* (faid he) *you thought to have gained a great Deal of Applaufe and Popularity by oppofing this Court, as you did the Court of Exchequer; but you have brought it to that Point, That either,* We muft go from the Bench, or you from the Barr: *Therefore We exclude you and Mr.* Alexander *from the Barr ;* and delivered a Paper to the Clerk, and ordered it be entered, which the Clerk entered accordingly, and returned the Paper to the Chief Juftice; after which the Chief Juftice ordered the Clerk to read publickly what he had written; an attefted Copy whereof follows.

At a Supream Court of Judicature held for the Province of *New-York,* at the City Hall of the City of *New-York,* on *Wednefday,* the 16th Day of *April,* 1735.

PRESENT,

The Honourable *James De Lancey,* Efq: Chief Juftice.
The Honourable *Frederick Philipfe,* Efq; Second Juftice.

---

* *This firft point is largely treated on, in the Arguments of* Van Dam's *Council, in fupport of their Plea to the Jurifdiction of the Supream Court, printed here above a Year before that, from Pag.* 14 *to* 35, *to which no Anfwer has as yet appeared; which Argument, contains alfo fome Part of the Arguments neceffary to fupport the* 2d. *Point.*

THE CASE AND TRIAL

' James Alexander, *Esq, and* William Smith, *Attornies of*
' *this Court, having presumed* (notwithftanding they were
' forewarned by the Court of their DISPLEASURE if
' they fhould do it) *to sign, and having actually signed, and*
' *put into Court, Exceptions, in the Name of* John Peter Zen-
' ger; *thereby denying the Legality of the Judges their Com-*
' *miffions; 'tho' in the ufual Form,* and the being of this Su-
' pream Court. *It is therefore ordered, that for the faid*
' *Contempt, the faid* James Alexander, *and* William Smith,
' *be excluded from any farther Practice in this Court, and that*
' *their Names be ftruck out of the Roll of Attornies of this*
' *Court.*

per. Cur'.   James Lyne, *Cl.*

After the Order of the Court was read, Mr. *Alexander*
afked whether it was the Order of Mr. Juftice *Philipfe* as
well as of the Chief Juftice? To which both anfwered, that
it was their Order; upon which Mr. *Alexander* added,
That it was proper to afk that Queftion, *That they might
know how to have their Relief*: He farther obferved to the
Court, upon reading of the Order, That they were mifta-
ken in their Wording of it, becaufe the Exceptions were
only to their Commiffions, and *not to the being of the Court,* as is
therein alledged; and prayed that the Order might be altered accordingly. The Chief Juftice faid, they conceived
the Exceptions were againft the Being of the Court. Both
Mr. *Alexander* and Mr. *Smith* denyed that they were, and
prayed the Chief Juftice to point to the Place that contained fuch Exception; and further added; That the Court
might well exift, tho' the Commiffions of all the Judges
were void; which the Chief Juftice confeffed to be true:
And therefore they prayed again that the Order in that
Point might be altered; but it was denied.
Then Mr. *Alexander* defired to know, whether they *over
ruled* or *rejected* the Exceptions; the Chief Juftice faid, he
did not underftand the Difference; to which faid *Alexander*
replied, that if he *rejected* the Exceptions, then they could

not appear upon the Proceedings, and in that Cafe the Defendant was entitled to have them made Part of the Proceedings, by Bill of Exceptions: But if they *over ruled* them, then by fo doing, they only declared them not fufficient, to hinder them from proceeding by virtue of thofe Commiffions, and the Exceptions would remain as Records of the Court, and ought to be entered on the Record of the Caufe as Part of the Proceedings. The Chief Juftice faid, they muft remain upon the File, to warrant what we have done; as to being Part of the Record of the Proceedings in that Caufe, he faid, you may fpeak to that Point to morrow.

Fryday, April 18th, 1735.

Mr. *Alexander* fignified to the Court, That on *Wednefday* laft their Honours had faid, That the Council for *Zenger* might fpeak to the Point, concerning the *Rejecting* or *Over ruling* of *Zenger's* Exceptions on the Morrow: To which the Chief Juftice anfwered. That he faid, *You may get fome Perfon to fpeak to that Point on the Morrow, not meaning that the faid* Alexander *fhould fpeak to it, that being contrary to the Order,* Both Mr. *Alexander* and Mr. *Smith* faid, they underftood it otherwife.

They both alfo mentioned, that it was a Doubt, whether by the Words of the Order they were debarred of their Practice as Council, as well as Attornies, whereas they practifed in both Capacities? To which the Chief Juftice anfwered, That the Order was plain, *That* James Alexander, *Efq; and* William Smith, *were debarred and excluded from their whole Practice at this Barr, and that the Order was intended to barr their acting both as Council and as Attornies, and that it could not be conftrued otherwife,* And it being afked Mr. *Philipfe,* Whether he underftood the Order fo; He anfwered, that he did.

Upon this Exclufion of my Council I petitioned the Court to order Council for my Defence, who thereon appointed *John Chambers,* Efq; who pleaded *Not Guilty* for me to the Information. But as to the Point. *Whether my Exceptions should be part of the Record as was moved by my former Council*, Mr. *Chambers* thought not proper to speak to it ; Mr. *Chambers* also moved, that a certain Day in the next Term, might be appointed for my Tryal, and for *a Struck Jury;* whereupon my Tryal was ordered to be on *Munday*, the 4*th* of *·August*, and the Court would consider till the first Day of next Term, whether I should have a Struck Jury or not, and ordered that the Sheriff should in the mean Time, at my Charge, return the Freeholders Book.

At a Supream Court of Judicature held for the Province of *New-York*, before The Honourable *James De Lancey*, Esq; Chief Justice of the said Province ; and The Honourable *Frederick Philipse*, Esq; second Justice of the said Province.

On *Tuesday* the 29*th* of *July*, 1735. The Court opened, and *on Motion of Mr.* Chambers *for a Struck Jury, pursuant to the Rule of the preceding Term, the Court were of Opinion that I was entitled to have a Struck Jury;* and that Evening at five of the Clock, some of my Friends attended the Clerk, for striking the Jury; when to their Surprize, the Clerk instead of producing the Freeholders Book, to Strike the Jury of it in their Presence as usual, he produced a List of 48 Persons, who, he said he had taken out of the Freeholders Book ; my Friends told him, that a great Number of these Persons were not Freeholders, that others were Persons holding Commissions and Offices at the Governour's Pleasure, that others were of the late displaced Magistrates of this City, who must be supposed to have Resentment against me, for what I had printed concerning them ; that others were the Governour's Baker, Taylor Shoemaker, Candlemaker, Joiner, *&c.* that as to the few indifferent Men that were upon that List, they had Reason to believe (as they had heard) that Mr. Attorney had a List of them, to strike them out ; and therefore requested that he would either bring the Freeholders Book, and chuse out of it 48 unexceptionable Men in their Prefence, as ufual or elfe, that he would hear their Objections particularly to the Lift he offered, and that he would put impartial Men in the Place of thofe againft whom they could fhew juft Objections. Notwithftanding this, the Clerk refufed to ftrike the Jury out of the Freeholders Book, and refufed to hear any Objections to the Perfons on his Lift; but told my Friends, if any Objections they had to any Perfons, they might ftrike those Perfons out; to which they anfwered, there would not remain a Jury, if they ftruck out all the exceptionable Men, and according to the Cuftom, they had only a Right to ftrike out 12.

But finding no Arguments could prevail with the Clerk to hear their Objections to his Lift, nor to ftrike the Jury as ufual, Mr. *Chambers* told him, he muft apply to the Court, which the next Morning he did, and the Court upon his Motion *Ordered, That the* 48 *fhould be ftruck out of the Freeholders Book as ufual, in the prefence of the Parties, and that the Clerk fhould hear Objections to Perfons propofed to be of the* 48, *and allow of fuch Exceptions as were juft.* In Purfuance of that Order, a Jury was that Evening ftruck, to the Satisfaction of both Parties, who my Friends and Council infifted on no Objections but *want of Freeholders;* and tho' they did not infift, that Mr. Attorney General (who was affifted by Mr. *Blagge,*) fhould fhew any particular Caufe, againft any Perfons he difliked, but acquiefced that *any perfon he defliked* fhould be out of the 48.

Before *James De Lancey,* Efq; Chief Juftice of the Province of *New-York,* and *Frederick Philipfe,* fecond Judge, came on my Tryal, on the fourth Day of *Auguft,* 1735. upon an Information for printing and publifhing two News Papers, which were called Libels againft our Governour and his Adminiftration.

The Defendant *John Peter Zenger* being called appeared.

And the Sherrif returned his *Venire* for the Tryal of the faid Caufe.

THE CASE AND TRIAL

Mr. *Chambers, of Council for the Defendant.* I humbly move Your Honours, that we may have Juftice done by the Sherrif, and that he may return the Names of the Jurors in the fame Order as they were ftruck.

Chief Juftice. *How is that? Are they not fo returned?*

Mr. *Ch.* No they are not: For fome of the Names that were laft fet down in the Pannel, are now placed firft.

Ch. J. *Make out that, and you fhall be righted.*

Mr. *Ch.* I have the Copy of the Pannel in my Hand, as the Jurors were ftruck, and if the Clerk will produce the Original figned by Mr. Attorney and my felf, Your Honour will fee our Complaint is juft.

Ch. J. *Clerk, is it fo? Look upon that Copy; is it a true Copy of the Pannel as it was ftruck?*

Clerk. Yes, I believe it is.

Ch. J. *How came the Names of the Jurors to be mifplaced in the Pannel annexed to the* Venire?

Sheriff. I have returned the Jurors in the fame Order in which the Clerk gave them to me.

Ch. J. *Let the Names of the Jurors be ranged in the Order they were ftruck, agreeable to the Copy here in Court.*

Which was done accordingly. And the Jury, whofe Names were as follows, were called and fworn.

Harmanus Rutgers,	*Samuel Weaver,*	*Benjamin Hildreth,*
Stanly Holmes,	*Andries Marfchalk,*	*Abraham Keteltas,*
Edward Man,	*Egbert van Borfom,*	*John Goelet,*
John Bell,	*Thomas Hunt, Form.*	*Hercules Wendover.*

Mr. Attorney General opened the Information, which was as follows.

Mr. *Attorney.* May it pleafe Your Honours, and you Gentlemen of the Jury; the Information now before the Court, and to which the Defendant *Zenger* has pleaded *Not Guilty,* is an Information for printing and publifhing *a falfe, fcandalous, and feditious Libel,* in which his Excellency the Governour of this Province, who is the King's immediate

Reprefentative here, is greatly and unjuftly fcandalized, as a Perfon that has no Regard to Law nor Juftice ; with much more, as will appear upon reading the Information. This of Libelling is what has always been difcouraged as a Thing that tends to create Differences among Men, ill Blood among the People, and oftentimes great Bloodfhed between the Party Libelling and the Party Libelled.   There can be no Doubt but you Gentlemen of the Jury will have the fame ill opinion of fuch practices, as the judges have always fhewn upon fuch Occafions : But I fhall fay no more at this Time, untill you hear the Information, which is as follows.

‘ *New-York*, Supream Court.
‘ of the Term of *January*, in the Eighth Year of the
‘ Reign of our Sovereign Lord King GEORGE the
‘ fecond, *&c.*

‘ *New-York, fs.* ‘ BE it remembered, That *Richard Bradly*,
‘ Efq: Attorney General of Our Sove-
‘ reign Lord the King, for the Province of *New-York*, who for
‘ Our faid Lord the King in this Part profecutes, in his own
‘ proper Perfon comes here into the Court of our faid Lord
‘ the King, and for our faid Lord the King gives the Court
‘ here to underftand and be informed, That *John Peter Zen-*
‘ *ger*, late of the City of *New-York*, Printer, (being a fedi-
‘ tious Perfon; and a frequent Printer and Publifher of falfe
‘ News and feditious Libels, and wickedly and malicioufly
‘ devifing the Government of Our faid Lord the King of this
‘ His Majefty's Province of *New-York*, under the Admin-
‘ iftration of His Excellency *William Cofby*, Efq ; Captain
‘ General and Governour, in Chief of the faid Province, to
‘ traduce, fcandalize and vilify, and His Excellency the faid
‘ Governour, and the Minifters and Officers of Our faid
‘ Lord, the King of and for the faid Province to bring into
‘ Sufpicion and the ill Opinion of the Subjects of Our faid
‘ Lord the King refiding within the Province) the Twenty
‘ eighth Day of *January*, in the feventh Year of the Reign

THE CASE AND TRIAL

' of Our Sovereign Lord *George* the fecond, by the Grace of
' God of *Great-Britain*, *France* and *Ireland*, King Defender
' of the Faith, *&c.* at the City of *New-York*, *did falſly, fedi-*
' *tiouſly and ſcandalouſly* print and publiſh, and caufe to be
' printed and publiſhed, a certain *falſe, malicious, ſeditious*
' *ſcandalous* Libel, entitled *The New-York Weekly Journal*,
' *containing the freſheſt Advices, foreign and domeſtick* ; in which
' Libel (of and concerning His excellency the faid Govern-
' our, and the Miniſters and Officers of Our faid Lord the
' king, of and for the faid Province) among other Things
' therein contained are thefe Words ; " *Your Appearance in*
" *Print at laſt*, gives a Pleafure to many, tho' moſt wiſh
" you had come fairly into the open Field, and not ap-
" peared behind *Retrenchments* made of the fuppofed Laws
" againſt Libelling, and of what other Men have faid and
" done before ; thefe *Retrenchments*, Gentlemen, may foon
" be ſhewn to you and all Men to be weak, and to have
" neither Law nor Reafon for their Foundation, fo cannot
" long ſtand you in ſtead : Therefore, you had much better
" as yet leave them, and come to what *the People of this City*
" *and Province* (the City and Province of *New-York* mean-
" ing) think are the Points in Queſtion (*to witt*) They (the
" People of the Ctiy and Province of *New-York* meaning)
" *think as Matters now ſtand, that their* LIBERTIES *and*
" PROPERTIES *are precarious, and that* SLAVERY *is like*
" *to be intailed on them and their Poſterity, if ſome paſt*
" *Things be not amended, and this they collect from many paſt*
" *Proceedings.*' (Meaning many of the paſt Proceedings of
' of His Excellency the faid Governour, and of the Minif-
' ters and Officers of our faid Lord the King, of and for the
' faid Province.) And faid the Attorney General of Our
' faid Lord the King, for Our faid Lord the King, like-
' wife gives the Court here to underſtand and be informed,
' that the faid *John Peter Zenger* afterwards (*to wit*) the
' eighth Day of *April*, in the feventh Year of the Reign of
' Our faid Lord the King, at the City of *New York* afore-
' faid, did *faſly, ſeditiouſly and ſcandalouſly* print and publiſh,

JOHN PETER ZENGER

' and cause to be printed and published, another *false mali-*
' *cious seditious and scandalous* Libel, entituled, *the New-York*
' *Weekly Journal, containing the freshest Advices, foreign and*
' *domestic.* In which Libel, (of and concerning the Govern-
' ment of the said Province of *New-York*, and of and con-
' cerning His Excellency the said Governour, and the Min-
' isters and Officers of Our said Lord the King, of and for
' the said Province) among other Things therein contained,
' are these Words " *One of our Neighbours* (one of the In-
" habitants of *New-Jersey* meaning) *being in Company, ob-*
" *serving the Strangers* (some of the Inhabitants of *New-*
" *York* meaning) *full of Complaints, endeavoured to perswade*
" *them to remove into* Jersey ; *to which it was replied, that*
" *would be leaping out of the Frying Pan into the Fire ; for,*
" *says he, we both are under the same Governour* (His Ex-
" cellency the said Governour meaning) *and your Assembly*
" *have shewn with a Witness what is to be expected from them;*
" *one that was then moving to* Pensilvania, (meaning one
" that was then removing from *New-York*, with intent to
" reside af *Pensilvania*) *to which Place it is reported several*
" *considerable Men are removing* (from *New-York* meaning)
" *expressed in Terms very moving, much Concern for the Cir-*
" *cumstances of* New-York (the bad Circumstances of the
" Province and People of *New-York* meaning) *seemed to*
" *think them very much owing to the Influence that some Men*
" (whom he called *Tools*) *had in the Administration* (meaning
" the Administration of Government of the said Province
" of *New-York*) *said he was now going from them, and was*
" *not to be hurt by any Measures they should take, but could*
" *not help having some Concern for the Welfare of his Coun-*
" *try-Men, and should be glad to hear that the Assembly* (mean-
" ing the General Assembly of the Province of *New-York*)
" *would exert themselves as became them, by shewing that they*
" *have the Interest of their Country more at Heart, than the*
" *Gratification of any private View of any of their Members,*
" *or being at all affected, by the Smiles or Frowns of a Gov-*
" *ernour,* (His Excellency the said Governour meaning)

THE CASE AND TRIAL

" *both which ought equally to be despised, when the Interest of*
" *their Country is at stake. You says he, complain of the Law-*
" *yers, but I think the Law it self is at an End,* WE (the
" People of the Province of *New-York* meaning) SEE
" MENS DEEDS DESTROYED, JUDGES ARBI-
" TRARILY DISPLACED, NEW COURTS ERECT-
" ED WITHOUT CONSENT OF THE LEGISLA-
" TURE (within the Province of *New-York* meaning) BY
" WHICH IT SEEMS TO ME, TRIALS BY JU-
" RIES ARE TAKEN AWAY WHEN A GOVERN-
" OUR PLEASES (His Excellency the said Governour
" meaning) MEN OF KNOWN ESTATES DENYED
" THEIR VOTES, CONTRARY TO THE RE-
" CEIVED PRACTICE, THE BEST EXPOSITOR
" OF ANY LAW : *Who is then in that Province* (meaning
" the Province of *New-York,*) *that call* (can call meaning)
" *any Thing his own, or enjoy any Libery* (Liberty meaning)
" *longer than those in the Administration* (meaning the Ad-
" ministration of Government of the said Province of *New-*
" *York*) *will condescend to let them do it, for which Reason I*
" *have left it,* (the Province of *New-York* meaning) *as I be-*
" *lieve more will.'* To the great Disturbance of the Peace
' of the said Province of *New-York,* to the Great Scandal
' of Our said Lord the King, of His Exceellency the said
' Governour, and of all others concerned in the Administra-
' tion of the Government of the said Province, and against
' the Peace of Our Sovereign Lord the King His Crown
' and Dignity, *&c.* Whereupon the said Attorney General
' of Our said Lord the King, for Our said Lord the King,
' prays the Advisement of the Court here, in the Premises,
' and the due Process of the Law, against him the said *John*
' *Peter Zenger,* in this Part to be done, to answer to Our
' said Lord the King of and in the Premises, *&c.*

' *R. Bradley,* Attorney General.

To this Information the Defendant has pleaded *Not
Guilty,* and we are ready to prove it.

JOHN PETER ZENGER

Mr. Chambers *has not been pleased to favour me with his Notes, so I cannot, for Fear of doing him Injustice, pretend to set down his Argument; But here Mr.* Chambers *set forth very clearly the Nature of a Libel, the great Allowances that ought to be made for what Men speak or write, That in all Libels there must be some particular Persons so clearly pointed out, that no Doubt must remain about who is meant; That he was in hopes Mr.* Attorney *would fail in his Proof, as to this Point; and therefore desired that he would go on to examine his Witnesses.*

Then Mr. *Hamilton*, who at the Request of some of my Friends, was so kind as to come from *Philadelphia* to assist me on the Tryal, spoke.

Mr. *Hamilton.* May it please your Honour; I am concerned in this Cause on the Part of Mr. *Zenger* the Defendant. The Information against my Client was sent me, a few Days before I left Home, with some Instructions to let me know how far I might rely upon the Truth of those Parts of the Papers set forth in the Information, and which are said to be libellous. And tho' I am perfectly of the Opinion with the Gentleman who has just now spoke, on the same Side with me, as to the common Course of Proceedings, I mean in putting Mr. Attorney upon proving, that my Client printed and published those Papers mentioned in the Information; yet I cannot think it proper for me (without doing Violence to my own Principles) to deny the Publication of a Complaint, which I think is the Right of every free-born Subject to make, when the Matters so published can be supported with Truth; and therefore I'll save Mr. Attorney the Trouble of Examining his Witnesses to that Point; and I do (for my Client) confess, that he both printed and published the two News Papers set forth in the Information, and I hope in so doing he has committed no Crime.

Mr. *Attorney.* Then if Your Honour pleases, since Mr. *Hamilton* has confessed the Fact, I think our Witnesses may be discharged; we have no further Occasion for them.

THE CASE AND TRIAL

Mr. Hamilton. If you brought them here, only to prove the Printing and Publishing of these News Papers, we have acknowledged that, and shall abide by it.

> *Here my Journeyman and two Sons (with several others subpœna'd by Mr. Attorney, to give Evidence against me) were discharged, and there was Silence in the Court for some Time.*

Mr. Chief justice. *Well Mr. Attorney, will you proceed?*

Mr. Attorney. Indeed Sir, as Mr. *Hamilton* has confessed the Printing and Publishing these Libels, I think the Jury must find a Verdict for the King ; for supposing they were true, the Law says that they are not the less libellous for that ; nay indeed the Law says, their being true is an Aggravation of the Crime.

Mr. *Hamilton.* Not so neither, Mr. Attorney, there are two Words to that Bargain. I hope it is not our bare Printing and Publishing a Paper, that will make it a Libel : You will have something more to do, before you make my Client a Libeller ; for the Words themselves must be libellous, that is, *false, scandalous, and seditious* or else we are not guilty.

> *As Mr. Attorney has not been pleased to favour us with his Argument, which he read, or with the Notes of it, we cannot take upon us to set down his Words, but only to shew the Book Cases he cited, and the general Scope of his Argument, which he drew from those Authorities. He observed upon the Excellency, as well as Use of Government, and the great Regard and Reverence, which had been constantly paid to it, both under the Law and Gospel. That by Government we were protected in our Lives, Religion and Properties ; and that for these Reasons, great Care had always been taken to prevent every Thing that might tend to scandalize Magistrates, and others concerned in the Administration of the Government, especially the supream Magistrate. And that there were many*

JOHN PETER ZENGER

Instances of very severe Judgments, and of Punishments inflicted upon such, as had attempted to bring the Government into Contempt ; by publishing false and scurrilous Libels against it, or by speaking evil and scandalous Words of Men in Authority ; to the great Disturbance of the publick Peace. And to support this, he cited 5 Coke 121. (suppose it should be 125.) Wood's Institut. 430. 2 Lilly 168. 1 Hawkins 73. 11. 6. From these Books he insisted, that a Libel was a malicious Defamation of any Person, expressed either in Printing or Writing, Signs or Pictures, to asperse the Reputation of one that is alive, or the Memory of one that is dead ; if he is a private Man, the Libeller deserves a severe Punishment, but if it is against a Magistrate or other publick Person, it is a greater Offence ; for this concerns not only the Breach of the Peace, but the Scandal of the Government ; for what greater Scandal of Government can there be, than to have corrupt or wicked Magistrates to be appointed by the King, to govern his Subjects under him ? And a greater Imputation to the State cannot be, than to suffer such corrupt Men to sit in the sacred Seat of Justice, or to have any Medling in, or concerning the Administration of Justice : And from the same Books Mr. Attorney insisted, that whether the Person defamed is a private Man or a Magistrate, whether living or Dead, whether the Libel is true or false, or if the Party against whom it is made is of good or evil Fame, it is nevertheless a Libel : For in a settled State of Government, the Party grieved ought to complain for every injury done him, in the ordinary Course of the Law. And as to its Publication, the Law had taken so great Care of Men's Reputations, that if one maliciously repeats it, or sings it in the Presence of an other, or delivers the Libel or a Copy of it over, to scandalize the Party, he is to be punished as a Publisher of a Libel. He said it was likewise evident, that Libelling was an Offence against the Law of God. Act. XXIII. 5. Then said Paul, I wiſt not Brethren, that he was the High Prieſt: For it is written, thou ſhalt not ſpeak evil of the Ruler of the People. 2 *Pet.* X. 11. Deſpiſe Government, preſumptuous are they, ſelf willed, they are not afraid to ſpeak evil of Dignities, &c. *He then inſiſted that it was clear, both by the Law God and Man, That it was a very great Offence to ſpeak evil of, or to revile thoſe in Authority over us; and that Mr.* Zenger *had offended in a moſt notorious and groſs Manner, in ſcandal-izing His Excellency our Governour, who is the King's immediate Repreſentative, and the Supream Magiſtrate of this Province: For can there be any Thing more ſcan-dalous ſaid of a Governour, than what is publiſhed in thoſe Papers? Nay, not only the Governour, but both the Council and Aſſembly are ſcandalized; for there it is plainly ſaid, That* as Matters now ſtand, their Liberties and Properties are precarious, and that Slavery is like to be entailed on them and their Poſterity. *And then again Mr.* Zenger *ſays,* The Aſſembly ought to de-ſpiſe the Smiles or Frowns of a Governour; That he thinks the Law is at an End; That we ſee Mens Deeds deſtroyed, Judges arbitrarily diſplaced, new Courts erected, without Conſent of the Legiſlature; *And* That it ſeems Tryals by Juries are taken away when a Governour pleaſes; That none can call any Thing their own, longer than thoſe in the Adminiſ-tration will condeſcend to let them do it.— — — — — — — — — — — — — — — *And Mr. Attorney added, that he did not know what could be ſaid in Defence of a Man, that had ſo notoriouſly ſcandalized the Governour and principal Magiſtrates and Officers of the Govern-ment, by charging them with depriving the People of their Rights and Liberties, and taking away Tryals by Juries, and in ſhort, putting an End to the Law itſelf.*— — — *If this was not a Libel, he ſaid, he did not know what was one. Such Perſons as will take thoſe Liberties with Governours and Magiſtrates, he thought ought to ſuf-*

JOHN PETER ZENGER

fer for stirring up Sedition and Discontent among the People. And concluded by saying, that the Government had been very much traduced and exposed by Mr. Zenger, before he was taken Notice of; that at last it was the Opinion of the Governour and Council, that he ought not to be suffered to go on, to disturb the Peace of the Government; by publishing such Libels against the Governour, and the chief Persons in the Government; And therefore they had directed this Prosecution, to put a Stop to this scandalous and wicked Practice, of libelling and defaming His Majesty's Government and disturbing his Majesty's Peace.

Mr. Chambers *then sum'd up to the Jury, observing with great Strength of Reason on Mr. Attorney's defect of Proof, that the Papers in the Information were* False, Malicious or Seditious, *which was incumbent on him to prove to the Jury, and without which they could not on their Oaths say,* That they were so, as charged.

Mr. *Hamilton.* May it please Your Honour; I agree with Mr. Attorney, that Government is a sacred Thing, but I differ very widely from him when he would insinuate, that the just Complaints of a Number of Men, who suffer under a bad Administration, is libelling that Administration. Had I believed that to be Law, I should not have given the Court the Trouble of hearing any Thing that I could say in this Cause. I own, when I read the Information, I had not the Art to find out (without the Help of Mr. Attorney's *Innuendo's*) that the Governor was the Person meant in every Period of that News Paper; and I was inclined to believe, that they were wrote by some, who from an extraordinary Zeal for Liberty, had misconstrued the Conduct of some Persons in Authority into Crimes; and that Mr. Attorney out of his too great Zeal for Power, had exhibited this Information, to correct the Indiscretion of my Client; and at the same Time, to shew his Superiors the great Concern he had, lest they should be treated with any undue

202

Freedom.   But from what Mr. Attorney has juft now faid, *to wit*, That this Profecution was directed by the Governor and Council, and from the Extraordinary Appearance of People of all Conditions, which I obferve in Court upon this Occafion, I have Reafon to think, that thofe in the Adminiftration have by this Profecution fomething more in View, and that the People believe they have a good deal more at ftake, than I apprehended : And therefore, as it is become my Duty, to be both plain and particular in this Caufe, I beg Leave to befpeak the Patience of the Court.

I was in hopes, as that terrible Court, where thofe dreadful Judgments were given, and that Law eftablifhed, which Mr. Attorney has produced for Authorities to fupport this Caufe, was long ago laid afide, as the moft dangerous Court to the Liberties of the People of *England*, that ever was known in that Kingdom ; that Mr. Attorney knowing this, would not have attempted to fet up a Star-Chamber here, nor to make their Judgments a Precedent to us : For it is well known, that what would have been judg'd Treafon in thofe Days for a Man to fpeak, I think, has fince not only been practiced as lawful, but the contrary Doctrine has been held to be Law.

In *Brewfter's* Cafe, for Printing, *That the Subjects might defend their Rights and Liberties by Arms, in cafe the King fhould go about to deftroy them*, he was told by the Chief Juftice that it was a great Mercy, he was not proceeded againft for his Life ; for that to fay, the King could be refifted by Arms in any Cafe whatfoever, was exprefs Treafon. And yet we fee fince that Time, Dr. *Sacheverell* was fentenced in the higheft Court in *Great Britain*, for faying, *That fuch a Refiftance was not lawful*. Befides, as Times have made very great Changes in the Laws of *England*, fo in my Opinion there is good Reafon that Places fhould do fo too.

Is it not furprizing to fee a Subject, upon his receiving a Commiffion from the King to be a Governor of a Colony in *America*, immediately imagining himfelf to be vefted with all the Prerogatives belonging to the facred Perfon of his

Prince? And which is yet more aftonifhing, to fee that a People can be fo wild as to allow of and acknowledge thofe Prerogatives and Exemptions, even to their own Deftruction? Is it fo hard a Matter to diftinguifh between the Majefty of our Sovereign, and the Power of a Governor of the Plantations? Is not this making very free with our Prince, to apply that Regard, Obedience and Allegiance to a Subject, which is due only to Our Sovereign? And yet in all the Cafes which Mr. Attorney has cited, to fhew the Duty and Obedience we owe to the Supreme Magiftrate, it is the King that is there meant and underftood, tho' Mr. Attorney is pleafed to urge them as Authorities to prove the Heinoufnefs of Mr. *Zenger's* Offence againft the Governor of *New-York*. The feveral Plantations are compared to fo many large Corporations, and perhaps not improperly; and can any one give an inftance, that the Mayor or Head of a Corporation, ever put in a Claim to the facred Rights of Majefty? Let us not (while we are pretending to pay a great Regard to our Prince and His Peace) make bold to transfer that Allegiance to a Subject, which we owe to our King only. What ftrange Doctrine is it, to prefs every Thing for Law here which is fo in *England*? I Believe we fhould not think it a Favour, at prefent at leaft, to eftablifh this
C. 3 Inft. 140. Practice. In *England* fo great a Regard and Reverence is had to the Judges, * that if any Man ftrikes another in *Weftminfter Hall*, while the Judges are fitting, he fhall lofe his Right Hand, and forfeit his Land and Goods, for fo doing. And tho' the Judges here claim all the Powers and Authorities within this Government, that a Court of King's Bench has in *England*, yet I believe Mr. Attorney will fcarcely fay, that fuch a Punifhment could be legally inflicted on a Man for committing fuch an Offence, in the Prefence of the Judges fitting in any Court within the Province of *New-York*. The Reafon is obvious; a Quarrel or Riot in *New-York*, cannot poffibly be attended with thofe dangerous Confequences that it might in *Weftminfter Hall*; nor (I hope) will it be alledged, that any Mifbehaviour to a

THE CASE AND TRIAL

Governor in the Plantations will, or ought to be, judged of or punished, as a like Undutifulness would be, to Our Sovereign. From all which, I hope Mr. Atttorney will not think it proper to apply his Law-Cases (to support the Cause of his Governor) which have only been judged, where the King's Safety or Honour was concerned. It will not be denied but that a Freeholder in the Province of *New-York*, has as good a Right to the sole and separate Use of his Lands, as a Freeholder in *England*, who has a Right to bring an Action of Trespass against his Neighbour, for suffering his Horse or Cow to come and feed upon his Land, or eat his Corn, whether inclosed or not inclused; and yet I believe it would be looked upon as a strange Attempt, for one Man here, to bring an Action against another, whose Cattle and Horses feed upon his Grounds not inclosed, or indeed for eating and treading down his Corn, if that were not inclosed. Numberless are the Instances of this Kind that might be given, to shew, that what is good Law at one Time and in one Place, is not so at another Time and in another Place; so that I think, the Law seems to expect, that in these Parts of the World Men should take Care, by a good Fence, to preserve their Property, from the Injury of unruly Beasts. And perhaps there may be a good Reason why Men should take the same Care, to make an honest and upright Conduct a Fence and Security against the Injury of unruly Tongues.

Mr. Attorney. I don't know what the Gentleman means, by comparing Cases of Freeholders in *England* with Freeholders here. What has this Case to do with Actions of Trespass, or Men's Fencing their Ground? The Case before the Court is, whether Mr. *Zenger* is guilty of Libelling His Excellency the Governor of *New-York*, and indeed the whole Administration of the Government? Mr. *Hamilton*, has confessed the Printing and Publishing, and I think nothing is plainer, than that the Words in the Information are *scandalous, and tend to sedition, and to disquiet the Minds of the People of this Province.* And if such Papers are not Libels,

JOHN PETER ZENGER

I think it may be said, there can be no such Thing as a Libel.

Mr. *Hamilton*. May it please Your Honour; I cannot agree with Mr. Attorney: For tho' I freely acknowledge, that there are such Things as Libels, yet I must insist at the same Time, that what my Client is charged with, is not a Libel; and I observed just now, that Mr. Attorney in defining a Libel, made use of the Words, *scandalous, seditious, and tend to disquiet the People*; but (whether with Design or not I will not say) he omitted the Word *false*.

Mr. Attorney. I think I did not omit the Word *false*: But it has been said already, that it may be a Libel, notwithstanding it may be true.

Mr. *Hamilton*. In this I must still differ with Mr. Attorney; for I depend upon it, we are to be tried upon this Information now before the Court and Jury, and to which we have pleaded *Not Guilty*, and by it we are charged with Printing and publishing *a certain false, malicious, seditious and scandalous Libel*. This Word *false* must have some Meaning, or else how came it there? I hope Mr. Attorney will not say, he put it there by Chance, and I am of Opinion his Information would not be good without it. But to shew that it is the principal Thing which, in my Opinion, makes a Libel, I put the Case, the Information had been for printing and publishing a certain *true* Libel, would that be the same Thing? Or could Mr. Attorney support such an Information by any Precedent in the *English* Law? No, the Falshood makes the Scandal, and both make the Libel. And to shew the Court that I am in good Earnest, and to save the Court's Time, and Mr. Attorney's Trouble, I will agree, that if he can prove the Facts charged upon us, to be *false*, I'll own them to be *scandalous, seditious* and *a Libel*. So the Work seems now to be pretty much shortned, and Mr. Attorney has now only to prove the Words *false*, in order to make us Guilty.

Mr. Attorney. We have nothing to prove; you have

confeſſed the Printing and Publiſhing; but if it was neceſ-
ſary (as I inſiſt it is not) how can we prove a Negative? But
I hope ſome Regard will be had to the Authorities that have
been produced, and that ſuppoſing all the Words to be true,
yet that will not help them, that Chief Juſtice *Holt* in his
Charge to the Jury, in the Caſe of *Tutchin*, made no Diſtinction, whether *Tutchin's* Paper's were *true* or *falſe*; and as
Chief Juſtice *Holt* has made no Diſtinction in that Caſe, ſo
none ought to be made here; nor can it be ſhewn in all that
Caſe, there was any Queſtion made about their being *falſe*
or *true*.

Mr. *Hamilton.* I did expect to hear, That a Negative
cannot be proved; But every Body knows there are many
Exceptions to that general Rule: For if a Man is charged
with killing another, or ſtealing his Neighbour's Horſe, if he
is innocent, in the one Caſe, he may prove the Man ſaid to
be killed, to be really alive; and the Horſe ſaid to be ſtoln,
never to have been out of his Maſter's Stable, &c. and this
I think is proving a Negative. But we will ſave Mr. Attorney the Trouble of proving a Negative, and take the
Onus probandi upon our ſelves, and prove thoſe very Papers
that are called Libels to be *true*.

Mr. *Ch. Juſtice.* You cannot be admitted, Mr. *Hamilton*,
to give the Truth of a Libel in Evidence. A Libel is not to
be juſtified; for it is neverthelefs a Libel that it is *true*.

Mr. *Hamilton.* I am ſorry the Court has ſo ſoon re-
ſolved upon that Piece of Law; I expected firſt to have
been heard to that Point. I have not in all my Reading
met with an Authority that ſays, we cannot be admitted
to give the Truth in Evidence, upon an Information for
a Libel.

Mr. *Ch. Juſtice.* The Law is clear, That you cannot
juſtify a Libel.

Mr. *Hamilton.* I own that, may it pleaſe Your Honour,
to be ſo; but, with Submiſſion, I underſtand the Word, *juſtify*,
there, to be a juſtification by Plea, as it is in the Caſe upon
an Indictment for *Murder*, or an *Aſſault and Battery*; there

the Prifoner cannot juftify, but plead *Not Guilty:* Yet it will
not be denied but he may, and always is admitted, to give the
Truth of the Fact, or any other Matter, in Evidence, which
goes to his Acquital; as in Murder, he may prove it was in
Defence of his Life, his Houfe, &c. and in Affault and Battery, he may give in Evidence, that the other Party ftruck
firft, and in both Cafes he will be acquitted. And in this
Senfe I underftand the Word *juftify*, when applied to the
Cafe before the Court.

Mr. *Ch. Juftice.* I Pray fhew that you can give the
Truth of a Libel in Evidence.

Mr. *Hamilton.* I am ready, both from what I underftand to be the Authorities in the Cafe, and from the Reafon
of the Thing, to fhew that we may lawfully do fo. But here
I beg leave to obferve, That Informations for Libels is a
Child, if not born, yet nurfed up, and brought to full Maturity, in the Court of Star-Chamber.

Mr. Ch. Juftice. Mr. *Hamilton* you'll find your felf mif-
taken; for in *Coke's Inftitutes* you'll find Informations for
Libels, long before the Court of Star-Chamber.

Mr. *Hamilton.* I thank Your Honour; that is an
Authority I did propofe to fpeak to by and by: But as you
have mention'd it, I'll read that Authority now. I think
it is in *3 Co. Inft.* under Title *Libel;* it is the Cafe of *John
de Northampton* for a Letter wrote to *Robert de Ferrers,* one
of the King's privy Council, *concerning Sir *William Scot,*
Chief Juftice, and his Fellows; but it does
not appear to have been upon Information; *Coke 3 Inft.* 174.
and I have good Grounds to fay it was
upon Indictment, as was the Cafe of *Adam de Ravenfworth,*
juft mentioned before by Lord *Coke,* under the fame
Title; and I think there cannot be a greater, at leaft a
plainer Authority for us, than the Judgment in the Cafe of
John de Northampton, which my Lord has fet down at large.
*Et quia prædictus Johannes cognovit dictam Litteram per fe
fcriptam Roberto de Ferrers, qui eft de Concilio Regis, qua littera
continet in fenullam veritatem, &c.* Now Sir, by this Judg-

ment it appears the libelous Words were utterly false, and there the Falshood was the Crime, and is the Ground of that Judgment: And is not that what we contend for? Do not we infist that the Falshood makes the Scandal, and both make the Libel? And how shall it be known whether the Words are libelous, *that is*, *true* or *false*, but by admitting us to prove them *true*, since Mr. Attorney will not undertake to prove them *false*? Besides, is it not against common Sense, that a Man should be punished in the same Degree for a *true Libel* (if any such Thing could be) as for a *false one*? I know it is said, *That Truth makes a Libel the more provoking, and therefore the Offence is the greater, and consequently the Judgment should be the heavier.* Well, suppose it were so, and let us agree for once, *That Truth is a greater Sin than Falshood*: Yet as the Offences are not equal, and as the Punishment is arbitrary, *that is*, according as the Judges in their Discretion shall direct to be inflicted; is it not absolutely necessary that they should know, whether the Libel is *true* or *false*, that they may by that Means be able to proportion the Punishment? For, would it not be a sad Case, if the Judges, for want of a due Information, should chance to give as severe a Judgment against a Man for writing or publishing a Lie, as for writing or publishing a Truth? And yet this (with submission) as monstrous and ridiculous as it may seem to be, is the natural Consequence of Mr. Attorney's Doctrine, *That Truth makes a worse Libel than Falshood*, and must follow from his not proving our Papers to be *false*, or not suffering us to prove them to be *true*. But this is only reasoning upon the Case, and I will now proceed to shew, what in my Opinion will be sufficient to induce the Court, to allow us to prove the Truth of the Words, which in the Information are called Libellous. And first, I think there cannot be a greater Authority for us, than the Judgment I just now mentioned, in the case of *John de Northampton*, and that was in early Times, and before the Star-Chamber came to its Fulness of Power and Wickedness. In that Judgment, as I observed, the *Falshood* of the

JOHN PETER ZENGER

Letter which was wrote, is affigned as the very Ground of the Sentence. And agreeable to this it was *State Tryals, urged by Sir *Robert Sawyer*, *in the Tryal of Vol. 4. the Seven Bifhops, *That the Falfity, the Malice, and Sedition of the Writing, were all Facts to be proved*. But here it may be faid, Sir *Robert* was one of the Bifhop's Council, and his Argument is not to be allowed for Law: But I offer it only to fhew that we are not the firft who have infifted, that to make a Writing a Libel, it muft be *falfe*. And if the Argument of a Council muft have no Weight, I hope there will be more Regard fhewn to the Opinion of a Judge, and therefore I mention the Words of Juftice *Powel* in the fame Tryal, where he fays (of the Petition of the Bifhops, which was called a Libel, and upon which they were profecuted by Information) That *to make it a Libel, it muft be falfe and malicious, and tend to Sedition*; and declared, *as he faw no Falfhood or Malice in it, he was of Opinion, that it was no Libel.* Now I fhould think this Opinion alone, in the Cafe of the King, and in a Cafe which that King had fo much at Heart, and which to this Day has never been contradicted, might be a fufficient Authority, to entitle us to the Liberty of proving the *Truth* of the Papers, which in the Information are called *falfe, malicious, feditious and fcandalous.* If it be objected, *that the Opinions of the other three Judges were againft him* ; I anfwer, That the Cenfures the Judgments of thefe Men have undergone, and the Approbation Juftice *Powel's* Opinion, his Judgment and Conduct upon that Tryal has met with, and the Honour he gained to himfelf, for daring to fpeak Truth at fuch a Time, upon fuch an Occafion, and in the Reign of fuch a King, is more than fufficient, in my humble Opinion, to warrant our infifting on his Judgment, as a full Authority to our Purpofe; and it will lye upon Mr. Attorney to fhew, that his Opinion has fince that Time been denied to be Law, or that Juftice *Powel* who delivered it, has ever been condemned or blamed for it, in any Law-Book extant at this Day, and this I will venture to fay,

Mr. Attorney cannot do. But to make this Point yet more clear, if any Thing can be clearer, I will on our Part proceed and shew, that in the Cafe of Sir *Samuel Barnardiston*. His Council, notwithstanding he stood before one of the greatest Monsters that ever presided in any *English* Court (Judge *Jefferies*) insisted on the Want of Proof, to the *Malice* and *seditious Intent* of the Author, of what was called a *Libel*. And in the Cafe of *Tutchin*, which seems to be Mr. Attorney's chief Authority, that Cafe is against him ; for he was, upon his Tryal put upon shewing the Truth of his Papers, but did not, at least the Prisoner was asked, by the King's Council, whether he would say they were *State Trials* true? And as he never pretended, that they *Vol. V. 549.* were true, the Chief Justice was not to say so.

But the Point will still be clearer on our Side from *Fuller's* Cafe, *For falsly and wickedly caufing to be printed a false and scandalous Libel,* *State Trials* *in which (amongst other Things) were contained* Vol. V. 445 *these Words,* 'Mr. Jones *has also made Oath,*
That he paid L.5000. *more, by the late King's Order, to several*
'*Persons in Places of Truft, that they might compleat my Ruin,*
'*and invalidate me forever. Nor is this all; for the same Mr.*
'*Jones will prove by undeniable Witnefs and Demonftration,*
'*that he has diftributed more than* L.180,000. *in Eight Years*
'*laft paft, by the French King's Order, to Perfons in publick*
'*Truft in this Kingdom.*' Here you see is a scandalous and infamous Charge against the late King ; here is a Charge no less than High Treason, against the *Men in publick Truft,* for receiving Money of the *French* King, then in actual War with the Crown of *Great Britain* ; and yet the Court were far from bearing him down with that Star Chamber Doctrine, *to wit, That it was no matter, whether what he faid was true or falfe* ; no, on the contrary, Lord Chief Justice *Holt* afks *Fuller, Can you make it appear, they are true? Have you any Witneffes? You might have had* Subpœna's *for your Witneffes against this Day. If you take upon you to write such Things as you are charged with, it lies upon you to prove them*

true, at your Peril. If you have any Witnesses, I will hear them. How came you to write those Books which are not true? If you have any Witnesses, produce them. If you can offer any Matter to prove what you have wrote, let us hear it. Thus said, and thus did, that great Man Lord Chief Justice *Holt*, upon a Tryal of the like Kind with ours, and the Rule laid down by him in this Case is, *That he who will take upon him to write Things, it lies upon him to prove them, at his Peril.* Now, Sir, we have acknowledged the Printing and Publishing of those Papers, set forth in the Information, and (with the Leave of the Court) agreeable to the Rule laid down by Chief Justice *Holt*, we are ready to prove them to be true, at our Peril.

Mr. Chief Justice. Let me see the Book.

Here the Court had the Case under Consideration, a considerable Time, and every one was silent.

Mr. Ch. Just. Mr. Attorney, you have heard what Mr. *Hamilton* has said, and the Cases he has cited, for having his Witnesses examined, to prove the Truth of the several Facts contained in the Papers set forth in the Information, what do you say to it?

Mr. Attorney. The Law in my Opinion is very clear; they cannot be admitted to justify a Libel; for, by the Authorities I have already read to the Court, it is not the less a Libel because it is true. I think I need not trouble the Court with reading the Cases over again; the Thing seems to be very plain, and I submit it to the Court.

Mr. Ch. Just. Mr. *Hamilton*, the Court is of Opinion, you ought not to be permitted to prove the Facts in the Papers: These are the Words of the Book, ' *It is far from* ' *being a Justification of a Libel, that the Contents thereof are* ' *true, or that the Person upon whom it is made, had a bad* ' *Reputation, since the greater Appearance there is of Truth in* ' *any malicious Invective, so much the more provoking it is.*'

Mr. Hamilton. These are Star Chamber Cases, and

I was in hopes, that Practice had been dead with the Court.

Mr. Ch. Just. Mr. *Hamilton*, the Court have delivered their Opinion, and we expect you will use us with good Manners; you are not to be permitted to argue against the Opinion of the Court.

Mr. *Hamilton.* With Submission, I have seen the Practice in very great Courts, and never heard it deemed unmannerly to - - - - - -

Mr. Ch. Just. After the Court have declared their Opinion, it is not good Manners to insist upon a Point, in which you are over-ruled.

Mr. *Hamilton.* I will say no more at this Time; the Court I see is against us in this Point; and that I hope I may be allowed to say.

Mr. Ch. Just. Use the Court with good Manners, and you shall be allowed all the Liberty you can reasonably desire.

Mr. *Hamilton.* I thank Your Honour. Then Gentlemen of the Jury, it is to you we must now appeal, for Witnesses to the Truth of the Facts we have offered, and are denied the Liberty to prove; and let it not seem strange, that I apply myself to you in this Manner, I am warranted so to do both by Law and Reason. The Law supposes you to be summoned, *out of the Neighbourhood where the Fact is alledged to be committed*; and the Reason of your being taken out of the Neighbourhood is, *because you are supposed to have the best Knowledge of the Fact that is to be tried.* And were you to find a Verdict against my Client, you must take upon you to say, the Papers referred to in the Information, and which we acknowledge we printed and published, are *false, scandalous and seditious*; but of this I can have no Apprehension. You are Citizens of *New York*; you are really what the Law supposes you to be, *honest and lawful Men*; and, according to my Brief, the Facts which we offer to prove were not committed in a Corner; they are notoriously known to be true; and therefore in your Justice lies

213

our Safety. And as we are denied the Liberty of giving Evidence, to prove the Truth of what we have publifhed, I will beg Leave to lay it down as a ftanding Rule in fuch Cafes, *That the fuppreffing of Evidence ought always to be taken for the ftrongest Evidence;* and I hope it will have that Weight with you. But fince we are not admitted to examine our Witneffes, I will endeavour to fhorten the Difpute with Mr. Attorney, and to that End, I defire he would favour us with fome Standard Definition of a Libel, by which it may be certainly known, whether a Writing be a Libel, yea or not.

Mr. Attorney. The Books, I think, have given a very full Definition of a Libel; they fay it is *in a* 1 *Hawk. Chap.* ftri& Senfe taken for a malicious Defamation, LXXIII. §. 1. & expreffed either in Printing or Writing, and feq. tending either to blacken the Memory of one *who is dead, or the Reputation of one who is alive, and to expofe him to public Hatred, Contempt or Ridicule.* § ?. *But it is faid, That in a larger Senfe, the Notion of a Libel may be applied to any Defamation whatfoever, expreffed either by Signs or Pictures, as by fixing up a Gallows againft a Man's Door, or by painting him in a fhameful and ignominious Manner.* §. 3. *And fince the chief Caufe for which the Law fo feverely punifhes all Offences of this Nature, is the dire& Tendency of them to a Breach of Publick Peace, by provoking the Parties injured, their Friends and Families to Acts of Revenge, which it would be impoffible to reftrain by the fevereft Laws, were there no Redrefs from Publick Juftice for Injuries of this kind, which of all others are moft fenfibly felt; and fince the plain Meaning of fuch Scandal as is expreffed by Signs or Pictures, is as obvious to common Senfe, and as eafily underftood by every common Capacity, and altogether as provoking as that which is expreffed by Writing or Printing, why fhould it not be equally criminal?* §. 4. *And from the fame Ground it feemeth alfo clearly to follow, That fuch fcandal as is expreffed in a fcoffing and ironical Manner, makes a Writing as properly a Libel, as that which is expreffed in direct Terms; as where a Writing,*

THE CASE AND TRIAL

in a taunting Manner reckoning up several Acts of publick Charity done by one, says You will not play the Jew, nor the Hypocrite, and so goes on in a Strain of Ridicule to insinuate, that what he did was owing to his Vain-Glory; or where a Writing, pretending to recommend to one the Characters of several great Men for his Imitation, instead of taking Notice of what they are generally esteemed famous for, pitched on such Qualities only which their Enemies charge them with the Want of, as by proposing such a one to be imitated for his Courage, who is known to be a great Statesman, but no Soldier, and another to be imitated for his Learning, who is known to be a great General, but no Scholar, &c. which Kind of Writing is as well understood to mean only to upbraid the Parties with the Want of these Qualities, as if it had directly and expressly done so.

Mr. Hamilton. Ay, Mr. Attorney; but what Standard Rule have the Books laid down, by which we can certainly know, whether the Words or the Signs are malicious? Whether they are defamatory? Whether they tend to the Breach of the Peace, and are a sufficient Ground to provoke a Man, his Family, or Friends to Acts of Revenge, especially those of the ironical sort of Words? And what Rule have you to know when I write ironically? I think it would be hard, when I say, *such a Man is a very worthy honest Gentleman, and of fine Understanding*, that therefore I meant *he was a Knave or a Fool.*

Mr. Attorney. I think the Books are very full; it is said in 1 *Hawk. p.* 193. just now read, *That such Scandal as is expressed in a scoffing and ironical Manner, makes a Writing as properly a Libel, as that which is expressed in direct Terms; as where a Writing, in a taunting Manner says, reckoning up several Acts of Charity done by one, says,* you will not play the Jew or the Hypocrite, *and so goes on to insinuate, that what he did was owing to his Vain-Glory, &c. Which Kind of Writing is as well understood to mean only to upbraid the Parties with the Want of these Qualities, as if it had directly and expressly done so.* I think nothing can be plainer or more full than these Words.

JOHN PETER ZENGER

Mr. Hamilton. I agree the Words are very plain, and I shall not scruple to allow (when we are agreed that the Words are *false and scandalous, and were spoken in an ironical and scoffing Manner, &c.*) that they are really *libellous;* but here still occurs the Uncertainty, which makes the Difficulty to know, what Words are *scandalous,* and what not; for you say, they may be *scandalous, true* or *false;* besides, how shall we know whether the Words were spoke in a *scoffing and ironical Manner,* or seriously? Or how can you know, whether the Man did not think as he wrote? For by your Rule, if he did, it is no *Irony,* and consequently no *Libel.* But under Favour, Mr. Attorney, I think the same Book, and the same Section will shew us the only Rule by which all these Things are to be known. The Words are these; *which Kind of Writing is as well* UNDERSTOOD *to mean only to upbraid the Parties with the Want of these Qualities, as if they had directly and expressly done so.* Here it is plain, the Words are *scandalous, scoffing and ironical,* only as they are UNDERSTOOD. I know no Rule laid down in the Books but this, I mean, as the Words are *understood.*

Mr. Ch. Just. Mr. *Hamilton,* do you think it so hard to know, when Words are ironical, or spoke in a scoffing Manner?

Mr. Hamilton. I own it may be known; but I insist, the only Rule to know is, as I do or can *understand* them; I have no other Rule to go by, but as I *understand* them.

Mr. Ch. Just. That is certain. All Words are libellous or not, as they are *understood.* Those who are to judge of the Words, must judge whether they *are scandalous* or *ironical, tend to the Breach of the Peace,* or are *seditious:* There can be no Doubt of it.

Mr. Hamilton. I thank Your Honour; I am glad to find the Court of this Opinion. Then it follows that those twelve Men must *understand* the Words in the Information to be *scandalous,* that is to say *false;* for I think it is not pretended they are of the *ironical* Sort; and when they understand the Words to be so, they will say we are guilty of Publishing a *false Libel,* and not otherwise.

Mr. Ch. Just. No, Mr. *Hamilton*; the Jury may find that *Zenger* printed and published those Papers, and leave it to the Court to judge whether they are libellous; you know this is very common; it is in the Nature of a special Verdict, where the Jury leave the Matter of Law to the Court.

Mr. *Hamilton.* I know, may it please Your Honour, the Jury may do so; but I do likewise know, they may do otherwise. I know they have the Right beyond all Dispute, to determine both the Law and the Fact, and where they do not doubt of the Law, they ought to do so. This of leaving it to Judgment of the Court, *whether the Words are libellous or not,* in Effect renders Juries useless (to say no worse) in many Cases; but this I shall have Occasion to speak to by and by; and I will with the Court's Leave proceed to examine the Inconveniences that must inevitably arise from the Doctrines Mr. Attorney has laid down; and I observe, in support of this Prosecution, he has frequently repeated the Words taken from the Case of *Libel. famosus,* in 5 *Co.* This is indeed the leading Case, and to which almost all the other Cases upon the Subject of Libels do refer; and I must insist upon saying, That according as this Case seems to be understood by the [Court *] and Mr. Attorney, it is not Law at this Day: For tho' I own it to be base and unworthy, to scandalize any Man, yet I think it is even vilainous to scandalize a Person of publick Character, and I will go so far into Mr. Attorney's Doctrine as to agree, that if the Faults, Mistakes, nav even the Vices of such a Person be private and personal, and don't affect the Peace of the Publick, or the Liberty or Property, of our Neighbour, it is unmanly and unmannerly to expose them either by Word or Writing. But when a Ruler of a People brings his personal Failings, but much more his Vices, into

---

* The word "Court" is written in a blank space in the original printed edition.

his Adminiftration, and the People find themfelves affected
by them, either in their Liberties or Properties, that will
alter the Cafe mightily; and all the high Things that are
faid in Favour of Rulers, and of Dignities, and upon the
fide of Power, will not be able to ftop People's Mouths
when they feel themfelves opprefled, I mean in a free Government.   It is true in Times paft it was a Crime to fpeak
Truth, and in that terrible Court of Star Chamber, many
worthy and brave Men fuffered for fo doing; and yet even
in that Court, and in thofe bad Times, a great and good
Man durft fay, what I hope will not be taken amifs of me
to fay in this Place, *to wit, The Practice of Informations for
Libels is a Sword in the Hands of a wicked King, and an ar-
rand Coward, to cut down and deftroy the innocent ; the one
cannot, becaufe of his high Station, and the other dares not, becaufe of his Want of Courage, revenge himfelf in another Manner.*

Mr. Attorney. Pray Mr. *Hamilton,* have a Care what
you fay, don't go too far neither, I don't like those Liberties.

Mr. Hamilton. Sure, Mr. Attorney, you won't make any
Applications ; all Men agree that we are governed by the
beft of Kings, and I cannot fee the Meaning of Mr. Attorney's Caution ; my well known Principles, and the Senfe I
have of the Blessings we enjoy under His prefent Majefty,
makes it impoffible for me to err, and I hope, even to be
fufpected, in that Point of Duty to my King.   May it
pleafe Your Honour, I was faying, that notwithftanding all
the Duty and reverence claimed by Mr. Attorney to Men
in Authority, they are not exempt from obferving the Rules
of common Juftice, either in their private or publick Capacities ; the Laws of our Mother Country know no Exemption.   It is true, Men in Power are harder to be come at for
wrongs they do, either to a private Perfon, or to the publick ; efpecially a Governour in the Plantations, where they
infift upon an Exemption from Anfwering Complaints of
any kind in their own Government.   We are indeed told,

and it is true they are obliged to anfwer a Suit in the King's Courts at *Weftminfter*, for a Wrong done to any Perfon here: But do we not know how impracticable this is to moft Men among us, to leave their Families (who depend upon their Labour and Care for their Livelihood) and carry Evidences to *Britain*, and at a great, nay, a far greater Expence than almoft any of us are able to bear, only to profecute a Governour for an Injury done here. But when the Oppreffion is general there is no Remedy even that Way, no, our Conftitution has (bleffed be God) given Us an Opportunity, if not to have fuch Wrongs redreffed, yet by our Prudence and Refolution we may in a great meafure prevent the committing of fuch Wrongs, by making a Governour fenfible that it is his intereft to be juft to those under his Care; for fuch is the Senfe that Men in General (I mean Freemen) have of common Juftice, that when they come to know, that a chief Magiftrate abufes the Power with which he is trufted, for the good of the People, and is attempting to turn that very Power againft the Innocent, whether of high or low degree, I fay, Mankind in general feldom fail to interpofe, and as far as they can, prevent the Deftruction of their fellow Subjects. And has it not often been feen (I hope it will always be feen) that when the Reprefentatives of a free People are by juft Reprefentations or Remonftrances, made fenfible of the fufferings of their Fellow-Subjects, by the Abufe of Power in the Hands of a Governour, they have declared (and loudly too) that they were not obliged by any Law to fupport a Governour who goes about to deftroy a Province or Colony, or their Privileges, which by His Majefty he was appointed, and by the Law he is bound to protect and encourage. But I pray it may be confidered, of what Ufe is this mighty Privilege, if every Man that fuffers muft be filent? And if a Man muft be taken up as a Libeller, for telling his fufferings to his Neighbour? I know it may be anfwered, *Have you not a Legiflature? Have you not a Houfe of Reprefentatives to whom you may complain?* And to this I anfwer, we have.

But what then? Is an Assembly to be troubled with every Injury done by a Governour? Or are they to hear of nothing but what those in the Administration will please to tell them? Or what Sort of a Tryal must a Man have? And how is he to be remedied; especially if the Case were, as I have known it to happen in *America* in my Time; That a Governour who has Places (I will not [say]* Pensions, for I believe they seldom give that to another which they can take to themselves) to bestow, and can or will keep the same Assembly (after he has modeled them so as to get a Majority of the House in his Interest) for near *twice Seven Years* together? I pray, what Redress is to be expected for a honest Man, who makes his Complaint against a Governour, to an Assembly who may properly enough be said, to be made by the same Governour against whom the Complaint is made? The Thing answers it self. No, it is natural, it is a Privilege, I will go farther, it is a Right which all Freemen claim, and are entitled to complain when they are hurt; they have a Right publickly to remonstrate the Abuses of Power, in the strongest Terms, to put their Neighbours upon their Guard, against the Craft or open Violence of Men in Authority, and to assert with Courage the Sense they have of the Blessings of Liberty, the Value they put upon it, and their Resolution at all Hazards to preserve it, as one of the greatest Blessings Heaven can bestow. And when a House of Assembly composed of honest Freemen sees the general Bent of the Peoples Inclinations, That is it which must and will (I'm sure it ought to) weigh with a Legislature, in Spite of all the Craft, Carressing and Cajoling, made use of by a Governour, to divert them from harkning to the Voice of their Country. As we all very well understand the true Reason, why Gentlemen take so much Pains and make such great Interest to be appointed Governours, so is the Design of their Appointment not less manifest. We know his Majesty's gracious Intentions to his Subjects; he desires no more than

---

* Supplied in contemporary manuscript in the original.

that his People in the Plantations fhould be kept up to their Duty and Allegiance to the Crown of *Great Britain*, that Peace may be preferved amongft them, and Juftice impartially adminiftred ; that we may he governed fo as to render us ufeful to our Mother Country, by encouraging us to make and raife fuch Commodities as may be ufeful to *Great Britain.* But will any one fay, that all or any of thefe good Ends are to be effected, by a Governour's fetting his People together by the Ears, and by the Affiftance of one Part of the People to plague and plunder the other ? The Commiffion which Governour's bear, while they execute the Powers given them, according to the Intent of the Royal Grantor, expreffed in their Commiffions, requires and deferved very great Reverence and Submiffion; but when a Governour departs from the Duty enjoyned him by his Sovereign, and acts as if he was lefs accountable than the Royal Hand that gave him all that Power and Honour that he is poffeffed of ; this fets People upon examining and enquiring into the Power, Authority and Duty of fuch a Magiftrate, and to compare thofe with his Conduct, and juft as far as they find he exceeds the Bounds of his Authority, or falls fhort in doing impartial Juftice to the People under his Adminiftration, fo far they very often, in return, come fhort in their Duty to fuch a Governour. For Power alone will not make a Man beloved, and I have heard it obferved, That the Man who was neither good nor wife before his being made a Governour, never mended upon his Preferment, but has been generally obferved to be worfe : For Men who are not endued with Wifdom and Virtue, can only be kept in Bounds by the Law; and by how much the further they think themfelves out of the Reach of the Law, by fo much the more wicked and cruel Men are. I wifh there were no Inftances of the Kind at this Day. And wherever this happens to be the Cafe of a Governour, unhappy are the People under his Adminiftration, and in the End he will find himfelf fo too ; for the People will neither love him nor fupport him. I make no Doubt but there are thofe here, who are zealoufly concerned for the Succefs of this Profecution, and yet I hope they are not many, and even fome of thofe, I am perfuaded (when they confider to what Lengths fuch Profecutions may be carried, and how deeply the Liberties of the People may be affected by fuch Means) will not all abide by their prefent Sentiments; I fay, *Not All:* For the Man who from an Intimacy and Acquaintance with a Governour has conceived a perfonal Regard for him, the Man who has felt none of the Strokes of his Power, the Man who believes that a Governour has a Regard for him and confides in him, it is natural for fuch Men to wifh well to the Affairs of fuch a Governour; and as they may be Men of Honour and Generofity, may, and no Doubt will, wifh him Succefs, fo far as the Rights and Privileges of their Fellow Citizens are not affected. But as Men of Honour, I can apprehend nothing from them ; they will never exceed that Point. There are others that are under ftronger Obligations, and thofe are fuch, as are in fome Sort engaged in Support of a Governour's Caufe, by their own or their Relations Dependance on his Favour, for fome Poft or Preferment ; fuch Men have what is commonly called Duty and Gratitude, to influence their Inclinations, and oblige them to go his Lengths. I know Men's Interests are very near to them, and they will do much rather than foregoe the Favour of a Governour, and a Livelihood at the fame Time ; but I can with very juft Grounds hope, even from thofe Men, whom I will fuppose to be Men of Honour and Confcience too, that when they fee, the Liberty of their Country is in Danger, either by their Concurrence, or even by their Silence, they will like *Englifhmen*, and like themfelves, freely make a Sacrifice of any Preferment or Favour rather than be acceffary to deftroying the Liberties of their Country, and entailing Slavery upon their Pofterity. There are indeed another fet of Men, of whom I have no Hopes, I mean fuch, who lay afide all other Confiderations, and are ready to joyn with Power in any Shapes, and with any Man or Sort of Men, by whofe Means or Intereft they may be affifted to gratify their Malice and Envy againft thofe whom they have been pleafed to hate; and that for no other Reafon, but becaufe they are Men of Abilities and Integrity, or at leaft are poffeffed of fome valuable Qualities, far fuperiour to their own. But as Envy is the Sin of the Devil, and therefore very hard, if at all, to be repented of, I will believe there are but few of this deteftable and worthlefs Sort of Men, nor will their Opinions or Inclinations have any influence upon this Tryal. But to proceed; I beg Leave to infift, That the Right of complaining or remonftrating is natural; And the Reftraint upon this natural Right is the Law only, and that thofe Reftraints can only extend to what is *falfe*: For as it is Truth alone which can excufe or juftify any Man for complaining of a bad Adminiftration, I as frankly agree, that nothing ought to excufe a Man who raifes a falfe Charge or Accufation, even againft a private Perfon, and that no manner of Allowance ought to be made to him, who does fo againft a publick Magiftrate. *Truth* ought to govern the whole Affair of Libels, and yet the Party accufed runs Rifque enough even then; for if he fails in proving every Tittle of what he has wrote, and to the Satisfaction of the Court and Jury too, he may find to his Coft, that when the Profecution is fet on Foot by Men in Power, it feldom wants Friends to Favour it. And from thence (it is faid) has arifen the great Diverfity of Opinions among Judges, about what Words were or were not fcandalous or libellous. I believe it will be granted, that there is not greater Uncertainty in any Part of the Law, than about Words of Scandal; it would be mifpending of the Court's Time to mention the Cafes; they may be faid to be numberlefs; and therefore the utmoft Care ought to be taken in following Precedents; and the Times when the Judgments were given, which are quoted for Authorities in the Cafe of Libels, are much to be regarded. I think it will be agreed, That ever fince the Time of the Star Chamber, where the moft arbitrary and deftructive Judgments and Opinions were given, that ever an *Englishman* heard of, at leaft in his own Country: I fay, Profecutions for Libels fince the Time of that arbitrary Court, and until the glorious Revolution, have generally been fet on Foot at the Inftance of the Crown or its Minifters; and it is no fmall Reproach to the Law, that thefe Profecutions were too often and too much countenanced by the Judges, who held their Places at Pleafure, (a difagreeable Tenure to any Officer, but a dangerous one in the Cafe of a Judge.) To fay more to this Point may not be proper. And yet I cannot think it unwarrantable, to fhew the unhappy influence that a Sovereign has fometimes had, not only upon Judges, but even upon Parliaments themfelves.

It has already been fhewn, how the Judges differed in their Opinions about the Nature of a Libel, in the Cafe of the feven Bifhops. There you fee three Judges of one Opinion, that is, of a wrong Opinion, in the Judgment of the beft Men in *England,* and one Judge of a right Opinion. How unhappy might it have been for all of us at this Day, if that Jury had underftood the Words in that Information as the Court did? Or if they had left it to the Court, to judge whether the Petition of the Bifhops was or was not a Libel? No they took upon them, to their immortal Honour! To determine both *Law* and *Fact,* and to *underftand* the Petition of the Bifhops *to be no Libel, that is, to contain no falfhood nor Sedition,* and therefore found them *Not Guilty.* And remarkable is the Cafe of Sir *Samuel Barnardifton,* who was fined 10,000*L.* for Writing a Letter, in which, it may be faid, none faw any Scandal or Falfhood but the Court and Jury; for that Judgment was afterwards looked upon as a cruel and deteftable Judgment, and therefore was reverfed by Parliament. Many more Inftances might be given of the Complaifance of Court-Judges, about thofe Times, and before; but I will mention only one Cafe more, and that is the Cafe of Sir *Edward Hales,* who tho' a *Roman Catholick,* was by King *James* II. prefered to be a Colonel of his Army, notwithftanding the Statute of 25 *Cha.* 2d

THE CASE AND TRIAL

Chap. 2. by which it is provided, *That every one that accepts of an Office, Civil or Military, &c. shall take the Oaths, subscribe the Declaration, and take the Sacrament, within three Months, &c. otherwise he is disabled to hold such Office, and the Grant for the same to be null and void, and the Party to forfeit* 500*l.* Sir *Edward Hales* did not take the Oaths or Sacrament, and was prosecuted for the 500*.l.* for exercising the Office of a Colonel by the Space of three Months, without conforming as in the Act is directed. Sir *Edward* pleads, *That the King by His Letters Patents did dispence with his taking the Oaths and Sacrament, and subscribing the Declaration, and had pardoned the forfeiture of* 500*.l.* And *whether the King's Dispensation was good, against the said Act of Parliament?* was the question. I shall mention no more of this Case, than to shew how in the Reign of an arbitrary Prince, where Judges hold their Seats at Pleasure, their Determinations have not always been such as to make Precedents of, but the Contrary ; and so it happened in this Case, where it was solemnly judged, *That, notwithstanding this Act of Parliament, made in the strongest Terms, for Preservation of the Protestant Religion, That yet the King had, by His Royal Prerogative, a Power to dispence with that Law* ; and Sir *Edward Hales* was acquitted by the Judges accordingly. So the King's Dispensing Power, being by the Judges set up above the Act of Parliament, this Law, which the People looked upon as their chief Security against Popery and Arbitrary Power, was by this Judgment rendred altogether ineffectual. But this Judgment is sufficiently exposed by Sir *Edward Atkins*, late one of the Judges of the Court of Common Pleas in his *Enquiry into the King's Power of dispensing with pœnal Statutes ;* where it is shewn, *Who it was that first invented Dispensations ; how they came into* England; *what ill Use has been made of them there; and all this principally owing to the Countenance given them by the Judges.* He says of the Dispensing Power, * *The Pope was the Inventor of it ; our Kings have bor-*

Sir *Edw. Atkins's* Enquiry into the Power of Dispensing with pœnal Statutes.

* Postscript to the Enquiry pag. 51.

rowed it from them; and the Judges have from Time to Time nursed and dressed it up, and given it Countenance; and it is still upon the Growth, and encroaching, 'till it has almost subverted all Law, and made the regal Power absolute if not dissolute. This seems not only to shew how far Judges have been influenced by Power, and how little Cases of this Sort, where the Prerogative has been in Question in former Reigns, are to be relied upon for Law: But I think it plainly shews too, that a Man may use a greater Freedom with the Power of His Sovereign and the Judges in *Great-Britain*, than it seems he may with the Power of a Governour in the Plantations, who is but a Fellow Subject. Are these Words with which we are charged, like these? Do Mr. *Zenger's* Papers contain any such Freedoms with his Governour or His Council, as Sir *Edward Atkins* has taken, with the Regal Power and the Judges in *England?* And yet I never heard of any Information brought against him for these Freedoms.

If then upon the whole there is so great an Uncertainty among Judges (learned and great Men) in Matters of this Kind; If Power has had so great an Influence on Judges; how cautious ought we to be in determining by their Judgments, especially in the Plantations, and in the Case of Libels? There is Heresy in Law, as well as in Religion, and both have changed very much; and we well know that it is not two Centuries ago that a Man would have been burnt as an Heretick, for owning such Opinions in Matters of Religion as are publickly wrote and printed at this Day. They were fallible Men, it seems, and we take the Liberty not only to differ from them in religious Opinions, but to condemn them and their Opinions too; and I must presume, that in taking these Freedoms in thinking and speaking about Matters of Faith or Religion, we are in the right: For tho' it is said there are very great Liberties of this Kind taken in *Newe York*, yet I have heard of no Information preferred by Mr. Attorney for any Offences of this Sort. From which I think it is pretty clear, That in *New-York*, a Man may

make very free with his God, but he muſt take ſpecial Care
what he ſays of his Governour. It is agreed upon by all
Men, that this is a Reign of Liberty ; and while Men
keep within the Bounds of Truth, I hope they may with
Safety both ſpeak and write their Sentiments of the Conduct
of Men in Power I me[a]n of that Part of their Conduct
only, which affects the Liberty or Property of the People
under their Adminiſtration ; were this to be denied, then the
next Step may make them Slaves: For what Notions can be
entertained of Slavery, beyond that of ſuffering the greateſt
injuries and Oppreſſions, without the Liberty of complaining;
or if they do, to be deſtroyed, Body and Eſtate, for ſo doing ?

It is ſaid and inſiſted on by Mr. Attorney, *That Government is a ſacred Thing ; That it is to be ſupported and reverenced; It is Government that protects our Perſons and Eſtates ;
That prevents Treaſons, Murders, Robberies, Riots, and all
the Train of Evils that overturns Kingdoms and States, and
ruins particular Perſons; and if thoſe in the Adminiſtration,
eſpecially the Supream Magiſtrate muſt have all their Conduct
cenſured by private Men, Government cannot ſubſiſt.* This is
called *a Licentiouſneſs not to be tollerated.* It is ſaid, *That it
brings the Rulers of the People into Contempt, and their Authority not to be regarded, and ſo in the End the Laws cannot
be put in Execution.* Theſe I ſay, and ſuch as theſe, are the
general Topicks inſiſted upon by Men in Power, and their
Advocates. But I wiſh it might be conſidered at the ſame
Time, How often it has happened, that the Abuſe of Power has
been the primary Cauſe of theſe Evils, and that it was the In-
juſtice and Oppreſſion of theſe great Men, which has commonly
brought them into Contempt with the People. The Craft
and Art of ſuch Men is great, and who, that is the leaſt
acquainted with Hiſtory or Law, can be ignorant of the
ſpecious Pretences, which have often been made uſe of by
Men in Power, to introduce arbitrary Rule, and deſtroy the
Liberties of a free People. I will give two Inſtances ; and
as they are Authorities not to be denied, nor can be miſun-
derſtood, I preſume they will be ſufficient.

JOHN PETER ZENGER

The *first* is the Statute of 3d of *Hen. 7. Cap.* 1. The Preamble of the Statute will prove all, and more than I have alledged. It begins, ' *The King Our Sovereign Lord re-*
' *membereth how by unlawful Maintenances, giving of Liveries,*
' *Signs and Tokens, &c. untrue Demeanings of Sheriffs in mak-*
' *ing of Pannels, and other untrue Returns, by taking of Money,*
' *by Injuries, by great Riots and unlawful Assemblies; the*
' *Policy and good Rule of this Realm is almost subdued; and for*
' *the not punishing these Inconveniences, and by Occasion of the*
' *Premisses, little or nothing may be found by Inquiry, &c. to*
' *the increase of Murders, &c. and unsureties of all Men living,*
' *and Losses of their Lands and Goods.*' Here is a fine and specious Pretence for introducing the Remedy, as it is called, which is provided by this Act, *that is*; instead of being lawfully accused by 24 good and lawful Men of the Neighbourhood, and afterwards tried by 12 like lawful Men, here is a Power given to the Lord Chancellor, Lord Treasurer, the Keeper of the King's privy Seal, or two of them, calling to them a Bishop, a temporal Lord, and other great Men mentioned in the Act, (whom, it is to be observed, were all to be Dependants on the Court) to receive Information against any Person for any of the Misbehaviours recited in that Act, and by their Discretion to examine, and to punish them according to their demerit.

The second Statute I proposed to mention, is the 11*th* of the same King, *Chap.* 3*d.* the Preamble of which Act has the like fair Pretences as the former; *for the King calling to his Remembrance the good Laws made against the receiving of Liveries, &c. unlawful Extortions, Maintenances, Embracery, &c. unlawful Games, &c. and many other great Enormitys, and Offences committed against many good Statutes, to the Displeasure of Almighty God, which,* the Act says, *could not, nor yet can, be conveniently punished by the due Order of the Law, except it were first found by* 12 *Men, &c. which, for the Causes aforesaid, will not find nor yet present the Truth.* And therefore the same Statute directs, *that the Justices of Assize, and Justices of the Peace, shall, upon Information for the King before*

228

them made, have full Power, by their Discretion, to hear and determine all such Offences. Here are two Statutes that are allowed to have given the deepest Wound to the Liberties of the People of *England* of any that I remember to have been made, unless it may be said, that the Statute made in the Time of *Henry 8th,* by which his Proclamations were to have the effect of Laws, might in its Consequence be worse. And yet we see the plausible Pretences found out by the great Men to procure these Acts. And it may justly be said, That by those Pretences the People of *England* were cheated or aw'd into the Delivering up their antient and sacred Rights of Tryals by Grand and Petit Juries. I hope to be excused for this Ex-   4. *Inst.* pression, seeing my Lord *Coke* calls it *an unjust and strange Act, that tended in its execution to the great Displeasure of Almighty God, and the utter subversion of the common Law.*

These, I think, make out what I alledged, and are flagrant Instances of the Influence of Men in Power, even upon the Representatives of a whole Kingdom. From all which I hope it will be agreed, that it is a Duty which all good Men owe to their Country, to guard against the unhappy Influence of ill Men when intrusted with Power; and especially against their Creatures and Dependants, who, as they are generally more necessitous, are surely more covetous and cruel. But it is worthy of Observation, that tho' the Spirit of Liberty was borne down and oppressed in *England* at that Time, yet it was not lost; for the Parliament laid hold of the first Opportunity to free the Subject from the many insufferable Oppressions and Outrages committed upon their Persons and Estates by Colour of these Acts, the last of which being deemed the most grievous, was repealed in the first Year of *Hen. 8th.* Tho' it is to be observed, that *Hen. 7th.* and his Creatures reap'd such great Advantages by the grievous Oppressions and Exactions, *grinding the Faces of the poor Subjects,* as my Lord *Coke* says, by Colour of this Statute by information only, that a Repeal of this Act could never be obtained during the Life of that Prince. The other Statute being the favourite Law for Supporting arbitrary Power, was continued much longer. The Execution of it was by the great Men of the Realm; and how they executed it, the Sense of the Kingdom, expressed in the 17*th* of *Charles* 1*st.* (by which the Court of Star-chamber, the soil where Informations grew rankest) will best declare. In that Statute *Magna Charta*, and the other Statutes made in the Time of *Edw.* 3*d.* which, I think, are no less than five, are particularly enumerated as Acts, by which the Liberties and Privileges of the People of *England* were secured to them, against such oppressive Courts as the Star Chamber and others of the like Jurisdiction. And the Reason assigned for their pulling down the Star Chamber, is *That the Proceedings, Censures and Decrees of the Court of Star Chamber, even tho' the great Men of the Realm, nay and a Bishop too* (holy Man) *were Judges, had by Experience been found to be an intolerable Burthen to the Subject, and the Means to introduce an arbitrary Power and Government.* And therefore that Court was taken away, with all the other Courts in that Statute mentioned, having like Jurisdiction.

I don't mention this Statute, as if by the taking away the Court of Star Chamber, the Remedy for many of the Abuses or Offences censured there, was likewise taken away; no, I only intend by it to shew, that the People of *England* saw clearly the Danger of trusting their Liberties and Properties to be tried, even by the greatest Men in the Kingdom, without the Judgment of a Jury of their Equals. They had felt the terrible effects of leaving it to the Judgment of these great Men to say what was *scandalous and seditious, false or ironical.* And if the Parliament of *England* thought this Power of judging was too great to be trusted with Men of the first Rank in the Kingdom, without the Aid of a Jury, how sacred soever their Characters might be, and therefore restored to the People their original Right of tryal by Juries, I hope to be excused for insisting, that by the Judgment of a Parliament, from whence an Appeal

THE CASE AND TRIAL

lies, the Jury are the proper Judges, of what is *false* at leaft, if not, of what is *fcandalous and feditious*. This is an Authority not to be denied, it is as plain as it is great, and to fay, that this Act indeed did reftore to the People Tryals by Juries, which was not the Practice of the Star Chamber, but that did not give the Jurors any new Authority, or any Right to try Matters of Law, I fay this Objection will not avail; for I muft infift, that where Matter of Law is complicated with Matter of Fact, the Jury have a Right to determine both. As for Inftance; upon Indictment for Murder, the Jury may, and almoft conftantly do, take upon them to Judge whether the Evidence will amount to Murder or Manslaughter, and find accordingly; and I muft fay I cannot fee, why in our Cafe the Jury have not at leaft as good a Right to fay, whether our News Papers are a Libel or no Libel as another Jury has to fay, whether killing of a Man is Murder or Manslaughter. The Right of the Jury, to find fuch a Ver- dict as they in their Confcience do think is agreeable to their Evidence, is fupported by the Authority of *Bufhel's* Cafe, in *Vaughan's Reports, pag.* 135. beyond any Doubt. For, in the Argument of that Cafe, the Chief Juftice who delivered the Opinion of the Court, lays it down for Law, *That in all General Iffues, as upon* Non Cul. *in* Tref- pafs, Non Tort. Nul Diffeizin *in* Affize, &c.   *Vaughan's Rep* *tho' it is Matter of Law, whether the De-*   p. 150. *fendant is a Trefpaffer, a Diffeizer,* &c. *in the particular Cafes in Iffue, yet the Jury find not* (*as in a fpecial Verdict*) *the fact of every Cafe, leaving the Law to the Court; but find for the Plaintiff or Defendant upon the Iffue to be tried, wherein they refolve both Law and Fact complicately.* It appears by the fame Cafe, that tho' the difcreet and lawful Affiftance of the Judge, by Way of Advice, to the Jury, may be ufeful; yet that Advice or Direction ought always to be upon *Suppofition, and not pofitive, and upon Coer-*   *pag.* 144. *fion.* The Reafon given in the fame Book is *be-* *caufe the Judge* (*as Judge*) *cannot know what the*   *pag.* 147. *Evidence is which the Jury have,* that is, *he can only know the*

231

JOHN PETER ZENGER

Evidence given in Court: but the Evidence which the Jury have, may be of their own Knowledge, as they are returned of the Neighbourhood. They may also know from their own Knowledge, that what is sworn in Court is not true; and they may know the Witnesses to be stigmatized, to which the Court may be strangers. But what is to my Purpose, is, that suppose the Court did really know all the Evidence which the Jury know, yet in that Case it is agreed, *That the Judge and Jury may differ in the Result of their Evidence as well as two Judges may,* which often happens. And in *pag.* 148. the Judge subjoins the Reason, why it is no Crime for a Jury to differ in Opinion from the Court, where he says, *That a Man cannot see with another's Eye, nor hear by another's Ear; no more can a Man conclude or infer the Thing by anothers Understanding or Reasoning.* From all which (I insist) it is very plain, *That the Jury are by Law at Liberty (without any affront to the Judgment of the Court) to find both the Law and the Fact, in our Case,* as they did in the case I am speaking to, which I will beg Leave just to mention, and it was this. Mr. *Penn* and *Mead* being Quakers, and having met in a peaceable Manner, after being shut out of their Meeting House, preached in *Grace Church Street* in *London,* to the People of their own Perswasion, and for this they were indicted; and it was said, *That they with other Persons, to the Number of* 300, *unlawfully and tumultuously assembled, to the Disturbance of the Peace, &c.* To which they pleaded, *Not Guilty.* And the Petit Jury being sworn to try the issue between the King and the Prisoners, that is, whether they were Guilty, according to the Form of the Indictment? Here there was no Dispute but they were assembled together, to the Number mentioned in the Indictment; But *whether that Meeting together was riotously, tumultuously, and to the Disturbance of the Peace?* was the question. And the Court told the Jury it was, and ordered the Jury to find it so; *For* (said the Court) *the Meeting was the Matter of Fact, and that is confessed, and we tell you it is unlawful, for it is against the Statute; and the Meeting being unlawful, it follows of Course that it was tumul-*

tuous, and to the Disturbance of the Peace.   But the Jury did not think fit to take the Court's Word for it, for they could neither find *Riot, Tumult*, or any Thing tending to the *Breach of the Peace* committed at that Meeting; and they acquitted Mr. *Penn* and *Mead.*   In doing of which they took upon them to judge both the *Law* and the *Fact*, at which the the Court (being themselves true Courtiers) were so much offended, that they fined the Jury 40 Marks a piece, and committed them till paid.   But Mr. *Bushel,* who valued the Right of a Juryman and the Liberty of his Country more than his own, refused to pay the Fine, and was resolved (tho' at great Expence and trouble too) to bring, and did bring, his *Habeas Corpus,* to be relieved from his Fine and Imprisonment, and he was released accordingly; and this being the Judgment in his Case, it is established for Law, *That the Judges, how great soever they be, have no Right to fine imprison or punish a Jury, for not finding a Verdict according to the Direction of the Court.* And this I hope is sufficient to prove, That Jurymen are to see with their own Eyes, to hear with their own Ears, and to make use of their own Consciences and Understandings, in judging of the Lives, Liberties or Estates of their fellow Subjects.   And so I have done with this Point.

This is the second information for Libelling of a Governour, that I have known in *America.*   And the first, tho' it may look like a Romance, yet as it is true, I will beg Leave to mention it.   Governour *Nicholson,* who happened to be offended with one [of]* his Clergy, met him one Day upon the Road, and as was usual with him (under the Protection of his Commission) used the poor Parson with the worst of Language, threatned to cut off his Ears, slit his Nose, and at last to shoot him through the Head.   The Parson being a reverend Man, continued all this Time uncovered in the Heat of the Sun, until he found an Opportunity to fly for it; and coming to a Neighbours House felt himself very ill of a

---

* The word "of" is missing in the original edition, but supplied in manuscript by a contemporary hand.

Feaver, and immediately writes for a Doctor; and that his Physician might the better judge of his Distemper, he acquainted him with the Usage he had received; concluding, that the Governour was certainly mad, for that no Man in his Senses would have behaved in that manner. The Doctor unhappily shews the Parsons Letter; the Governour came to hear of it; and so an Information was prefered against the poor Man for saying *he believed the Governour was mad*; and it was laid in the Information to be *false, scandalous* and *wicked, and wrote with Intent to move Sedition among the People, and bring His Excellency into Contempt.* But by an Order from the late Queen *Anne,* there was a Stop put to that Prosecution, with sundry others set on foot by the same Governour, against Gentlemen of the greatest Worth and Honour in that Government.

And may not I be allowed, after all this, to say, That by a little Countenance, almost any Thing which a Man writes, may with the Help of that useful Term of Art, called an *Innuendo,* be construed to be a Libel, according to Mr. Attorney's Definition of it, That *whether the Words are spoke of a Person of a publick Character, or of a private Man, whether dead or Living, good or bad, true or false* all make a Libel; for according to Mr. Attorney, *after a Man hears a Writing read, or reads and repeats it, or laughs at it, they are all punishable.* It is true, Mr. Attorney is so good as to allow, *after the Party knows it to be a Libel,* but he is not so kind as to take the Man's Word for it.

> Here were several Cases put to shew, That tho' what a Man writes of a Governour was true, proper and necessary, yet according to the foregoing Doctrine it might be construed to be a Libel: But Mr. *Hamilton* after the Tryal was over, being informed, That some of the Cases he had put, had really happened in this Government, he declared he had never heard of any such; and as he meant no personal Reflections he was sorry he had mentioned them, and therefore they are omitted here.

Mr. *Hamilton.* If a Libel is understood in the large and unlimited Sense urged by Mr. Attorney, there is scarce a Writing I know that may not be called a Libel, or scarce

any Perfon fafe from being called to an Account as a Libeller: For *Mofes*, meek as he was, libelled *Cain*; and who is
it that has not libelled the Devil? For according to Mr. Attorney it is no Juftification to fay one has a bad Name. *Ecb-
ard* has libelled our good King *William*: *Burnet* has libelled
among many others King *Charles* and King *James*; and
Rapin has libelled them all. How muft a Man fpeak or
write, or what muft he hear, read or fing? Or when muft he
laugh, fo as be fecure from being taken up as a Libeller? I
fincerely believe, that were fome Perfons to go thro' the
Streets of *New-York* now-a-days, and read a Part of the
Bible, if it was not known to be fuch, Mr. Attorney, with
the help of his *Innuendo's*, would eafily turn it into a Libel.
As for inftance, *If*. IX. 16. *The Leaders of the People caufe
them to err, and they that are led by them are deftroyed.* But
fhould Mr. Attorney go about to make this a Libel, he would
read it thus; *The Leaders of the People* [*innuendo*, the Governour and Council of *New-York*] *caufe them* [*innuendo*, the
People of this Province] *to err, and they* [the People of this
Province meaning] *that are led by them* [the Governour and
Council meaning] *are deftroyed* [*innuendo*, are deceived
into the Lofs of their Liberty] which is the worft Kind of
Deftruction. Or if fome Perfons fhould publickly repeat, in
a Manner not pleafing to his Betters, the 10*th* and 11*th*
Verfes of the LVI. *Chap.* of the fame Book, there Mr. Attorney would have a large Field to difplay his Skill, in the artful Application of his *Innuendo's*. The Words are, *His
Watchmen are all blind, they are ignorant, &c. Yea, they are
greedy dogs, that can never have enough.* But to make them
a Libel, there is according to Mr. Attorney's Doctrine, no
more wanting but the Aid of his Skill, in the right adapting
his *Innuendo's*. As for Inftance; *His Watchmen* [*innuendo*, the
Governour's Council and Affembly] *are* [all]* *blind, they are
ignorant* [*innuendo*, will not fee the dangerous Defigns of His
Excellency] *Yea, they* [the Governour and Council mean-

* This word is fupplied in the original in manuscript by a contemporary
hand.

ing] *are greedy Dogs, which can never have enough* [*innuendo*, enough of Riches and Power.*]   Such an Inftance as this is feems only only fit to be laugh'd at ; but I may appeal to Mr. Attorney himfelf, whether thefe are not at leaft equally proper to be applied to His Excellency and His Minifters, as fome of the Inferences and *Innuendo's* in his Information againft my Client.   Then if Mr. Attorney is at Liberty to come into Court, and file an Information in the King's Name, without Leave, who is fecure, whom he is pleafed to profecute as a Libeller ? And as the Crown Law is con-tended for in bad Times, there is no Remedy for the greateft Oppreffion of this Sort, even tho the Party profecuted is ac-quitted with Honour.   And give me Leave to fay, as great Men as any in *Britain*, have boldly afferted, That the Mode of Profecuting by Information (when a Grand Jury will not find *Billa vera*) is a national Grievance, and greatly inconfiftent with that Freedom, which the Subjects of *England* enjoy in moft other Cafes. But if we are fo unhappy as not to be able to ward off this Stroke of Power directly, yet let us take Care not to be cheated out of our Liberties, by Forms and Ap-pearances ; let us always be fure that the Charge in the In-formation is made out clearly even beyond a Doubt ; for tho Matters in the Information may be called *Form* upon Tryal, yet they may be, and often have been found to be *Matters of Subftance* upon giving Judgment.

  Gentlemen ; The Danger is great, in Proportion to the Mifchief that may happen, through our too great Credulity. A proper Confidence in a Court, is commendable ; but as the Verdict (what ever it is) will be yours, you ought to re-fer no Part of your Duty to the Difcretion of other Perfons. If you fhould be of the Opinion, that there is no Falfhood in Mr. *Zenger's* Papers, you will, nay (pardon me for the Expreffion) you ought to fay fo ; becaufe you don't know whether others (I mean the Court) may be of that Opinion. It is your Right to do fo, and there is much depending upon your Refolution, as well as upon your Integrity.

  The lofs of liberty to a generous Mind, is worfe than

Death ; and yet we know there have been thofe in all Ages, who for the fake of Preferment, or fome imaginary Honour, have freely lent a helping Hand, to opprefs, nay to deftroy their Country. This brings to my Mind that faying of the immortal *Brutus*, when he look'd upon the Creatures of *Cæfar*, who were very great Men, but by no Means good Men. "*You* Romans *faid* Brutus, *if yet I may call you fo,* " *confider what you are doing; remember that you are affifting* " *Cæfar to forge thofe very Chains, which one day he will make* " *your felves wear.*" This is what every Man (that values Freedom) ought to confider: He fhould act by Judgment and not by Affection or Self-Intereft ; for, where thofe pre-vail, No Ties of either Country or Kindred are regarded ; as upon the other Hand, the Man, who loves his Country, prefers it's Liberty to all other Confiderations, well knowing that without Liberty, Life is a Mifery.

A famous Inftance of this you will find in the Hiftory of another brave *Roman* of the fame Name, I mean *Lucius Junius Brutus*, whofe ftory is well known and therefore I fhall mention no more of it, than only to fhew the Value he put upon the Freedom of his Country. After this great Man, with his Fellow Citizens whom he had engag'd in the Caufe, had banifh'd *Tarquin* the Proud, the laft King of *Rome*, from a Throne which he afcended by inhuman Murders and poffefs'd by the moft dreadful Tyranny and Profcriptions, and had by this Means, amafs'd incredible Riches, even fuf-ficient to bribe to his Intereft, many of the young Nobility of *Rome*, to affift him in recovering the Crown ; but the Plot being difcovered, the principal Confpirators were appre-hended, among whom were two of the Sons of *Junius Brutus*. It was abfolutely neceffary that fome fhould be made Ex-amples of, to deter others from attempting the reftoring of *Tarquin* and deftroying the Liberty of *Rome*. And to effect this it was, that *Lucius Junius Brutus*, one of the Con-fuls of *Rome*, in the Prefence of the *Roman* People, fat Judge and condemned his own Sons, as Traitors to their Country : And to give the laft Proof of his exalted Virtue, and his

JOHN PETER ZENGER

Love of Liberty : He with a Firmnefs of Mind, (only becoming fo great a Man) caus'd their Heads to be ftruck off
in his own Prefence ; and when he obferv'd that his rigid
Virtue, occafion'd a fort of Horror among the People, it is
obferv'd he only faid. " *My Fellow-Citizens, do not think that*
" *this Proceeds from any Want of natural Affection* : *No, The*
" *Death of the Sons of* Brutus *can affect* Brutus *only* ; *but the*
" *Lofs of Liberty will affect my Country.*" Thus highly was
Liberty efteem'd in thofe Days that a Father could facri-
fice his Sons to fave his Country, But why do I go to
Heathen *Rome*, to bring Inftances of the Love of Liberty, the
beft Blood in *Britain* has been fhed in the Caufe of Liberty ;
and the Freedom we enjoy at this Day, may be faid to be
(in a great Meafure) owing to the glorious Stand the famous
Hamden, and other of our Countrymen, made againft the
arbitrary Demands, and illegal Impofitions, of the Times
in which they lived ; who rather than give up the Rights of
Englifhmen, and fubmit to pay an iIlegal Tax, of no more,
I think, than 3 shillings, refolv'd to undergo, and for their
Liberty of their Country did undergo the greateft Extremities, in that arbitrary and terrible Court of Star Chamber,
to whofe arbitrary Proceedings, (it being compos'd of the
principal Men of the Realm, and calculated to fupport arbitrary Government) no Bounds or Limits could be fet, nor
could any other Hand remove the Evil but a Parliament.

Power may juftly be compar'd to a great River, while
kept within it's due Bounds, is both Beautiful and Ufeful ;
but when it overflows, it's Banks, it is then too impetuous
to be ftemm'd, it bears down all before it, and brings Deftruction and Defolation wherever it comes. If then this is
the Nature of Power, let us at leaft do our Duty, and like
wife Men (who value Freedom) ufe our utmoft Care
to fupport Liberty, the only Bulwark againft lawlefs Power,
which in all Ages has facrificed to it's wild Luft and bound-
lefs Ambition, the Blood of the beft Men that ever liv'd.

I hope to be pardon'd Sir for my Zeal upon this Occafion ; it is an old and wife Caution. *That when our Neigh-*

bours Houſe is on Fire, we ought to take Care of our own. For tho' Bleſſed be God, I live in a Government where Liberty is well underſtood, and freely enjoy'd : yet Experience has ſhewn us all (I'm ſure it has to me) that a bad Precedent in one Government, is ſoon ſet up for an Authority in another; and therefore I cannot but think it mine, and every Honeſt Man's Duty, that (while we pay all due Obedience to Men in Authority) we ought at the ſame Time to be upon our Guard againſt Power, wherever we apprehend that it may affect ourſelves or our Fellow-Subjects.

I am truly very unequal to ſuch an Undertaking on many Accounts. And you ſee I labour under the Weight of many Years, and am born down with great Infirmities of Body ; yet Old and Weak as I am, I ſhould think it my Duty if required, to go to the utmoſt Part of the Land, where my Service cou'd be of any Uſe in aſſiſting to quench the Flame of Proſecutions upon Informations, ſet on Foot by the Government, to deprive a People of the Right of Remonſtrating, (and complaining too) of the arbitrary Attempts of Men in Power. Men who injure and oppreſs the People under their Adminiſtration provoke them to cry out and complain ; and then make that very Complaint the Foundation for new Oppreſſions and Proſecutions. I wiſh I could ſay there were no Inſtances of this Kind. But to conclude; the Queſtion before the Court and you Gentlemen of the Jury, is not of ſmall nor private Concern, it is not the Cauſe of the poor Printer, nor of *New-York* alone, which you are now trying: No! It may in it's Conſequence, affect every Freeman that lives under a Britiſh Government on the main of *America*. It is the beſt Cauſe. It is the Cauſe of Liberty ; and I make no Doubt but your upright Conduct, this Day, will not only entitle you to the Love and Eſteem of your Fellow-Citizens ; but every Man who prefers Freedom to a Life of slavery will bleſs and honour You, as Men who have baffled the Attempt of Tyranny; and by an impartial and uncorrupt Verdict, have laid a noble Foundation for ſecuring to ourſelves, our Poſ-

JOHN PETER ZENGER

terity, and our Neighbours, That, to which Nature and the Laws of our Country have given us a Right,--the Liberty ----both of expofing and oppofing arbitrary Power (in thefe Parts of the World, at leaft) by fpeaking and writing Truth.

Here Mr. Attorney obferv'd, that Mr. Hamilton had gone very much out of the Way, and had made himfelf and the People very merry : But that he had been citing Cafes, not at all to the Purpofe ; he faid, there was no fuch Caufe as Mr. Bufhel's or Sir Edward Hales before the Court ; and he could not find out what the Court or Jury had to do with Difpenfations, Riots or unlawful Affemblies : All that the Jury had to confider of was Mrs. Zenger's Printing and Publifhing two fcandalous Libels, which very highly reflected on his Excellency and the principal Men concern'd in the Adminiftration of this Government, which is confefs'd. That is, the Printing and Publifhing of the Journals fet forth in the Information is confefs'd. And concluded that as Mr. Hamilton had confefs'd the Printing, and there could be no doubt but they were fcandalous Papers, highly reflecting upon his Excellency, and the principal Magiftrates in the Province. And therefore he made no Doubt but the Jury would find the Defendant Guilty, and would refer to the Court for their Direction.

Mr. Ch. Juft. Gentlemen of the Jury. The great Pains Mr. *Hamilton* has taken, to fhew how little Regard Juries are to Pay to the Opinion of the Judges ; and his infifting fo much upon the Conduct of fome Judges in Tryals of this kind ; is done no doubt, with a Defign that you fhould take but very little Notice, of what I might fay upon this Occafion. I fhall therefore only obferve to you that, as the Facts or Words in the Information are confeffed : The only Thing that can come in Queftion before you is, whether the Words as fet forth in the Information make a Lybel. And that is a Matter of Law, no Doubt, and which you may leave to the Court. But I fhall trouble you no further with any Thing

more of my own, but read to you the Words of a learned
and upright Judge * in a cafe of the like Nature.

' *To fay that corrupt Officers are appointed to adminifter Af-*
' *fairs, is certainly a Reflection on the Government. If People*
' *fhould not be called to account for poffeffing the People with an*
' *ill Opinion of the Government, no Government can fubfift, For*
' *it is very neceffary for all Governments that the People fhould*
' *have a good Opinion of it. And nothing can be worfe to any*
' *Government, than to endeavour to procure Animofities; as to the*
' *Management of it, this has been always look'd upon as a Crime,*
' *and no Government can be fafe without it be punifhed.*

' *Now you are to confider, whether thefe Words I have read*
' *to you, do not tend to beget an ill Opinion of the Adminiftra-*
' *tion of the Government? To tell us, that thofe that are em-*
' *ployed know nothing of the Matter, and thofe that do know*
' *are not employed. Men are not adapted to Offices, but Offices, to*
' *Men, out of a particular Regard to their Intereft, and not to*
' *their Fitnefs for the Places; this is the Purport of thefe*
' *Papers.*

Mr. *Hamilton.* I humbly beg Your Honours Pardon:
I am very much misapprehended, if you fuppofe what I faid
was fo defigned.

Sir, you know; I made an Apology for the Freedom I
found my felf under a Neceffity of ufing upon this Occafion.
I faid, there was Nothing perfonal defigned; it arofe from the
Nature of our Defence.

The Jury withdrew and in a fmall Time returned and
being afked by the Clerk whether they were agreed of their
Verdict, and whether *John Peter Zenger* was guilty of Printing and Publifhing the Libels in the Information mentioned?
They anfwered by *Thomas Hunt*, their Foreman, *Not Guilty*,
Upon which there were three Huzzas in the Hall, which
was crowded with People and the next Day I was difcharged
from my Imprifonment.

* Ch. J. *Holt* in *Tutchin's* Cafe.

JOHN PETER ZENGER

✤✤✤✤✤✤✤✤✤✤✤✤✤✤✤✤✤✤✤✤

APPENDIX.

City of New-York } *ſs.* **A**T a Common Council, held at the City— Hall of the ſaid City, on *Tueſday* the Sixteenth Day of *September*, Anno Dom. 1735.

PRESENT.

Paul Richards Eſq; Mayor.
Gerardus Stuyveſant Eſq; Deputy-Mayor.
Daniel Horſmanden, Eſq; Recorder.

ALDERMEN.

William Roome Eſq; *John Walter* Eſq; *Stephen Bayard* Eſq; *Simon Johnſon* Eſq; *Chriſtopher Fell* Eſq; *Johannes Burger* Eſq;

ASSISTANTS.

Mr. *Johannes Waldron.* Mr. *John Moore.* Mr. *Charles Le Roux.*
Mr. *Ede Myer.*　　　Mr. *John Fred. Evert Byvanck.*

Ordered, *That* Andrew Hamilton, *Eſq; of* Philadelphia, *Barriſter at Law, be preſented with the Freedom of this Corporation; and that Alderman* Bayard, *Alderman* Johnſon, *and Alderman* Fell, *be a Committee to bring in a Draught thereof,*

City of New-York. } *ſs.* **A**T a Common-Council, held at the City- Hall of the ſaid City on *Monday* the twenty Ninth Day of *September*, being the Feaſt Day of St. *Michael* the Archangel *Anno Dom.* 1735.

PRESENT.

Paul Richards Eſq; Mayor.
Daniel Horſmanden, Eſq; Recorder.

THE CASE AND TRIAL

Stephen Bayard Simon Johnfon *and* Chriftopher Fell,
Efqrs. *Alderman, to whom it was referred to prepare the
Draught of the Freedom of this Corporation, to be prefented to*
Andrew Hamilton *Efq; make their Report thereon, in the
Words following* (to wit) *That they have prepared the Form
of the Grant, to the faid* Andrew Hamilton, *Efq; of the Free-
dom of the City of* New-York, *in thefe words* (to wit).

City of   *PAUL RICHARDS* Efq; the Recorder Al-
New-York. $\}$ *fs.* dermen and Affiftants of the City of *New-
York*, convened in Common-Council, To
all whom thefe Prefents fhall come Greeting. *WHEREAS*,
Honour is the Juft Reward of Virtue, and publick Benefits demand a publick Acknowledgment. We therefore, under
a grateful Senfe of the remarkable Service, done to the Inhabitants of this City and Colony, by *Andrew Hamilton*, Efq;
of *Pennfilvania*, Barrifter at Law, by his Learned and generous Defence of the Rights of Mankind, and the Liberty of
the Prefs, in the Cafe of *John Peter Zenger*, lately tried on an
Information exhibited in the Supream-Court of this Colony,
do by thefe Prefents, bear to the faid *Andrew Hamilton*
Efq; the publick Thanks of the Freemen of this Corporation for that fignal Service, which he Chearfully undertook
under great Indifpofition of Body, and generoufly performed,
refufing any Fee or Reward : And in Teftimony of our great
Eeem* for his Perfon, and Senfe of his Merit, do hereby
prefent him with the Freedom of this Corporation. Thefe
are therefore to Certify and Declare, that the faid *Andrew*

---

* So printed in the original for " Efteem."

JOHN PETER ZENGER

Hamilton Efq ; is hereby admitted, received and allowed a Freedom* and Citizen of the faid City: To Have, Hold, Enjoy and Partake of all the Benefits Liberties, Priviledges, Freedoms and Immunities whatfoever granted or belonging to a Freeman and Citizen of the fame City. *In Teftimony*, whereof the Common Council of the faid City, in Common Council affembled, have caufed the Seal of the faid City to be hereunto affixed this Twenty Ninth Day of *September. Anno Domini One Thousand Seven Hundred and Thirty Five.*

By Order of the Common Council
William Sharpas. Clerk

And we do further Report, that fundry of the Members of this Corporation and Gentlemen of this City have voluntarily Contributed fufficent for a Gold Box of five Ounces, aud a half for Inclofing the Seal of the faid Freedom ; Upon the Lid of which, we are of Opinion fhould be engraved the Arms of the City of New-York : *Witnefs Our Hands this Twenty Ninth day of* September, 1735.

Stephen Bayard·
Simon Johnfon.
Chriftopher Fell.

Which Report is approved by this Court, and Ordered, *That the Freedom and Box be forthwith made, purfuant to the faid Report, and that Mr.* Sharpas, *the Common Clerk of this City, do affix the Seal to the fame Freedom, and inclofe it in the faid Box.*

Mr. Alderman *Bayard going to* Philadelphia *and offering to be the Bearer of the faid Freedom to Mr.* Hamilton, Ordered, *That Mr.* Sharpas, *deliver it to Alderman* Bayard *for that Purpoje ; and that Alderman* Bayard *do deliver it to Mr.* Hamilton, *with Affurances of the great Efteem, that this Corporation have for his Perfon and Merit.*

---

* So given in the original for "Freeman."

244

THE CASE AND TRIAL

City of   ⎱ _ſs._   At a Common-Council, held at the City-
New-York ⎰   Hall of the ſaid City, on _Wedneſday_ the
fifteenth Day of _October_, Anno Domini
1735.

PRESENT.

Paul Richards, Eſq; Mayor.
Daniel Horſemanden, Eſq; Recorder.

ALDERMEN.

John Walter, Eſq;   _William Roome_, Eſq;
Simon Johnſon, Eſq;   _Johannes Burger_, Eſq;

ASSISTANTS.

Mr. _Johannes Waldron_, Mr. _Gerrardus Beekman_, Mr. _Henry_
Mr. _Abraham de Peyſter_, Mr. _Peter Stoutenburgh_. _Bogart_.

Ordered, _That the Freedom, granted by this Corporation,
to_ Andrew Hamilton, _Eſq; with the Report of the Committee, for preparing a Draught of the ſame and the Order of this
Court, thereon, may be printed._

William Sharpas.

Round on the Lid of the Box mentioned in the above ſaid Report and Order,
there is engraved not only the Arms of the City of _New-York_, but alſo this Motto
in a Garter;

DEMERSÆ LEGES-TIMEFACTA LIBERTAS-HÆC TANDEM
EMERGUNT.

On the inner Side of the Lid of the Box ſhewing it ſelf at the ſame Time with
the Certificate of the Freedom; There is Engraven in a flying Garter, theſe Words.

NON NUMMIS,—VIRTUTE PARATUR.

As an Incentive to publick Virtue, on the Front of the Rim of the ſaid
Box, there is Engraven a Part of _Tully's_ Wiſh;

ITA CUIQUE EVENIAT, UT DE REPUBLICA MERUIT.

Which Freedom and Box was preſented in the Manner that had been
directed, and gratefully accepted by the ſaid _Andrew Hamilton_, Eſq;

JOHN PETER ZENGER

ERRATA.

Pag. 12 Lin. 8. *for* Who *read* tho'. The same Page, Lin. 9. for *Freeholders* read *Freehold*. The same Page, Lin. 11. *for* be out *read* be left out. Pag. 13. Lin. *penult. for* said the *read* the said.

New-York, Printed and fold by *John Peter Zenger*. MDCCXXXVI.

A brief Narrative of the Case and Tryal of *John Peter Zenger*, Printer of the *New-York weekly Journal.*

AS There was but one Printer in the Province of *New-York*, that printed a publick News Paper, I was in Hopes, if I undertook to publish another, I might make it worth my while; and I soon found my Hopes were not groundless: My first Paper was printed. *Nov. 5th, 1733.* and I continued printing and publishing of them, I thought to the Satisfaction of every Body, till the *January* following; when the Chief Justice was pleased to animadvert upon the Doctrine of Libels, in a long Charge given in that Term to the Grand Jury, and afterwards on the third *Tuesday* of *October, 1734.* was again pleased to charge the Grand Jury in the following Words.

'*Gentlemen*; I shall conclude with reading a Paragraph or two out of the same Book, concerning Libels; they are arrived to that Height, than they call loudly for your Animadversion; it is high Time to put a Stop to them; for at the rate Things are now carried on, when all Order and Government is endeavoured to be trampled on; Reflections are cast upon Persons of all Degrees, must not these Things end in Sedition, if not timely prevented? Lenity, you have seen will not avail, it becomes you then to enquire after the Offenders, that we may in a due Course of Law be enabled to punish them. If you, *Gentlemen*, do not interpose, consider whether the ill Consequences that may arise from any Disturbances of the publick Peace, may not in part, lye at your Door?

'*Hawkins*, in his Chapter of Libels, considers three Points, 1*st*. What shall be said to be a Libel. 2*dly*. Who are liable to be punished for it. 3*dly*. In what Manner they are to be punished. Under the 1*st*. he says, §. 7. *Nor can there be any Doubt, but that a Writing which defames a private Person only, is as much a Libel as that which defames Persons intrusted in a publick Capacity, in as much as it manifestly tends to create ill Blood, and to cause a Disturbance of the publick Peace; however, it is certain, that it is a very high Aggravation of a Libel, that it tends to scandalize the Government, by reflecting on those who are entrusted with the administration of publick Affairs, which does not only endanger the publick Peace, as all other Libels do, by stirring up the Parties immediately concerned in it, to Acts of Revenge, but also has a direct Tendency to breed in the People a Dislike of their Governours, and incline them to Faction and Sedition.* As to the 2d. Point he says §. 10. It is certain, not only he who composes or procures another to compose it, but also that he who publishes, or procures another to publish it, are in Danger of being punished for it; and it is said not to be material whether he who disperses a Libel, knew any Thing of the Contents or Effects of it or not; for nothing could be more easy

A BIBLIOGRAPHY

OF THE

TRIAL

OF

JOHN PETER ZENGER

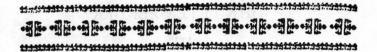

BIBLIOGRAPHY

OF THE TRIAL OF JOHN PETER ZENGER

1736

HREE rows of printer's ornaments. A brief Narrative of the Case and Try-/al of *John Peter Zenger*, Printer of the/*New-York weekly Journal.*/ [One row of ornaments.]

[Colophon:] New-York, Printed and sold by *John Peter Zenger*, MDCCXXXVI./

Folio, 20 leaves.

Collation : No separate title-page. Text, pages 1 to [40], 15–40 being wrongly numbered 17–42.

This is the first edition of the "Trial."

1737

[Two rows of printer's ornaments.] /REMARKS/ON/*Zenger's* TRYAL,/Taken out of the *Barbados* Gazette's./For the Benefit of the Students in/*Law*, and others in *North America.*/ [1737.]

12mo, 36 leaves.

Collation : No separate title-page. Above heading at top of page 1. Letter, signed "Anglo Americanus," dated "Bridge-Town, June 24, 1737," pages 1–5; text, with heading, "From the Barbados Gazette, Nº 439 | Remarks on Zenger's Trial," pages 6–39; letter, beginning "Mr. Keimer,"—signed "Anglo Americanus," dated "Bridge-Town, | July 20, | 1737," page 40; part 2, with heading, "Remarks | on | Zenger's Tryal, | Taken out of the Barbados Gazette, | Nº 446, &c | Part II." signed "Indus Britannicus." dated "Bridge-Town, | July 29, 1737." pages [41]–71; blank page [72].

Nos. 466, 467, 468 and 469 of the *Pennsylvania Gazette* contain a reply to this written by James Alexander.

JOHN PETER ZENGER

1738

[Two rows of printer's ornaments.]/A brief NARRATIVE of the Case/and Tryal of *John Peter Zenger*, Printer,/of the *New-York weekly Journal.*/

[Colophon :] BOSTON :/Printed and Sold by THOMAS FLEET, at the *Heart* and *Crown* in/Cornhill, 1738./

4to, 24 leaves.

Collation : No separate title-page; text and Appendix, pages 1–48.

THE/TRYAL/OF/*John Peter Zenger*,/OF/NEW-YORK, PRINTER,/Who was lately Try'd and Acquitted for PRINTING and/PUBLISHING a LIBEL against the Government./ With the PLEADINGS and ARGUMENTS on both Sides./*Ita CUIQUE eveniat, ut de REPUBLICA meruit.* (Cicero.)/[Printer's ornament.]/*London :* Printed for J. WILFORD, behind the Chapter-House, *St.* Paul's/Church-Yard. 1738./

4to, 17 leaves.

Collation : Title, 1 page ; blank, 1 page; text and Appendix, pages 1–32.

THE/TRYAL/OF/*John Peter Zenger*,/OF/NEW-YORK, PRINTER,/Who was lately Try'd and Acquitted for PRINTING and/PUBLISHING a LIBEL against the Government./ With the PLEADINGS and ARGUMENTS on both Sides./*Ita CUIQUE eveniat, ut de REPUBLICA meruit.* (Cicero) / THE SECOND EDITION./[Printer's ornament.] *London :* Printed for J. WILFORD, behind the Chapter-House, St. *Paul's*/Church-Yard, 1738./

4to, 17 leaves.

Collation : Title, 1 page; blank, 1 page; text and Appendix, pages 1–32,

THE/TRYAL/OF/*John Peter Zenger*,/OF/NEW-YORK, PRINTER,/Who was lately Try'd and Acquitted for PRINTING and/PUBLISHING a LIBEL against the Government./With the PLEADINGS and ARGUMENTS on both Sides./*Ita CUIQUE eveniat, ut de REPUBLICA meruit.* (Cicero)/The THIRD EDITION./[Printer's ornament.]/*London;* Printed for J.WILFORD, behind the Chapter-House, St. *Paul's*/Church-Yard, 1738./

4to, 17 leaves.

Collation: Title, 1 page; blank, 1 page; text and Appendix, pages 1–32.

BIBLIOGRAPHY

THE/TRYAL/OF/*John Peter Zenger*,/OF/NEW-YORK,
PRINTER,/Who was lately Try'd and Acquitted for PRINTING
and/PUBLISHING a LIBEL against the Government./With the
PLEADINGS and ARGUMENTS on both Sides./*Ita* CUIQUE
eveniat, ut de REPUBLICA *meruit.* (Cicero)/The FOURTH
EDITION./.[Printer's Ornament.]/*London:* Printed for J. WIL-
FORD, behind the Chapter-House, St. *Paul's*/Church-Yard, 1738./

4to, 17 leaves.

Collation: Title, 1 page; blank, 1 page; text and Appendix, pages 1–32.

REMARKS/ ON THE/TRIAL/ OF/ John-Peter Zenger,/
PRINTER of the/NEW-YORK Weekly Journal,/Who was
lately Try'd and Acquitted for/Printing and Publishing TWO
LIBELS/Against the/Government of that PROVINCE./LON-
DON:/Printed for J. ROBERTS in *Warwick-Lane.* MDCC-
XXXVIII./(Price One Shilling)/

4to, 16 leaves.

Collation: Title 1 page; blank, 1 page; Preface, 2 pages; text, signed at
end "Indus Britannicus," pages [1]–27; blank, page [28].

[Two rows of printer's ornaments.]/A BRIEF/NARRATIVE
/OF THE/CASE *and* TRIAL *of* JOHN PETER ZENGER,/
Printer of the NEW-YORK *Weekly Journal.*/

4to, 16 leaves.

Collation: No separate title-page. Text and Appendix, pages 1–32.
This edition of the trial is apparently an English one; it strongly resembles
Wilford s editions, but is as yet unidentified.

1750

THE/CASE and TRYAL/OF/JOHN PETER ZENGER,/
OF/NEW-YORK,/PRINTER,/Who was lately tryed and acquitted for PRINT-/ING and PUBLISHING a LIBEL against
the/GOVERNMENT./WITH/The PLEADINGS and AR-
GUMENTS on both Sides./*Ita* CUIQUE *eveniat, ut de* REPUB-
LICA *meruit.* CICERO./LONDON:/Printed for J. WILFORD,
behind the Chapter-House, St./*Paul's* Church-Yard, 1750./[Price
a *British* Sixpence.]/

8vo, 30 leaves.

Collation: Title, page [1]; blank, page [2]; text and Appendix, pages 3–60.

JOHN PETER ZENGER

1752

THE/TRIAL/OF/*John Peter Zenger*,/OF/NEW-YORK,
PRINTER;/Who was Tried and Acquitted,/For PRINTING
and PUBLISHING a LIBEL/against the Government./WITH/
The PLEADINGS and ARGUMENTS on both Sides./*Ita*
CUIQUE *eveniat, ut de* REPUBLICA *meruit*. Cic./[Printer's or-
nament.]/LONDON :/Printed for P. BROWN, in *Fleet-Street*.
MDCCLII./(Price One Shilling and Sixpence.)/

8vo, 40 leaves.

Collation: Title, 1 page; blank, 1 page; Preface, 2 pages; text and Appendix, pages [1]–[76].

1756

A BRIEF/NARRATIVE/OF THE/CASE AND TRIAL/
OF/JOHN PETER ZENGER, Printer of the/NEW-YORK
WEEKLY-JOURNAL. / [Printer's ornament.] NEW-YORK
Printed:/LANCASTER Re-printed, and Sold by W. DUN-
LAP,/at the *New Printing-Office*, in *Queen-Street*, 1756./

Folio, 20 leaves.

Collation: Title, page [1] ; blank, p. [2]; text and Appendix, pages [3]–
[40].

1765

THE/TRIAL/OF/JOHN PETER ZENGER,/OF NEW
YORK, PRINTER:/Who was charged with having printed and
published/a LIBEL against the Government; and acquitted./
WITH/A NARRATIVE OF HIS CASE./To which is now added,
being never printed before,/THE TRIAL/OF/MR. WILLIAM
OWEN,/BOOKSELLER, near TEMPLE-BAR,/Who was also
Charged with the Publication of a LIBEL/against the GOVERN-
MENT ; of which he was honour-/ably acquitted by a Jury of
Free-born Englishmen,/Citizens of London./[Printer's ornament.]/
LONDON :/Printed for J. ALMON, opposite Burlington-House,
Piccadilly./MDCCLXV./(Price One Shilling.)/

8vo, 30 leaves.

Collation: Title, page [1]; notice of the new edition, 10 lines, pages [2];
text, page [3]–48 ; text of trial of Mr. William Owen, 11 pages; publisher's
advertisements, 1 page.

BIBLIOGRAPHY

1770

A BRIEF/NARRATIVE/OF THE/CASE and TRIAL/ OF / JOHN PETER ZENGER, / PRINTER / OF THE/ NEW-YORK WEEKLY JOURNAL,/FOR A/LIBEL./In a free State, such as our's is, all Men ought to/enjoy, and express their Minds freely./ TIBERIUS CAESAR./NEW-YORK :/Reprinted, by JOHN HOLT, at the *Exchange.* 1770/

4to, 28 leaves.

Collation: Title, 1 page; blank, 1 page; text and Appendix, pages [1]–46, "Summary Account of the trial of Mr. Willim Owen, Bookseller," pages 47–49; "From the Political Register," etc., pages 50–53; blank, page [54].

1784

THE TRIAL/OF JOHN PETER ZENGER,/OF NEW-YORK, PRINTER ;/FOR A LIBEL/AGAINST THE GOVERNMENT, / ON THE FOURTH OF AUGUST, / MDCCXXXV./ INSCRIBED/TO THE HONORABLE T. ERSKINE./"God and Reason made the Law, and have placed Con-/science within you to determine, not like an Asiatic/ Cadi, according to the Ebbs and Flows of his own Pas-/sions, but like a British Judge, in this Land of Liberty/and good Sense, who makes *no new Law*, but faithfully/declares that Law which *he knows* already written."/STERNE/LONDON : PRINTED FOR FLEXNEY, HOLBORN ; DAVIES, RUSSELL-/STREET ; MERRIL, CAMBRIDGE ; AND/EDDOWES, SHREWSBURY. 1784./

8vo, 34 leaves.

Title, 1 page; blank, 1 page; dedication, 2 pages; text, pages [1]–64.

1799

[Printer's ornament.]/A/BRIEF NARRATIVE/OF THE/ CASE AND TRYAL/OF/*John Peter Zenger,*/Printer of the *New-York Weekly Journal.*/[Colophon :]/Reprinted and Sold at the *Bible* and *Heart*, Cornhill, Boston,/MDCCXCIX./

8vo, 24 leaves.

Collation : No separate title-page. Text and Appendix, pages 1–48.

1841

AMERICAN / CRIMINAL TRIALS/By PELEG W.

JOHN PETER ZENGER

CHANDLER./VOLUME I./BOSTON:/CHARLES C. LITTLE
AND JAMES BROWN./LONDON : / A. MAXWELL, 32,
BELL YARD, LINCOLN'S INN./MDCCCXLI./

8vo, 2 volumes.

The "Trial of John Peter Zenger" fills pages [151]–209 of Vol. I.

1741

CARIBBEANA. / CONTAINING / LETTERS and DIS-
SERTATIONS,/ Together with / POETICAL ESSAYS, / On
various SUBJECTS and OCCASIONS ;/Chiefly wrote by several
Hands in the/WEST-INDIES./And some of them to Gentlemen
residing there./Now collected together in/TWO VOLUMES./
Wherein are also comprised, divers Papers relating to TRADE,/
GOVERNMENT, and LAWS in general; but more especially,/
to those of the *British* Sugar-Colonies, and of *Barbados* in parti-/
cular: As Likewise the Characters of the most eminent Men that/
have died, of late Years, in that Island./To which are added in an/
APPENDIX,/Some Pieces never before Published./Vol. II./LON-
DON :/Printed for T. OSBORNE, in *Gray's-Inn* ; J. CLARKE,
at the *Royal Ex-/change* ; S. AUSTIN, in *St. Paul's Church-
Yard*; G. HAWKINS, at/*Temple-Bar* ; R. DODSLEY, in *Pall-
Mall*, and W. LEWIS in *Covent-/Garden*. M.DCC.XLI.

4to, 2 vols.

Vol. II. contains "Remarks on Zenger's Trial," signed "Anglo-Americanus," in five letters, pages 198–221; also "Remarks on Zenger's Trial by
another Hand," signed "Indus Britannicus," pages 225–241; "Letters from |
Anglo-Americanus | with an article from the Pensilvania Gazette of Dec. 8,
1737," pages 264–271; and "Letter to Anglo-Americanus and Indus-Britanni-
cus," signed "P. C.," pages 272–273.

1816

A/COMPLETE COLLECTION/OF/State Trials/AND/
PROCEEDINGS FOR HIGH TREASON AND OTHER/
CRIMES AND MISDEMEANORS / FROM THE / EARL-
IEST PERIOD TO THE YEAR 1783,/WITH NOTES AND
OTHER ILLUSTRATIONS : / COMPILED BY / T. B.
HOWELL, ESQ., F.R.S., F.SA./INCLUDING,/IN ADDI-
TION TO THE WHOLE OF THE MATTER CON-
TAINED IN THE/FOLIO EDITION OF HARGRAVE,/

BIBLIOGRAPHY

UPWARDS OF TWO HUNDRED CASES NEVER BE-
FORE COLLECTED:/ TO WHICH IS SUBJOINED/A
TABLE OF PARALLEL REFERENCE, / RENDERING
THIS EDITION APPLICABLE TO THOSE BOOKS OF
AUTHORITY IN/WHICH REFERENCES ARE MADE
TO THE FOLIO EDITION./In TWENTY-ONE VOL-
UMES./VOL. XVII./12 GEORGE I TO 17 GEORGE II
1726–1743./LONDON :/Printed by T. C. Hansard, Peter-
borough-Court, Fleet-Street : / FOR LONGMAN, HURST,
REES, ORME, and BROWN; J. M. RICHARDSON;/BLACK,
PARBURY AND ALLEN ; BALDWIN, CRADOCK AND
JOY;/E. JEFFREY ; J. HATCHARD ; R. H. EVANS ; J.
BOOKER; E. LLOYD;/J. BOOTH ; BUDD AND CALKIN;
AND T. C. HANSARD./1816./

8vo, 21 vols.

Vol. XVIII contains an account of Zenger's trial, filling columns 675 to
764, with the following heading :

"490./The Trial of MR. JOHN PETER ZENGER, of New-York, Printer
/for printing and publishing a Libel against the Government,/before the Hon.
James de Lancey Esq. Chief Justice of the/Province of New-York, and the
Hon. Frederick Phillipse, Esq./second Judge, at New-York, on August 4th. 9
George II,/A.D. 1735."

LIST OF ISSUES
OF THE
NEW YORK WEEKLY JOURNAL
WITH THE LIBRARIES
POSSESSING SAME

LIST OF ISSUES
OF THE
NEW YORK WEEKLY JOURNAL
WITH THE LIBRARIES POSSESSING SAME

EXPLANATION OF ABBREVIATIONS

A.—American Antiquarian Society, Worcester, Mass.
D.—Edward H. DeLancey, New York.
L.—New York Public Library, Lenox Collection.

N.—New York Historical Society.
P.—Historical Society of Pennsylvania.
R.—Public Records Office, London.
W.—John David Wolfe, New York.

Each number, so far as seen, consists of four pages, except where indicated.

No. 1—Oct. 5. 1733. .... P. N. L. A. (Should be Nov. 5).	No. 26—April 29. 1734. .... P. N. L. A.
	No. 27—May 6. " .... P. N. L. A. (2 pages only).
No. 2—Nov. 12. " .... P. N. L. A.	No. 28—May 13. " .... P. N. L. A.
No. 3—Nov. 19. " .... P. N. L. A.	No. 29—May 20. " .... P. N. L. A.
No. 4—Nov. 26. " .... P. N. L. A.	No. 30—May 27. " .... P. N. L. A.
No. 5—Dec. 3. " .... P. N. L. A.	No. 31—June 3. " .... P. N. L. A.
No. 6—Dec. 10. " .... R. P. N. L. A.	No. 32—June 10. " .... P. N. L. A.
No. 7—Dec. 17. " .... R. P. N. L. A.	No. 33—June 17. " .... P. N. L. A.
No. 8—Dec. 24. " .... P. N. L. A.	No. 34—June 24. " .... P. N. L. A.
No. 9—Dec. 31. " .... P. N. L. A.	No. 35—July 1. " .... P. N. L. A.
	No. 36—July 8. " .... P. N. L. A.
No. 10—Jan. 7. 1733-[4]. .... P. N. L. A.	No. 37—July 15. " .... P. N. L. A.
No. 11—Jan. 14. " .... P. N. L. A.	No. 38—July 22. " .... P. N. L. A.
No. 12—Jan. 21. " .... P. N. L. A.	No. 39—July 29. " .... P. N. L. A.
No. 13—Jan. 28. " .... P. N. L. A.	No. 40—Aug. 5. " .... P. N. L. A.
No. 14—Feb. 4. " .... P. N. L. A.	No. 41—Aug. 12. " .... P. N. L. A.
No. 15—Feb. 11. " .... P. N. L. A.	No. 42—Aug. 19. " .... P. N. L. A.
No. 16—Feb. 18. " .... P. N. L. A.	No. 43—Aug. 26. " .... P. N. L. A.
No. 17—Feb. 25. " .... P. N. L. A.	No. 44—Sept. 2. " .... P. N. L. A.
No. 18—Mar. 4. " .... P. N. L. A.	No. 45—Sept. 9. " .... P. N. L. A.
No. 19—Mar. 11. " .... P. N. L. A.	No. 46—Sept. 16. " .... P. N. L. A.
No. 20—Mar. 18. " .... P. N. L. A.	No. 47—Sept. 23. " .... R. P. N. L. A.
No. 21—Mar. 25. 1734. .... P. N. L. A. (6 pages).	No. 48—Sept. 30. " .... R. P. N. L. A.
No. 22—April 1. " .... P. N. L. A.	No. 49—Oct. 7. " .... R. P. N. L. A.
No. 23—April 8. " .... P. N. L. A.	No. 50—Oct. 14. " .... P. N. L. A.
No. 24—April 15. " .... P. N. L. A.	No. 51—Oct. 21. " .... P. N. L. A.
No. 25—April 22. " .... P. N. L. A.	No. 52—Oct. 28. " .... P. N. L. A.

JOHN PETER ZENGER

No. 53—Nov. 4. 1734. .... P. N. L. A.
No. 54—Nov. 11. " .... P. N. L. A.
(Printer arrested. Paper not published on Nov. 18).
No. 55—Nov. 25. 1734. .... P. N. L. A.
No. 56—Dec. 2. " .... P. N. L. A.
No. 57—Dec. 9. " .... P. N. L. A.
No. 58—Dec. 16. " .... P. N. L. A.
No. 59—Dec. 23. " .... P. N. L. A.
No. 60—Dec. 30. " .... P. N. L. A.

No. 61—Jan. 6. 1734-[5]. ...... P. N. L. A.
No. 62—Jan. 13. " .... P. L. A.
No. 63—Jan. 20. " .... P. L. A.
No. 64—Jan. 27. " .... P. L. A.
No. 65—Feb. 3. " .... P. N. L. A.
No. 66—Feb. 10. " .... P. L. A.
No. 67—Feb. 17. " .... P. N. L. A.
No. 68—Feb. 24. " .... P. N. L. A.
No. 69—Mar. 3. " .... P. L. A.
No. 70—Mar. 10. " .... P. L. A.
No. 71—Mar. 17. " .... P. N. L. A.
No. 72—Mar. 24. " .... P. L. A.
No. 73—Mar. 31. 1735. .... P. L. A.
No. 74—April 7. " .... P. L. A.
No. 75—April 14. " .... P. N. L. A.
No. 76—April 21. " .... L. A.
No. 77—April 28. " .... L. A.
No. 78—May 5. " .... N. L. A.
No. 79—May 12. " .... L. A.
No. 80—May 19. " .... L. A.
No. 81—May 26. " .... L. A.
No. 82—June 2. " .... L. A.
No. 83—June 9. " .... N. L. A.
No. 84—June 16. " .... N. L. A.
No. 85—June 23. " .... N. L. A.
No. 86—June 30. " .... N. L. A.
No. 87—July 7. " .... L. A.
No. 88—July 14. " .... L. A.
No. 89—July 21. " .... N. L. A.
No. 90—July 28. " .... L. A.
No. 91—Aug. 2. " .... L. A.
No. 92—Aug. 11. " .... L. A.
No. 93—Aug. 18. " .... L. A.
No. 94—Aug. 25. " .... L. A.
No. 95—Sept. 1. " .... L. A.
No. 96—Sept. 8. " .... P. L. A.
No. 97—Sept. 15. " .... P. L. A.
No. 98—Sept. 23. " .... P. L. A.
No. 99—Sept. 27. " .... P. N. L. A.
(2 pages only).
No. 100—Oct. 6. " .... P. N. L. A.
No. 101—Oct. 13. " .... P. L. A.
No. 102—Oct. 20. " .... P. L. A.
No. 103—Oct. 27. " .... P. L. A.
No. 104—Nov. 3. " .... P. L. A.

No. 105—Nov. 10. 1735. .... P. N. L. A.
No. 106—Nov. 17. " .... P. L. A.
No. 107—Nov. 24. " .... P. L. A.
No. 108—Dec. 1. " .... P. L. A.
No. 109—Dec. 8. " .... P. L. A.
No. 110—Dec. 15. " .... P. L. A.
No. 111—Dec. 22. " .... P. L. A.
No. 112—Dec. 29. " .... P. N. L. A.

No. 113—Jan. 5. 1735-[6] ...... P. L. A.
No. 114—Jan. 12. " .... P. L. A.
No. 115—Jan. 19. " .... P. L. A.
No. 116—Jan. 26. " .... N. L. A.
No. 117—Feb. 2. " ...... R. P. L. A.
No. 118—Feb. 9. " .... L. N. A.
No. 119—Feb. 16. " .... L. A.
No. 120—Feb. 23. " .... N. L. A.
No. 121—Mar. 1. " .... N. L. A.
No. 122—Mar. 8. " .... R. N. L. A.
No. 123—Mar. 15. " .... N. L. A.
No. 124—Mar. 22. " .... N. L. A.
No. 125—Mar. 29. 1736. ...... R. L. A.
No. 126—April 5. " .... A.
No. 127—April 12. " .... L. A.
No. 128—April 19. " .... L. A.
No. 129—April 26. " .... L. A.
No. 130—May 3. " .... L. A.
No. 131—May 10. " .... L. A.
No. 132—May 17. " .... L. A.
No. 133—May 24. " .... L. A.
No. 134—May 31. " .... L. A.
No. 135—June 7. " .... L. A.
No. 136—June 14. " .... L. A.
No. 137—June 21. " .... L. A.
No. 138—June 28. " .... L. A.
No. 139—July 5. " .... L. A.
No. 140—July 12. " .... L. A.
No. 141—July 19. " .... A.
No. 142—July 26. " .... A.
No. 143—Aug. 2. " .... L. A.
No. 144—Aug. 9. " .... L. A.
No. 145—Aug. 16. " .... L. A.
No. 146—Aug. 23. " .... A.
No. 147—Aug. 30. " .... A.
No. 148—Sept. 6. " .... A.
No. 149—Sept. 13 " ...... R. L. A.
No. 150—Sept. 20. " .... A.
No. 151—Sept. 27. " .... A.
No. 152—Oct. 4. " .... A.
No. 153—Oct. 11. " .... A.
No. 154—Oct. 18. " .... A.
No. 155—Oct. 25. " .... A.
No. 156—Nov. 1. " .... A.
No. 157—Nov. 8. " .... A.
No. 158—Nov. 15. " .... A.
No. 159—Nov. 22. " .... L. A.

ISSUES OF NEW YORK WEEKLY JOURNAL

No. 160—Nov. 29. 1736. .... L. A.
No. 161—Dec. 6. " .... L. A.
No. 162—Dec. 13. " .... L. A.
No. 163—Dec. 20. " .... A.
No. 164—Dec. 27. " .... L. A.

No. 165—Jan. 10. 1736-[7] .... A.
No. 166—Jan. 17. " .... A.
No. 167—Jan. 24. " .... L. A.
No. 168—Jan. 31. " .... L. A.
No. 169—
No. 170—Feb. 14. " .... A.
No. 171—Feb. 21. " .... L. A.
No. 172—Feb. 28. " .... L. A.
No. 173—Mar. 7. " .... L. A.
No. 174—Mar. 14. " .... L. A.
No. 175—Mar. 21. " .... L. A.
No. 176—Mar. 28. 1737. .... L. A.
No. 177—April 4. " .... L. A.
No. 178—April 11. " .... L.
No. 179—April 18. " .... L. A.
No. 180—April 25. " .... L. A.
No. 181—May 2. " .... L. A.
No. 182—May 9. " .... L. A.
No. 183—May 16. " .... L. A.
No. 184—May 23. " .... A.
No. 185—May 30. " .... A.
No. 186—June 6. " .... L. A.
No. 187—June 13. " .... A.
No. 188—June 20. " .... A.
No. 189—June 27. " .... A.
No. 190—June 27. " .... L. A.
No. 191—July 4. " .... L. A.
No. 192—July 11. " .... L. A.
No. 193—July 18. " .... L. A.
No. 194—July 25. " .... L. A.
No. 195—Aug. 1. " .... L. A.
No. 196—Aug. 8. " .... A.
No. 197—Aug. 15. " .... L. A.
No. 198—Aug. 22. " .... L. A.
No. 199—Aug. 29. " .... L. A.
No. 200—Sept. 5. " .... A.
No. 201—Sept. 13. " .... L. A.
No. 202—Sept. 20. " .... L. A.
No. 203—Sept. 26. " .... L. A.
No. 204—Oct. 3. " .... A.
No. 205—Oct. 10. " .... A.
No. 206—Oct. 17. " .... A.
No. 207—Oct. 24. " .... A.
No. 208—Oct. 31. " .... A.
No. 209—Nov. 7. " .... A.
No. 210—Nov. 14. " .... A.
No. 211—Nov. 21. " .... A.
No. 212—Nov. 28. " .... A.
No. 213—Dec. 5. " .... A.
No. 214—Dec. 12. " .... A.

No. 215—Dec. 19. 1737. .... A.
No. 216—Dec. 26. " .... A.

No. 217—
No. 218—
No. 219—Jan. 17. 1737-[8] .... L. A.
No. 220—Jan. 24. " .... A.
No. 221—Jan. 30. " .... L. A.
No. 222—Feb. 6. " .... L. A.
No. 223—Feb. 13. " .... L. A.
No. 224—Feb. 20. " .... A.
No. 225—Mar. 6. " .... L. A.
No. 226—Mar. 13. " .... L. A.
No. 227—Mar. 21. " .... L. A.
No. 228—Mar. 27. 1738. .... L. A.
No. 229—April 3. " .... L. A.
No. 230—April 10. " .... L. A.
No. 231—April 17. " .... L. A.
No. 232—April 24. " .... L. A.
No. 233—May 1. " .... L. A.
No. 234—May 8. " .... L. A.
No. 235—May 15. " .... L. A.
No. 236—May 22. " .... L. A.
No. 237—May 29. " .... A.
No. 238—June 5. " .... L. A.
No. 239—June 12. " .... N. L. A.
No. 240—June 19. " .... N. L. A.
No. 241—June 26. " .... N. L. A.
No. 242—July 3. " .... N. L. A.
No. 243—July 10. " .... N. L. A.
No. 244—July 17. " .... N. L. A.
No. 245—July 24. " .... N. L. A.
No. 246—July 31. " .... N. L. A.
No. 247—Aug. 7. " .... N. L. A.
No. 248—Aug. 14. " .... L. A.
(The date is misprinted "Aug. 41"
in one of the Lenox copies).
No. 249—Aug. 21. " .... N. L. A.
No. 205—Aug. 28. " .... N. L. A.
No. 260—Sept. 4. " .... N. L. A.
No. 261—Sept. 11. " .... L. A.
No. 262—Sept. 18. " .... L. A.
No. 262—Sept. 25. " .... L. A.
No. 263—Oct. 2. " .... N. L. A.
No. 264—Oct. 9. " .... L. A.
(There are two issues with variations).
No. 255—Oct. 15. " .... L. A.
No. 257—Oct. 23. " .... A.
No. 258—Oct. 30. " .... L. A.
No. 257—Nov. 6. " .... L. A.
No. 258—Nov. 13. " .... L. A.
No. —[Nov. 20.]
No. 259—Nov. 27. " .... L. A.
(6 pages).
No. 260—Dec. 4. " .... L. A.
No. —[Dec. 11.]

JOHN PETER ZENGER

No. 263—Dec. 18. 1738.	N. L. A.	No. 316—Jan. 1. 1739-[40].	D.
No. 263—Dec. 25. "	N. L. A.	No. 317—Jan. 7. "	D.
		No. 318—Jan. 14. "	D.
No. 264—Jan. 1. 1738-[9].	N. L. A.	No. 319—Jan. 21. "	D.
No. 265—Jan. 8. "	N. L. A.	No. 320—Jan. 28. "	D.
No. 266—Jan. 15. "	N. L. A.	No. 321—Feb. 5. "	D. N.
No. 267—Jan. 22. "	L. A.	No. 322—Feb. 11. "	D.
No. 268—Jan. 29. "	N. L. A.	No. 323—Feb. 18. "	D.
No. 269—Feb. 5. "	N. L. A.	No. 324—Feb. 25. "	D.
No. 270—Feb. 12. "	N. L. A.	No. 325—Mar. 3. "	D. L.
No. 271—Feb. 19. "	N. L. A.	No. 326—Mar. 10. "	D. L.
No. 272—Feb. 19. "	L.	No. 327—Mar. 17. "	D. L.
No. 272—Feb. 26. "	L.	No. 328—Mar. 24. "	D.
No. 273—Mar. 5. "	L.	No. 329—Mar. 31. 1740.	D.
No. 274—Mar. 10. "	L.	No. 330—April 7. "	D.
No. 275—Mar. 19. "	L.	No. 331—April 14. "	D.
No. 276—Mar. 26. 1739.	L.	No. 332—April 21. "	D.
No. 277—April 2. "	N. L.	No. 333—April 28. "	D.
No. 278—April 9. "	N. L.	No. 334—May 5. "	D.
No. 279—April 16. "	N. L.	No. 336—May 12. "	D.
No. 280—April 21. "	N. L.	No. 337—May 19. "	D.
No. 281—April 30. "	N. L.	No. 338—May 26. "	D.
No. 282—May 8. "	N. L.	No. 339—June 2. "	D.
No. 283—May 15. "	N. L.	No. 340—June 9. "	D.
No. 284—May 21. "	L.	No. 341—June 16. "	D.
No. 285—May 28. "	L.	No. 342—June 23. "	D.
No. 286—June 4. "	L.	No. 343—June 30. "	D.
No. 287—June 11. "	L.	No. 344—July 7. "	D.
No. 288—		No. 345—July 14. "	D.
No. 289—June 25. "	L.	No. 346—July 21. "	D.
No. 290—July 2. "	L.	No. 347—July 28. "	D.
No. 291—July 9. "	L.	No. 348—Aug. 4. "	D.
No. 292—		No. 349—Aug. 11. "	D.
No. 293—		No. 350—Aug. 18. "	D.
No. 294—		No 351—Aug. 25. "	D.
No. 295—		No. 352—Sept. 1. "	D
No. 296—		No. 353—Sept. 8. "	D.
No. 297—		No. 354—Sept. 15. "	D.
No. 298—Aug. 27. "	L. N.	No. 355—Sept. 22. "	D.
No. 299—		No. 356—Sept. 29. "	D.
No. 300—		No. 357—Oct. 6. "	N. D. L.
No. 301—		No. 358—Oct. 13. "	D.
No. 302—		No. 359—Oct. 20. "	D.
No. 303—		No. 360—Oct. 27. "	D.
No. 304—		No. 361—Nov. 3. "	D.
No. 305—		No. 262—Nov. 10. "	D.
No. 306—Oct. 22. "	D.	No. 363—Nov. 17. "	D.
No. 307—Oct. 29. "	D.	No. 364—Nov. 24. "	D.
No. 308—Nov. 5. "	D.	No. 365—Dec. 1. "	D.
No. 309—Nov. 12. "	D.	No. 366—Dec. 8. "	D.
No. 310—Nov. 19. "	D.	No. 367—Dec. 15. "	D.
No. 311—		No. 368—Dec. 22. "	D.
No. 312—Dec. 3. "	D.	No. 369—Dec. 29. "	D.
No. 313—Dec. 10. "	D.		
No. 314—Dec. 17. "	D.	No. 370—Jan. 5. 1740-[1].	D. L.
No. 315—Dec. 24. "	D. A.	No. 371—Jan. 12. "	D.

ISSUES OF NEW YORK WEEKLY JOURNAL

No. 372—Jan. 19. 1740-[1] .... N. D. L.
No. 373—Jan. 26. " .... D.
No. 374—Feb. 2. " .... D.
No. 375—Feb. 9. " .... D.
No. 376—Feb. 16. " .... D.
No. 377—Feb. 23. " .... D.
No. 378—Mar. 2. " .... D.
No. 379—Mar. 9. " .... D.
No. 380—Mar. 16. " .... D.
No. 381—Mar. 23. " .... D.
No. 382—Mar. 30. 1741. .... D.
No. 383—April 6. " .... D.
No. 384—April 13. " .... D.
No. 385—April 20. " .... D. A.
No. 386—April 27. " .... D.
No. 387—May 4. " .... D.
No. 388—May 11. " .... D.
No. 389—May 18. " .... D.
No. 390—May 25. " .... D.
No. 391—May 31. " .... D.
No. 392—June 8. " .... D.
No. 393—June 15. " .... D.
No. 394—June 22. " .... D.
No. 395—June 29. " .... D.
No. 396—July 6. " .... D.
No. 397—July 13. " .... D.
No. 398—July 20. " .... D.
No. 399—July 27. " .... D.
No. 400—Aug. 3. " .... D.
No. 401—Aug. 10. " .... D.
No. 402—Aug. 17. " .... D.
No. 403—Aug. 24. " .... D.
No. 404—
No. 405—Sept. 7. " .... D.
No. 406—Sept. 14. " .... D.
No. 407—Sept. 21. " .... D.
No. 409—Sept. 28. " .... D. L.
No. 410—Oct. 5. " .... D.
No. 411—Oct. 12. " .... D.
No. 412—Oct. 18. " .... D. A.
No. 413—Oct. 26. " .... D.
No. 414—Nov. 2. " .... D.
No. 415—Nov. 9. " .... D.
No. 416—Nov. 16. " .... D.
No. 417—Nov. 23. " .... D.
No. 148—Nov. 30. " .... D.
No. 419—Dec. 8. " .... D.
No. 420—Dec. 14. " .... D. L.
No. 421—Dec. 21. " .... D. L.
No. 422—Dec. 28. " .... D. L.

No. 423—Jan. 4. 1741-[2] .... L.
No. 424—Jan. 11. " .... L.
No. 425—Jan. 18. " .... L.
No. 426—Jan. 25. " .... L.
No. 427—Feb. 1. " .... L.

No. 428—Feb. 8. 1741-[2] .... L.
No. 429—Feb. 15. " .... L.
No. 430—Feb. 22. " .... N. L.
No. 431—Mar. 1. " .... L.
No. 432—Mar. 8. " .... L.
No. 433—Mar. 15. " .... L.
No. 434—Mar. 22. " .... L.
No. 435—Mar. 29. 1742. .... L.
No. 436—April 5. " .... L.
No. 437—April 12. " .... L.
No. 438—April 19. " .... L.
No. 439—April 26. " .... L.
No. 440—May 3. " .... L.
No. 441—May 10. " .... L.
No. 442—May 17. " .... L.
No. 443—May 24. " .... L.
No. 444—May 31. " .... L.
No. 445—
No. 446—June 14. " .... L.
No. 447—June 21. " .... L.
No. 448—June 28. " .... L.
No. 449—July 5. " .... L.
No. 450—July 12. " .... L.
No. 451—July 19. " .... L.
No. 452—July 26. " .... L.
No. 453—Aug. 2. " .... L.
No. 454—Aug. 9. " .... L.
No. 455—Aug. 16. " .... L.
No. 456—Aug. 23. " .... L.
No. 457—Aug. 30. " .... L.
No. 458—Sept. 6. " .... L.
No. 459—Sept. 13. " .... L.
No. 460—
No. 461—Sept. 27. " .... L.
No. 462—Oct. 4. " .... L.
No. 463—Oct. 11. " .... L.
No. 464—Oct. 18. " .... L.
No. 465—
No. 466—
No. 457—Nov. 1. " .... L.
No. 458—Nov. 8. " .... L.
No. 469—Nov. 15. " .... L.
No. 470—Nov. 22. " .... L.
No. 471—Nov. 29. " .... L.
No. 472—Dec. 6. " .... L.
No. 473—Dec. 13. " .... L.
No. 474—Dec. 20. " .... L.
No. 475—Dec. 27. " .... L.

No. 476—Jan. 3. 1742-[3]. .... L.
No. 477—Jan. 10. " .... L.
No. 478—Jan. 17. " .... L.
No. 479—Jan. 24. " .... L.
No. 480—Jan. 31. " .... L.
No. 481—Feb. 7 " .... L.
No. 482—Feb. 14. " .... L.

JOHN PETER ZENGER

No. 483—Feb. 21 1742-[3]............ L.
No 484—Feb. 28. " .... L.
No. 485—Mar. 7. " .... L.
No. 486—
No. 487—Mar. 21. " .... L.
No. 488—Mar. 28. 1743. .... L.
No. 489—April 4. " .... L.
No. 490—April 11. " .... L.
No. 491—April 18. " .... L.
No. 492—April 25. " .... L.
No. 493—May 2. " .... L.
No. 494—May 9. " .... L.
No. 495—May 16. " .... L.
No. 496—May 23. " .... L.
No. 497—May 30. " .... L.
No. 497—May 30. " .... L.
(Number is misprinted 497 for 498,
and date is misprinted May 30
for June 6).
No. 499—June 13. " .... L.
No. 500—June 20. " .... L.
No. 501—June 27. " .... L.
No. 502—July 4. " .... L.
No. 503—July 11. " .... L.
No. 504—July 18. " .... L.
No. 505—July 25. " .... L.
No. 506—Aug. 1. " .... L.
No. 507—Aug. 8. " .... L.
No. 508—Aug. 15. " .... L.
No. 509—
No. 510—Aug. 29. " .... L.
No. 511—Sept. 5. " .... L.
No. 512—Sept. 12. " .... L.
No. 513—Sept. 19. " .... L.
No. 514—Sept. 26. " .... L.
No. 515—Oct. 3. " .... L.
No. 516—Oct. 10. " .... L.
No. 517—Oct. 17. " .... L.
No. 518—Oct. 24. " .... L.
No. 519—Oct. 31. " .... L.
No. 520—Nov. 7. " .... L.
No. 521—Nov. 14. " .... L.
No. 522—Nov. 21. " .... L.
No. 523—Nov. 28. " .... L.
No. 524—
No. 525—Dec. 11. " .... L.
No. 526—Dec. 19. " .... L.
No. 527—Dec. 26. " .... L.

No. 528—Jan. 2. 1743-[4]............ L.
No. 529—Jan. 9. " .... L.
No. 530—Jan. 16. " .... L.
No. 531—Jan. 23. " .... L.
No. 532—Jan. 30. " .... L.
No. 533—Feb. 6. " .... L.
No. 534—Feb. 13. " .... L.

No. 535—Feb. 20. 1743-[4]............ L.
No. 536—Feb. 27. " .... L.
No. 537—Mar. 5. " .... L. A.
No. 538—
No. 539—
No. 540—
No. 541—April 2. 1744. ....N.
No. 543—
No. 544—
No. 545—April 30. " .... A.
No. 546—
No. 547—
No. 548—
No. 549—
No. 550—
No. 551—
No. 552—
No. 553—
No. 554—
No. 555—
No. 556—
No. 557—
No. 558—
No. 559—
No. 560—
No. 561—
No. 562—
No. 563—
No. 564—Sept. 3. " ....N.
No. 565—
No. 566—
No. 567—
No. 568—
No. 569—
No. 570—
No. 571—
No. 572—
No. 573—
No. 574—
No. 575—Nov. 19. " ....N.
No. 576—
No. 577—
No. 578—
No. 579—Dec. 17. " ....N.
No. 580—
No. 581—
No. 582—
No. 583—
No. 584—

No. 585—Jan. 28. 1744-[5].......... N.
No. 586—Feb. 4. " ....N.
No. 587—
No. 588—
No. 589—Feb. 25. " ....N.
No. 590—

ISSUES OF NEW YORK WEEKLY JOURNAL

No. 591—Mar. 11. 1744-[5]..............N.
No. 592—
No. 593—Mar. 25. 1745...................N.
No. 594—April 1. " ....N.
No. 595—April 8. " ....N.
No. 596—
No. 597—
No. 598—
No. 599—
No. 600—
No. 601—
No. 602—
No. 603—June 3. " ....N.
No. 604—June 10. " ....N.
No. 605—
No. 606—
No. 607—
No. 608—
No. 609—
No. 610—
No. 611—
No. 612—Aug. 5. " ....N.
No. 613—
No. 614—
No. 615—Aug. 27. " ....N.
No. 616—Sept. 2. " ....N.
No. 617—
No. 618—
No. 619—
No. 620— Sept. 30. " ....N.
No. 621—
No. 622—
No 623—
No. 624—
No. 625—
No. 626—
No. 627—
No. 628—Dec. 16. " ....N.
No. 629—
No. 630—
No. 631—
No. 632—
No. 633—

No. 634.—Jan 27. 1745-[6]......... N.
No. 635—
No. 636—Feb. 10. " ....N.
No. 636—Feb. 17. " ....N.
No. 638—Mar. 3. " ....N.
No. 639—
No. 640—
No. 641—
No. 642—
No. 643—
No. 644—
No. 645—

No. 646—April 28. 1746...................N
No. 647—
No. 648—
No. 649—May 19. " ....N.
No. 650—
No. 651—
No. 652—June 9. " ....N.
No. 653—June 16. " ....N.
No. 654—June 23. " ....N.
No. 655—July 14. " ... . A.
No. 656—
No. 657—
No. 658—
No. 659—July 28. " ....N.
No. 660—
No. 661—
No. 662—
No. 663—
No. 664—Sept. 1. " ....N.
No. 665—
No. 666—
No. 667—
No. 668—
No. 669—Oct. 3. " .... A.
No. 670—
No. 608—Oct. 27. " ....
No. 672—
No. 673—
No. 674—
No. 675—Nov. 24. " ....N.
No. 676—
No. 677—
No. 678—
No. 679—
No. 680—Dec. 29. " ....N.

No. 681—Jan. 5. 1746-[7]..............N.
No. 682—
No. 683—
No. 684—
No. 685—Feb. 2. " ....N.
No. 686—
No. 687—Feb. 17. " .... A.
No. 688—
No. 689—
No. 690—
No. 691—
No. 692—Mar. 23. " ....N. A.
No. 693—Mar. 30. 1747...................N.
No. 694—April 6. " ....N.
No. 695—
No. 696—
No. 697—April 27. " ....N.
No. 698—
No. 699—
No. 700—May 18. " ....N.

JOHN PETER ZENGER

No. 701—May 25. 1747. ....N.
No. 702—
No. 703—
No. 704—
No. 705—
No. 706—
No. 707—July 6. " ....N.
No. 708—
No. 709—
No. 710—
No. 711—Aug. 3. " .... W.
No. 712—
No. 713—
No. 714—Aug. 24. " ....N.
No. 715—Aug. 31. " ....N.
No. 716—
No. 717—Sept. 14. " .... A.
No. 718—
No. 719—Sept. 28. " ....N.
No. 720—
No. 721—Oct. 12. " ....N.
No. 722—Oct. 19. " .... A.
No. 723—
No. 724—
No. 725—Nov. 9. " ....N. A
No. 726—
No. 727—
No. 728—
No. 729—Dec. 7. " .... A.
No. 730—
No. 731—Dec. 21. " ....N. A.
No. 732—
No. 733—
No. 734—
No. 735—

No. 736—Jan. 25. 1747-[48]. .... A.
No. 737—Feb. 1. " ....N. A.
No. 738—Feb. 8. " ....N.
No. 739—Feb. 15. " ....N.
No. 740—
No. 741—
No. 742—Mar. 7. " .... A.
No. 743—Mar. 14. " ....N.
No. 744—
No. 745—
No. 746—April 4. 1748. ....N.
No. 747—
No. 748—
No. 749—
No. 750—
No. 751—May 9. " ....N. A.
No. 752—
No. 753—May 23. " .... A.
No. 754—May 30. " .... A.
No. 755—

No. 756—
No. 757—June 20. 1748. .... A.
No. 758—June 27. " ....N. A.
No. 759—July 4. " .... A.
No. 760—
No. 761—July 18. " ....N. A.
No. 762—July 25. " .... A.
No. 763—Aug. 1. " ....N. A.
No. 764—Aug. 8. " .... A.
No. 765—Aug. 15. " .... A.
No. 766—Aug. 22. " ....N. A.
No. 767—
No. 768—Sept. 5. " .... A.
No. 769—Sept. 12. " .... A.
No. 770—Sept. 19. " ....N. A.
No. 771—Sept. 26. " .... A.
No. 772—
No. 773—
No. 774—Oct. 17. " .... A.

No. 775—Oct. 24. " .... A.
No. 776—Oct. 31. " .... A.
No. 777—Nov. 7. " .... A.
No. 778—Nov. 14. " .... A.
No. 779—
No. 780—
No. 781—
No. 782—Dec. 12. " ....N. A.
No. 783—
No. 784—Dec. 26. " .... A.
No. 785—Jan. 2. " ....N.
No. 786—Jan. 9. " ....N. A.
(A Supplement was issued).

No. 787—Jan. 13. 1748-[49]. .... A.
No. 788—
No. 789—Jan. 30. " ....N.
No. 790—
No. 891—Feb. 13. " ....N.
No. 792—
No. 793—Feb. 27. " ....N.
No. 794—
No. 795—
No. 796—Mar. 20. " ....N. L.
No. 797—
No. 798—
(A Supplement was issued).
No. 799—
No. 800—
No. 801—
No. 802—May 1. 1749. ....N.
No. 803—May 8. " ....N.
No. 804—May 10. " .... A.
No. 805—May 22. " .... A.
No. 806—
No. 807—June 5. " .... A.

No. 708—June 12. 1749. ....N.　A.
No. 871—June 19. " ....N.
No. 810—June 26. " .... A.
No. 811—July 3. " ....N.　A.
No. 812—July 10. " .... A.
No. 813—July 17. " .... A.
No. 814—July 24. " .... A.
No. 815—July 30. " .... A.
No. 816—Aug. 7. " .... A.
No. 817—Aug. 14. " .... A.
No. 818—Aug. 21. " .... A.
No. 802—Aug. 28. " ....N.　A.
No. 820—
No. 821—
No. 822—Sept. 18. " ....N.　A.
No. 823—Sept. 25. " .... A.
No. 824—
No. 825—
No. 826—Oct. 16. " .... A.
No. 827—
No. 828—
No. 829—
No. 830—
No. 831—
No. 832—
No. 833—
No. 834—
No. 835—
No. 836—

No. 837—Jan. 2. 1749-[50]. ....N.
No. 838—
No. 839—
No. 840—
No. 841—
No. 842—
No. 843—
No. 844—Feb. 19. " ....N.
No. 845—Feb. 27. " ....N.　A.
No. 845—Mar. 5. " .... A.
No. 846—Mar. 12. " .... A.
No. 847—Mar. 19. " .... A.
No. 848—
No. 849—April 2. 1750. ....N.　A.
No. 850—April 9. " ....N.　A.
No. 851—April 15. " ....N.　A.
No. 852—

No. 853—April 31. 1750. .... A.
No. 854—May 9. " ....N.　A.
No. 855—
No. 856—
No. 857—May 28. " ....N.
No. 858—June 4. " ....N.　A.
No. 859—June 11. " .... A.
No. 860—
No. 861—
No. 862—July 2. " ....N.
No. 863—July 9. " ....N.
No. 864—
No. 865—
No. 866—
No. 867—Aug. 6. " .... A.
No. 868—
No. 869—Aug. 20. " ....N.　A.
No. 870—
No. 871—Sept. 3. " ....N.
No. 872—
No. 873—Sept. 17. " .... A.
No. 874—Sept. 24. " .... A.
No. 875—
No. 876—Oct. 8. " .... A.
No. 877—Oct. 15. " .... A.
No. 878—Oct. 22. " .... A.
No. 888—Oct. 29. " .... A.
No. 880—
No. 881—
No. 882—
No. 1001—Nov. 26. 1750. .... A.
No. 1002—Dec. 3. " .... A.
No. 1003—
No. 1004—
No. 1005—
No. 1006—
No. 1007—
No. 1008—Jan. 14. 1750-[1] ....N.　A.
No. 1009—
No. 1010—
No. 1011—Feb. 4. 1750-[1] ....N.
No. 1012—
No. 1013—
No. 1014—
No. 1015—
No. 1016—
No. 1017—Mar. 18. ....N.

INDEX

INDEX

JOHN PETER ZENGER

INDEX

JOHN PETER ZENGER

INDEX

LIVINGSTON RUTHERFURD (d. 1940) was a descendant of colonial New York politician James Alexander, one of the principal editors of Zenger's *New-York Weekly Journal.* In addition to his compilation on the Zenger press and trial, he wrote a historical work on the Rutherfurd family.

STANLEY N. KATZ is Class of 1921 Bicentennial Professor of the History of American Law and Liberty at Princeton University. He is the author of *Newcastle's New York: Anglo-American Politics, 1732-1753,* and the editor of *Colonial America: Essays in Politics and Social Development,* among other works.